D0882156

Ecologies of Faith in
New York City

POLIS CENTER SERIES ON RELIGION AND URBAN CULTURE

David J. Bodenhamer and Arthur E. Farnsley II, editors

Ecologies of Faith in New York City

The Evolution of Religious Institutions

EDITED BY RICHARD CIMINO, NADIA A. MIAN,
AND WEISHAN HUANG

FOREWORD BY NANCY T. AMMERMAN

INDIANA UNIVERSITY PRESS

Bloomington & Indianapolis

This book is a publication of

INDIANA UNIVERSITY PRESS
601 North Morton Street
Bloomington, Indiana 47404-3797 USA

iupress.indiana.edu

Telephone orders 800-842-6796
Fax orders 812-855-7931

© 2013 by Indiana University Press

Manufactured in the
United States of America

Library of Congress
Cataloging-in-Publication Data

Ecologies of faith in New York City : the
evolution of religious institutions / edited
by Richard Cimino, Nadia A. Mian, and
Weishan Huang ; foreword by Nancy T.
Ammerman.
  p. cm. – (Polis Center series on religion and urban culture)
  Includes bibliographical references and
index.
  ISBN 978-0-253-00684-4 (cloth : alk.
paper) – ISBN 978-0-253-00690-5 (pbk. :
alk. paper) – ISBN 978-0-253-00694-3
e-book) 1. New York (N.Y.) – Religion.
2. Religions – Relations. I. Cimino,
Richard P. II. Mian, Nadia A., [date]
III. Huang, Weishan, [date]
  BL2527.N7E26 2013
  200.9747′1 – dc23

                    2012026047

1 2 3 4 5   18 17 16 15 14 13

For Lowell Livezey

Contents

Foreword

Nancy T. Ammerman

After pioneering research by H. Paul Douglass in the 1920s and 1930s, the questions surrounding what congregations do and how they are related to the larger society faded from view for half a century.[1] Social scientists were preoccupied with the notion that religion was a dying force, a story line interrupted only by macro social forces like the civil rights movement, not by the ordinary religious lives carried on in local communities. Local communities of faith were simply not on the radar screen, either of sociologists or of denominational leaders. The religious heroes of the day were theologians (such as the Niebuhrs) and movement leaders (like Martin Luther King, Jr.). If religion changed the world – or was changed by the world – the changes would involve seismic cultural shifts, not alterations in local landscapes.

When a small group of sociologists and church leaders met at the Lilly Endowment in the early 1980s, the notion of studying congregations was something of a dare.[2] Would anyone pay attention? But an informal group, known as the Congregational Studies Project Team, emerged, and it produced *The Handbook for Congregational Studies* in 1986.[3] The *Handbook* struck a responsive chord, and attention to congregations began to gather momentum in both seminaries and among social scientists. One of the key analytical moves advocated by the *Handbook*'s authors was attention to what they called "context." They spoke of congregations as in a constant state of flux. "The sources of change are primarily environmental, forcing the religious institution to adjust to what is going on around it," they wrote (p. 48). As the team was steeped in an activist liberal Protestant tradition, the well-being of society was a critical concern, and the embodiment of the gospel in human cultures was taken for granted.

By the early 1990s, it was not just liberal Protestants doing the studying or being studied. My own earliest work had focused on American Fundamentalism through the lens of life in a local congregation,[4] but Peter Berger had challenged me to devise a plan for studying key social trends affecting American religion. My answer was that we should look at local communities where those trends were especially visible and examine the work of the congregations in those communities. The resulting book, *Congregation and Community*, was among the first attempts to provide a systematic mapping of the relationships between religious institutions and their geographic locations.[5] While the project started with assumptions about how those institutions were shaped by changing local communities, the reality on the ground pushed toward a different, more interactive perspective.

As the work on that project moved forward, I joined the Congregational Studies Project Team, and the team as a whole was at work on a revision of the *Handbook*. Rather than seeing congregations as situated in a "context," we began to talk about them in an ecological framework, looking for the ways in which congregations competed for resources (such as people, money, space) and established themselves as legitimate, mutually dependent participants in the environment, with the necessary habits for surviving. We also noted the particular symbioses that sometimes created niches in which a particular, specialized way of relating to the population could thrive. Indeed, one of the most important findings of *Congregation and Community* was that congregations need not be local at all. Some respond to the loss of a symbiotic relationship with their immediate neighborhood by establishing a niche identity sufficiently strong to draw members and resources from a broad geographic area.

The *Congregation and Community* research team, spread out in communities across the country, spawned a rich next generation of work that expanded what we know about the ecological world of congregations. Art Farnsley went on to direct a series of projects in Indianapolis in which the civic contributions and social services of congregations were a special focus.[6] Nancy Eiesland widened the urban lens to include the exurbs, writing about the way rural and urban sensibilities intermingled in the congregations of the "particular place" of Dacula, Georgia.[7] She drew our attention especially to the way congregations are lodged in shifting networks of people and institutions. Beyond that core group, Omar McRoberts was completing a Harvard dissertation that would become *Streets of Glory*, and he would insist that we take seriously the theological differences that shape congregational responses to the urban realities of "the street."[8] Each of these (and a growing cadre of others) expanded both the congregations about which we knew and the ideas we had for thinking about the social ecology in which those congregations are actors.

Alongside this work, a parallel young generation of social scientists was being nurtured in Stephen Warner's "New Ethnic and Immigrant Congregations" project. Recognizing that immigrants were reshaping American society and that religion was a big part of that experience, Warner commissioned a group of young scholars to pay attention. Their collection of case studies, *Gatherings in Diaspora*,[9] was the seed for an enormous harvest of attention to immigrant congregations, a harvest that continues in the pages of this book. The study of immigration pushed the ecological perspective out to the global level at the same time that it built on a tradition of urban neighborhood studies from the past. Warner's insight from that project joined with Eiesland's study of exurban networks to inform the chapter they produced for *Studying Congregations*. It was a defining statement about what it means to think about congregations ecologically, and it is a resource on which many of this book's authors draw.[10]

By the time Congress passed "Charitable Choice" legislation in 1996, then, the study of congregations was no longer in its infancy, and in the years that followed, it has become a veritable industry. Two waves of a national representative survey of congregations have established a rich base of data from which many researchers are writing, and policy makers from local to national know that congregations are a critical part of the social safety net.[11] Putnam and Campbell's massive study of American religion, in contrast to what might have been written in earlier decades, puts congregations squarely in the picture. Even as old, established churches and synagogues struggle, new immigrant congregations are popping up, and entrepreneurs are experimenting with new forms of "emerging" church.[12] Congregations remain central to any account of American religion, and this *Ecologies of Faith* collection is a welcome exploration of some of the questions that remain to be answered.

Inspired and led by Lowell Livezey, the "Ecologies of Learning" multidisciplinary team has turned its attention here to one of the largest and most complex social ecologies in the world – New York City. This is a city connected to every other corner of the world, yet it is also a city of neighborhoods. Livezey began his work on urban congregations in Chicago, later taking it to Boston and beyond, in each place challenging seminaries and researchers to look at the broad range of religious traditions and the vibrant array of ministries he found.[13] As the authors here note, Livezey was not content with the talk about "adaptation." That sounded too passive to him; he was convinced that congregations could and should be agents having an impact on their surroundings. As a result, this collection of studies attends to the active engagement of congregations in their own destiny – creating new connections and spaces and community organizations that shape the urban social landscape at the same time that they are being shaped by it.

Livezey and his team were themselves committed to facilitating that agency, offering their expertise and the fruits of their insight back to the congregations. As can be seen in Nadia Mian's account of Trinity Lutheran's deliberations on redevelopment, the ecological perspective has come full circle. Not only does it help analysts understand the interaction between congregations and their "contexts," but it also helps congregations assess their own possible futures and act back on the environment accordingly. The emphasis on congregational agency is one of the consistent themes running through the book's accounts of gentrification, immigration, and entrepreneurialism.

Gentrification is a form of neighborhood change that has been addressed in earlier work, but it is given important new definition and scope here. Hans Tokke's account of the transformation of Times Square reminds us that residential areas are not the only ones to be gentrified, and individual "urban pioneers" are sometimes aided by aggressive governmental and commercial initiatives. Here, too, congregations – like Times Square Church – exist as part of the shifting mix of populations and spaces. In Flushing the population mix is very different, but the push of economic change is still present. There it is Chinese entrepreneurs who are altering the financial and real estate picture, leaving both residents and immigrant congregations to scramble.

Gentrification, of course, is not just about money. It is also about different kinds of people occupying urban spaces, often alongside older populations long settled. As Richard Cimino points out in his essay on Williamsburg and Greenpoint, this process "can activate communities of faith even as their neighborhood functions are drastically changed." The ministries and styles of worship that met the needs of a bygone population can be transformed through the efforts of pastors, denominations, and religious entrepreneurs, resulting in multiple new niches in which lifestyles and religious styles shape each other. Cimino writes about the resulting flux and experimentation and introduces the notion of "niche switching."

Not every experiment will survive, however; populations of hipsters provide both windows of religious opportunity and ceilings imposed by the limits of their willingness to broach any religious participation at all. In other communities the windows and ceilings are shaped in different ways, but the essays in this book help us to recognize the play of opportunity and constraint in the changes forever reshaping urban landscapes. Congregations can creatively draw on a variety of theologies, knowledge, and resources, but the constraints of zoning, politics, and the economy are also very real.

While Williamsburg's shifting ecology is more economic and lifestyle-oriented than ethnic, Cimino's opening anecdote reminds us of the amazing cultural and religious pluralism that is New York City. His twenty-something hipster shouts into a cellphone that there is a parade for "our lady of cara-mel." And other cultural and religious divides, with equally amusing mis-understandings, lurk around nearly every corner. New York City has been religiously plural almost from its beginnings, and it has long had a strong secular cosmopolitan population, as well. Still, it has also always had ethnic and religious enclaves where a singular set of religious habits and institu-tions dominates the culture (most famously, perhaps, the Jewish population in sections of Crown Heights). These essays on the religious ecology of this particular city add immense richness to the American religious catalog.

Some of the interaction along religious divides is not, of course, so amus-ing. As the essays in this book address the challenges faced by immigrant religious communities, the difficulties described are sometimes acute. The Korean Protestants who want places to worship in Flushing have to deal with high property values, lack of parking, and complicated zoning laws; and the Falun Gong practitioners who want to participate in community parades have to face the global political reach of the Chinese government. The African im-migrants described by Moses Biney are often relegated by American racism to high-crime neighborhoods where members dread attending. Establishing a foothold in American society involves these and similar struggles to establish a place for one's religious community.

As these essays also make clear, there are niches within niches, arenas of competition, and sometimes conflict not just between old and new but also among different groups of newcomers. An ecology is not simply a homogenous space altered by the presence of a single "other." Weishan Huang shows us that immigrants from Taiwan can imagine Falun Gong as part of their com-munity in ways that immigrants from mainland China cannot. Biney writes about African American churchgoers who may share some experiences with African immigrants, but resent immigrants who speak and sing in Twi, while those same immigrants wish they could incorporate drums and dancing in their worship. This set of New York City congregational cases provides an important addition to the ecological toolkit, pointing us to the competition *within* niches, as well as between newcomers and older residents.

The places immigrants establish for themselves are, of course, both potential bridges to the larger community and welcome havens where language and custom are nurtured and economic and emotional supports are available. They are critical enough, as Keun-Joo Christine Pae's essay makes clear, that immigrants brave crowded conditions and anti-Korean feelings to have a place of their own. Like the Asians, Brazilians are also rapidly making their presence felt – with at least eighty-six congregations in Queens by Donizete Rodrigues's count. In his essay, we see the intersection of the immigration theme with this book's attention to entrepreneurialism. The amazing Bishop Zeny Tinouco seems ever on the lookout for ways to expand the reach of his ministry. Like other Pentecostals, Bishop Zeny believes God wants his flock to grow, and now there are branches of his movement in Manhattan and New Jersey, as well as in Portugal and Brazil. Initially nested in Portuguese enclaves, Brazilian immigrants are now spreading throughout New York and New Jersey, and some pastors use ethnic parades as a "space" more efficient for gathering and recruiting than neighborhoods.

Transnational ties and ethnic organizations are two of the many kinds of community networks we encounter in this book. Ecological theorists have long given attention to partnerships and resources as necessary elements in the social environment. This book considerably expands our focus to a much broader range of partners and kinds of resources – including the ingenuity of religious leaders like Bishop Zeny. We see in these complex New York cases how entrepreneurs have to do more than come up with a good idea and some cash. They have to talk to (and sometimes organize) neighborhood activists. They have to lobby city hall to change or interpret zoning laws their way. They have to convince police to support the effort. They have to learn from other experiments, scanning the religious horizon for wisdom: Biney's African immigrants know from the experience of Koreans, for instance, that the needs of the second generation will transform how congregations are formed. They have to write grants and hire marketing experts. And sometimes, like The Father's Heart Church's first attempt at starting an ice cream parlor, they may just have to wait for the utility construction outside the front door to be completed. The richness of the New York City organizational, physical, and political environment and the careful attention of this book's observers mean that readers will come away with a much longer checklist of players in the organizational ecology.

The particular realities of NYC property values, along with the age of many of the city's congregational buildings, create acute economic pressures in the environment of many congregations. That environment seems to provide a ready-packaged economic solution: redevelop the property in ways that will generate revenue and preserve space for the congregation and its ministries. At Trinity Lutheran, Mian writes, that model was challenged by the congregation's own careful assessment of its mission and its place in the neighborhood. And at Father's Heart Church, on the Lower East Side, Alphabet Scoop Ice Creamery is a for-profit spin-off that expresses the congregation's long commitment to families and at-risk youth (who form the core employee pool). Entrepreneurial economic activity became part of the mission-visioning of both churches, with different strategies emerging; in both cases, doing religious work required engaging with neighborhood organizations and fighting economic and political battles. Thinking ecologically about congregations requires attention to just such action.

The picture of a church engaging in for-profit economic activity rightly prompts Sheila Johnson to ask about the boundary between sacred and profane. That question is not named as one of the themes of this collection, but it is nevertheless persistently present, especially in the closing section. Matthew Weiner describes the community organizer who was the catalyst for a Hindu nonprofit aimed at caring for elderly people in the community. "While she commonly says her work is secular, and is seen in that way by most civic leaders, she also understands herself and her work as Hindu." Like so much else of the work described in these pages, this organizer's efforts are secular and sacred at the same time. Ideas and practices shaped by relationships with the divine move beyond the boundaries of religious communities into the streets of the neighborhood. Johnson writes about the genesis of the ice cream parlor: "Population shifts inevitably alter meaning systems, values, and symbols, but in the case of Alphabet Scoop, the ministry was able to incorporate the ethos of Alphabet City without compromising its ethical principles." Similarly, Brazilian churches exist in a symbiotic relationship with Brazilian ethnic culture, and Trinity Lutheran "navigated the world of real estate and negotiated its options in discussions with the congregation, community, experts in the development field, and other churches." Even the worship in Midtown churches reflected, respectively, off-Broadway sensibilities (at Lamb's) and the world of tourist-attraction Broadway glitz (at the Times Square Church).

Have these congregations merely accommodated or adapted to a persistent secular social ecology? The answer this book offers is "no." An older framework for studying congregational "contexts" reflected unwittingly the secularization paradigm of the day: the congregation (the sacred) is subject to the dictates of the society (the secular). It can adjust to accommodate society, sometimes quite creatively, but the walls are there, with all the pressure coming from outside in. As the secularization paradigm itself has crumbled over the last two decades,[14] more and more of us have pointed to the reality that religion is never a neat and tightly bounded cultural category. Like other identities, it always has permeable boundaries. Religious identities and religious action take place in the midst of everyday life.[15] Sacred things are present in everyday mundane places – from ethnic parades, to Saturday night jazz liturgies, to gourmet ice cream scooped by a kid who really needs that job. This religious cultural turn to the study of lived religion paves the way for the kinds of congregational studies represented in this book. Here the scope of social action being studied is expanded to include the economic and political along with neighborhood organizing, social services, zoning, policing, and the gathering of religious communities themselves for worship, fellowship, and mutual support.

These essays, then, challenge students of congregational ecology to broaden the range of partners we pay attention to and to take seriously the actions of the congregations themselves in shaping their environment. But the essays are also really good stories. They take us to dozens of neighborhoods in a fascinating city and tell us about the people who are creating and re-creating the religious life of that city. Ecologies of faith are, after all, populated by people, and this book introduces us to fascinating stories about those people and the communities they inhabit.

NOTES

1. Based at the National Council of Churches, Douglass amassed impressive survey data on the activities of congregations in an increasingly urban nation. See Douglass, *The Church in the Changing City*; Douglass and Brunner, *The Protestant Church as a Social Institution*.

2. William McKinney, who was at the meeting, has recounted this encounter (personal communication).

3. Carroll, Dudley, and McKinney, *Handbook for Congregational Studies*.

4. Ammerman, *Bible Believers*.

5. Ammerman, *Congregation and Community*.

6. Farnsley, *Rising Expectations*; Farnsley et al., *Sacred Circles, Public Squares*.

7. Eiesland, *A Particular Place*.

8. McRoberts, *Streets of Glory*.

9. Warner and Wittner, *Gatherings in Diaspora*.

10. Eiesland and Warner, "Ecology: Seeing the Congregation in Context."

11. Chaves, *Congregations in America*; Chaves et al., "The National Congregational Study"; Chaves and Tsitsos, "Congregations and Social Services."

12. Putnam and Campbell, *American Grace*.

13. Livezey, *Public Religion and Urban Transformation*.

14. Gorski and Altinordu, "After Secularization?"; Warner, "Work in Progress toward a New Paradigm for the Sociological Study of Religion in the United States."

15. Ammerman, *Everyday Religion*; McGuire, *Lived Religion*.

REFERENCES

Ammerman, Nancy T, ed. *Everyday Religion: Observing Modern Religious Lives.* New York: Oxford University Press, 2006.

Ammerman, Nancy T. *Bible Believers: Fundamentalists in the Modern World.* New Brunswick, NJ: Rutgers University Press, 1987.

———. *Congregation and Community.* New Brunswick, NJ: Rutgers University Press, 1997.

Carroll, Jackson W., Carl S. Dudley, and William McKinney. *Handbook for Congregational Studies.* Nashville: Abingdon Press, 1986.

Chaves, Mark. *Congregations in America.* Cambridge, Mass.: Harvard University Press, 2004.

Chaves, Mark, Mary Ellen Koneiczny, Kraig Beyerlein, and Emily Barman. "The National Congregational Study: Background, Methods, and Selected Results." *Journal for the Scientific Study of Religion* 38, no. 4 (1999): 458–76.

Chaves, Mark, and William Tsitsos. "Congregations and Social Services: What They Do, How They Do It, and with Whom." *Nonprofit and Voluntary Sector Quarterly* 30 (2001): 660–83.

Douglass, H. Paul. *The Church in the Changing City.* New York: Doran, 1927.

Douglass, H. Paul, and Edmund de S. Brunner. *The Protestant Church as a Social Institution.* New York: Harper and Row, 1935.

Eiesland, Nancy. *A Particular Place: Urban Restructuring and Religious Ecology.* New Brunswick, NJ: Rutgers University Press, 2000.

Eiesland, Nancy L., and R. Stephen Warner. "Ecology: Seeing the Congregation in Context." In *Studying Congregations: A New Handbook,* edited by Nancy T. Ammerman, Jackson Carroll, Carl Dudley, and William McKinney, 78–104. Nashville: Abingdon Press, 1998.

Farnsley, Arthur Emery, II. *Rising Expectations: Urban Congregations, Welfare Reform, and Civic Life.* Bloomington: Indiana University Press, 2003.

Farnsley, Arthur Emery, II, N. J. Demerath III, Etan Diamond, Mary L. Mapes, and Elfriede Wedam. *Sacred Circles, Public Squares: The Multi-centering of American Religion.* Bloomington: Indiana University Press, 2004.

Gorski, Philip S., and Ateş Altınordu. "After Secularization?" *Annual Review of Sociology* 34 (2008): 55–85.

Livezey, Lowell W., ed. *Public Religion and Urban Transformation: Faith in the City.* New York: New York University Press, 2000.

McGuire, Meredith B. *Lived Religion: Faith and Practice in Everyday Life.* New York: Oxford University Press, 2008.

McRoberts, Omar Maurice. *Streets of Glory: Church and Community in a Black Urban Neighborhood.* Chicago: University of Chicago Press, 2003.

Putnam, Robert D., and David E. Campbell. *American Grace: How Religion Divides and Unites Us.* New York: Simon & Schuster, 2010.

Warner, R. Stephen. "Work in Progress toward a New Paradigm for the Sociological Study of Religion in the United States." *American Journal of Sociology* 98, no. 5 (1993): 1044–93.

Warner, R. Stephen, and Judith G. Wittner, eds. *Gatherings in Diaspora: Religious Communities and the New Immigration*. Philadelphia: Temple University Press, 1998.

Acknowledgments

When we began working at the Ecologies of Learning (EOL) Project as research fellows, we had no idea that our academic endeavors would end with the publication of this book. Founded in 2004 by Lowell Livezey, Professor of Urban and Religious Studies, EOL was established to study the relation of New York's religious institutions to their neighborhoods and larger urban structures and dynamics. After Lowell's untimely death in 2007, we worked to compile all the data and research that had been conducted, as a tribute to his dedication to social justice, religious communities, and scholarship in urban religions. We only wish we had had more time to learn from him. This book is the culmination of those efforts.

It has been a long and difficult journey to publication, and we are very grateful and appreciative of those who have helped us along the way. We would also like to acknowledge the Lilly Endowment for its generous grant, as well as EOL's project sponsor, New York Theological Seminary, for its moral and institutional support as we brought this book to fruition.

Within EOL, we are particularly indebted to our Director of Administration and Development, Shirvahna Gobin. In addition to being a constant source of support and stability, Shirvahna worked tirelessly to help us organize the more practical details of publishing and continued to do so even after EOL dissolved and transitioned into the Center for the Study and Practice of Urban Religion in 2009.

Along our journey, many people encouraged and assisted us with this project, including Nancy Ammerman, Courtney Bender, David Bodenhamer, Art Farnsley, Lois Livezey, Peter Paris, and Robert Sloan of Indiana University Press. Their guidance and support have been incalculable.

We would like to thank our contributors for the time and talents that they put into their chapters, and for remaining dedicated participants through the writing and publication process.

We are also appreciative and grateful to the congregations, pastors, groups, and individuals who opened the doors to their houses of worship, organizations, and homes to assist us in our research. Last but not least, this book would not have been possible without the love and support of our families and friends.

As editors, we assume responsibility for any errors or omissions that may be found in the following chapters.

Ecologies of Faith in
New York City

Introduction

The Ecology of Religious Institutions in New York City

Richard Cimino and Nadia A. Mian, with Weishan Huang

On a cold, winter morning, West Park Presbyterian Church, on the corner of 86th and Amsterdam on the Upper West Side of Manhattan, finally reopened its doors. As the church having been closed since 2007, community groups, congregants, and local residents gathered to sweep, mop, and dust the building. Cooperation between the church and community was not always easy. For years, the church had battled the community over plans to redevelop the church property. With an aging building in desperate need of repairs and a dwindling congregation with little endowment, West Park had hoped to tear down its historic house of worship and replace it with a modern mixed-use facility. There would be room for condominiums on the top floors and space for the church on the first few floors. Hoping to adapt to the ever-shifting religious landscape of New York City, the congregation believed that altering its building would ensure the survival of the church. They would be less focused and worried about a building that no longer suited their needs, and revenue from the development would allow the congregation to continue with its mission work. The community, however, felt differently, and viewed the large, red sandstone structure as a part of the neighborhood. In the summer of 2010, after a lengthy and public dispute, West Park Presbyterian was designated a New York City landmark. Now, through continuing cooperation and negotiation with the city and community members, West Park must find new ways of survival, which includes not only maintaining the property but keeping the congregation together.

West Park is an example of how religious institutions shape and are shaped by a wide range of actors, processes, and movements. The interactions between religious institutions and their surrounding environments are most clearly seen in a post-industrial, global city such as New York. Established American religions are pressed to find new niches when they encounter the changed patterns of religious and urban identity brought on by gentrification. "Old World" religions brought by immigrants are renewed when they come into contact with the new pluralism of urban centers. Religious organizations are challenged to broaden their offerings, find new ways of cooperating in their neighborhoods and the wider city, and take on new roles and responsibilities as they engage in entrepreneurial activities, such as real estate development.

This book rests on the premise that the shifting terrain of religion in urban America can best be understood through an ecological perspective. This approach examines the way religious institutions adapt to their environments through patterns of interdependence with other religious groups, as well as neighborhood and city organizations and structures. Such adaptation does not rule out conflict, as change often creates challenges. However, challenges can be mitigated, as ecological models focus on cooperation as much as competition.

Other themes in the organizational ecology model are also effective in explaining the dynamics of urban religion. The failure of religious organizations to adapt to changing environments can lead to institutional demise or replacement, based in part on the kinds of social and theological resources available. Since interdependence, rather than autonomy, drives religious ecology, this book argues that more is at stake than the fortunes or failures of particular institutions; religion actually contributes to the welfare of neighborhoods and the wider city. As Nancy Eiesland and R. Stephen Warner (1998, 40) write:

> The ecological frame . . . assumes that [any] congregation is one among many. Other congregations have their place in the community, their own visions, and their particular constituents, and . . . they influence each other for good and for ill. Congregations can consciously cooperate and compete; they can hinder (and help) one another without intending to do so; they affect each other by their very presence.

The challenges of urban religious institutions in contributing to the common good of cities are especially pressing for congregations and other institutions involved in commercial and entrepreneurial activities. This volume contributes to the expanding role of religious institutions in a diverse and increasingly pluralistic society by examining how sociostructural challenges, such as gentrification, immigration, and entrepreneurialism, affect congregations. It further studies how congregations go through the process of coping with change, how they grow, adapt, and exhibit agency and how their actions affect their neighborhoods. The religious institutions in this book are all from the New York City area, a large metropolitan center constantly in a state of flux. We examined a diverse cross-section of congregations – Christian, Hindu, new Asian religious movements, African, Korean, and Brazilian – to demonstrate that the key to their survival lies in understanding the urban context in which they reside while utilizing resources to aid in that survival.

URBAN ECOLOGY AND RELIGIOUS ECOLOGY

Religious ecology can be traced back to the origins of urban sociology at the University of Chicago's sociology department, often referred to as the "Chicago School." Scholars of the Chicago School, such as Ernest W. Burgess, Robert E. Park, and Roderick McKenzie, advanced theories of urban ecology as lenses through which city life and human nature could be examined and analyzed. Within the Chicago School, "biological metaphor and ecological models were apt framing devices for the discussion of urban social relations" (Lutters and Ackerman 1996, 3–4). Forces at work in nature could be used to explain forces shaping city life, such as supply and demand of resources, competition, cooperation, evolution, niches, and the interconnected web of networks that sustain the urban environment. The Chicago School considered the city a laboratory in which theories regarding the city could be tested. As Vasishth and Sloane (2002, 349) write, "The particulars of urban change – the waves of immigrants arriving, concentrating, and dispersing in patterned succession – and of ecological processes – invasion, assimilation, adaptation, cooperation, competition, and local migration – shaped [Chicago sociologists'] theoretical structures and the questions they asked in their research." Shifts and changes in the urban environment were sufficient to help explain and understand city life. However, the importance lay not in the patterns that emerged as a result of change; rather, the *process* of change itself was key to understanding communities.

Amos Hawley expanded the theory of human ecology by stressing the role of differentiation and adaptation of the population to its environment to explain sociospatial arrangements in the urban milieu. In his examination of the structure of communities, Hawley studied how populations interact with their environment to change, develop, and organize society. Hawley's theory of human ecology acts as the intellectual foundation on which organizational ecology theorists such as Carroll, Hannan, and Freeman based their work (Carroll 1984; Hannan and Freeman 1989; Singh and Lumsden 1990). In building a theory of organizational ecology, Hannan and Freeman asked, "why are there so many different kinds of organizations? And what processes lead to diversity?" (Hannan and Freeman 1989). Theorists were interested in understanding what leads to the birth, death, growth, and change of organizations. Change is inevitable if an organization is to survive. According to one of the theory's major tenets, even though organizations are affected by social and environmental conditions, those that resist change are considered inert. Inert organizations are strong structurally, but when change occurs, they cannot handle the process and may die.

Organizational ecology did not focus on adaptation of an organization to its environment, but on the succession of change, the process of an organization being replaced by a new one. Selection in this case becomes important. According to the evolutionary stage of selection, there is a "mechanism for the elimination of certain types of organizations. Elimination can occur through any type of organizational mortality: dissolution, absorption by merger, or radical transformation" (Carroll 1984, 74). To survive, organizations sometimes create a niche that allows them to fulfill a certain need within a community. Niche theory distinguishes between specialist and generalist organizations. As DiMaggio (1998, 16) defines them, "specialists are organizations that intensively exploit very narrow niches, relatively small entities that do one thing very well. . . . Generalist organizations occupy broader niches, for example, offering several products in several markets."

Building upon the foundation of organizational analysis, the theory known as new institutionalism gives greater consideration to the external environment and how it shapes the structure and processes of organizations. The theory also pays special attention to the role that culture (organizational, professional, industrial, and societal) plays in an organization (DiMaggio 1998, 14). In *Sacred Companies* (1998), Demerath and colleagues explore the application of organizational theory to religious organizations using new institutionalism theory. Religious institutions are inherently cultural. Stout and Cormode (1998, 64) define an institution as "an embedded social structure of rules and hierarchies created to embody and perpetuate a set of cultural norms and values among its members. Any definition of institution that limits the usage to social structures, hierarchies, and bureaucracies is incomplete and misleading. . . . Culture, values, symbols, and ideas must be added for they are the springs on which institutions rest." Physical structures also play a part in how an institution functions. Stout and Cormode (1998, 66) go on to argue that "religious institutions are not merely the cultures of prayer, confession, festas, and so on. They are also structures – buildings, budgets, and tax exemptions." Therefore, for Stout and Cormode, religious institutions are both a "structure and a culture."

Stemming from the discipline of congregational studies, religious ecology pays heed to the internal organizational structure of an organization (including its history, culture, and networks), its interactions with the urban environment, and the effects of socioeconomic and political issues on religious organizations. Interdependence, adaptation, cooperation, migration, niche, and culture become important characteristics distinguishing the theory.

Religious organizations are viewed as participatory actors that shape and are shaped by city life. Eiesland (2000) defines religious ecology as the "patterns of relations, status, and interaction among religious organizations within a locality . . . religious groups may not relate to those nearby, but they are nonetheless part of an ecology because of their physical proximity and by virtue of common environmental factors, for example, economic, educational, or infrastructural changes" (xi, 11). The common issues create a bond, based on which cooperation between secular and nonsecular institutions becomes important. While this is not to say that there is no competition, the sharing of resources, such as information, is vital to the health and survival of one's local ecology.

Understanding the local religious ecology includes examining the "scope" and "layers" of a community. As Eiesland and Warner (1998) explain:

> By wide scope, we mean the open-ended character of the congregation's environment . . . a congregation is linked to networks and events across geographic and temporal space. . . . [Congregations] are also characterized by shared conversations, common practices, and structures that promote cooperation and exchange. . . . Layers refers to the fact that the interaction between a congregation, or any institution, and its environment occurs at different levels. (40)

The open-ended scope of an institution through its networks and events across time and space sheds light on the fact that institutions do not reside in a bubble. Traditions, practices, languages – essentially culture – bridges and bonds institutions through time and space.

In her pioneering research on the religious ecologies of nine communities across the United States, Nancy Ammerman (1997) found that congregational adaptation is assisted as much by local coalitions, member networks, and even governmental partnerships as by denominations and theological heritage. Through an analysis of a congregation's local demography, culture, and organizational structure, the context of the congregation becomes clearer. Race, age, ethnicity, income, housing, and family structure, among other factors in the area, are taken into consideration when analyzing both the church and community. The culture of the neighborhood – it's shared practices, traditions, norms, and values – are explored. The congregation's organizational hierarchy – whether it is nondenominational, without a pastor, or governed by a hierarchical structure – may affect its relationship and interaction with its community.

Within a local religious ecology, cooperation and competition among congregations are not uncommon as each attempts to survive. As religious institutions are affected by their external surroundings, they adapt their internal organizational structure and alter their congregational identity as they struggle to remain viable. Adaptation and interdependence among religious and civic groups is central to the ecological framework. Providing new services, amending their mission, refocusing on a new cause, or attracting one specific demographic group are all strategies of survival. Some institutions may leave their community and migrate to where the majority of the congregation lives, or they may consider planting a new church elsewhere.

We have discovered this pattern in the religious geography in New York City, in the past and today. As the chapters by Weishan Huang, Donizete Rodrigues, and Moses Biney reveal, language and culture drew many of these newcomers together in ethnic neighborhoods, while racism or social-economic attraction ensured that many new ethnic Chinese and Koreans would live and worship in immigrant communities.

As noted above, organizations are either generalists or specialists; generalists have a broad appeal, while specialists focus on "concentrating their resources on tightly focused populations, forms, or identities" (Eiesland 2000, 15). It can be argued that a "niche" congregation falls within the category of a specialist organization. The ecological approach stresses that congregations fill niches and adapt to their environment to meet the needs of different groups rather than engaging in direct competition with each other, as in market theories of religious change and growth. Institutions unable to adapt to change die and are replaced by a new organization.

However, while the tenets of the theory are, for the most part, representative of what we found occurring in communities and institutions throughout the New York City area, our research allows us the opportunity to extend and develop the theory. In our research, we find that while religious institutions adapt to their environment, the term "adaptation" connotes passivity. We argue that religious institutions are active agents in adapting to circumstance; they are not bystanders, altering without resistance or restraint. Nadia Mian's chapter on Trinity Lutheran Church tells how the congregation must choose whether or not to redevelop its property in the midst of increasing gentrification and structural concerns regarding its building. Trinity actively engages the community in order to understand and decide which course of action to take. In the end, the church decides not to redevelop its house of worship, which goes against the current trend of church redevelopment projects in New York City and other large, metropolitan areas. Instead, the members adapt by diversifying their revenue stream and sharing their space. Sheila Johnson further illustrates the role of agency in adaptation. To work within the religious ecology of the Lower East Side, The Father's Heart Ministries chooses which small business it wants to pursue. Even after having failed, the Father's Heart still actively pursues community development until it is successful. As previously mentioned, congregations fill niches to adapt to their environment, and Richard Cimino's chapter finds that especially under the segmenting effect of gentrification, different niches can exist within a single neighborhood. The same environment encourages "niche-switching" (or attempts at switching) by congregations on a fairly regular basis. In contrast to previous treatments of religion and gentrification, such attention to niche formation and activity implies a significant degree of agency by organizations during neighborhood change. The theory of religious ecology is still in its primary stages of exploration, and the aim of our research is to improve and expand upon work that has already been conducted, particularly as we apply these concepts to three key areas of urban transformation: gentrification, immigration, and entrepreneurial innovation.

THE RELIGIOUS ECOLOGY OF NEW YORK CITY

If a religious ecology evolves through a complex interaction of local environments with different congregational cultures, it is obvious that the ecology of

New York is quite different from that of other cities. Because New York is a city of myriad neighborhoods and thousands of congregations, it would be a daunting task to outline a specific religious ecology for such a vast metropolis. The whole concept of urban ecology, focusing on neighborhood interactions, seems to rule against a wide-angle analysis of a metropolitan region. The postmodern city and the religious sphere are decentered, defined not only by local economic and political realities but also by global flows and virtual and social networks that transcend spatial boundaries (Blokland and Savage 2008). But even taking into account local and global realities, we believe New York City has a "macro-ecology" that sets the stage for interactions on the neighborhood and congregational levels.

A common theme running through historical and contemporary treatments of New York is ethnic, cultural, and religious pluralism. As Tony Carnes (2001) writes, "The history of religion in New York has always been framed by a higher degree of tolerance, secularization of public institutions, and pluralism than usually found elsewhere in the United States." The lack of official establishments of churches (though there was the unofficial establishment of the Dutch Reformed and Episcopal churches) in New York (and the Middle Atlantic colonies in general) permitted a greater range of diversity early on in a nation marked by either state-sanctioned religion or regional strongholds of particular faiths. But New York is not representative of the diversities of American religion. New York City has a considerably higher proportion of Catholics and Jews than does the United States as a whole. Churches of the American heartland and Bible Belt, such as those of Baptists, Methodists, and Lutherans, are considerably underrepresented in New York (Klaff 2001). Using 1991 – and thus low-end – figures, the same analysis suggests that more non-Christian religions are found in New York than in the nation in general. As Carnes (2001) echoes, "New York City has more Roman Catholics, Muslims, Hindus, Rastafarians, Jehovah's Witnesses, Greek Orthodox, Russian Orthodox, and religious Jews than any other city in the United States." An examination of the numbers of houses of worship in New York from 1960 to 1990 finds that Christian churches slowly declined and non-Christian religious institutions rose in number during the postindustrial period (Mian 2008). New York–style pluralism also has a distinct "secular cosmopolitan" element. David Martin (2010) writes that the Dutch founding of New York (or New Amsterdam) can be considered a stage in a "secular mutation" within Protestantism, culminating in the "ascendency of the commercial over the religious." Manhattan's reputation as a global capital of finance, the media, entertainment, fashion, the arts, and publishing has drawn many cultural pilgrims to the city who have distanced themselves from the perceived "provincialism" of their religious backgrounds.

The diversity of religions in New York tells us little about how such pluralism is fleshed out in the city's neighborhoods. New York experienced a massive influx of Roman Catholics and Jews in the early twentieth century, but these immigrants and their religious institutions were often based in enclaves geographically separated from one another. The expansion of religious diversity after the relaxation of immigration laws in 1965 (allowing more non-Western immigrants into the country) has brought faith groups into greater proximity, if not interaction.

Today, congregations, parishes, temples, and mosques can still be at the centers of ethnic enclaves, or just as likely coexist side by side with one another in mixed neighborhoods. They can compete for members, seek out particular niches and ignore each other, or cooperate with one another through coalitions and other neighborhood organizations. Such patterns are determined both by neighborhood realities and by religious organizations' theological and social resources and repertoires. The strongly Catholic structure of much of New York religion, with the parish representing and seeking to serve those within particular neighborhood boundaries, has created a large measure of stability in the religious ecology of New York. Even if modern-day Catholics seek to override such parish boundaries and choose their place of worship, the parish model discourages the movement of churches (not all of them Catholic) outside of the city (Gamm 1999). Yet many congregations show higher mobility, following their members who migrate to other parts of the city or beyond – a pattern evident even among religions that traditionally have given little place to congregational structures and activities (Warner 1999; Carnes 2001). The new immigration adds not only to the diversity of the religious ecology but also to its volatility. Today, as newcomers settle in one area while older waves of immigrants leave for the suburbs or other parts of the city, it is more difficult to identify a particular neighborhood as having a specific religious complexion or concentration. The recycling of buildings among increasingly diverse religious congregations has created a new neighborhood-based pluralism throughout much of the city.

While competition is always a reality, this new pluralism can also be channeled in cooperative directions through the agency and leadership of the many ecumenical and interfaith organizations and coalitions that are based in New York. National and international organizations, such as the Interchurch

Center (including the National Council of Churches and a growing number of interfaith groups) and the United Nations, both coordinate and set the tone for local cooperative efforts.

The cooperative dimension of New York religion was brought home to the city and the whole nation after 9/11. An interfaith prayer service was organized at Yankee Stadium shortly after the attacks in which the local leader of the conservative Lutheran Church – Missouri Synod, Rev. David Benke, publicly offered a prayer along with the other clerics. When news of Benke's participation in the service reached the denomination's leadership in the Midwest, he was publicly reproved and charged with engaging in syncretism (or mixing the faith with non-Christian, "pagan" elements). The response of New Yorkers, including Missouri Synod Lutheran New Yorkers, to the disciplining and suspension of Benke amounted to a collective Bronx cheer, as they rallied to his defense, eventually resulting in the lifting of the suspension (Balmer 2006).

Migration is another theme that figures more highly in the religious ecology of New York than in other cities. Although most U.S. cities depend on the global movement of people and resources, New York, along with other key cities, has long functioned as a "gateway city" for immigrants. New York not only attracts immigrants but also hosts church planters, missionaries, gurus, and religious innovators who view the world's financial and cultural capital as a staging ground for their own ministries and movements. In this book, several chapters illustrate how church planters target specific sections of the city for evangelization. It further explores how the Falun Gong, an Asian new religious movement, established headquarters in New York to facilitate its global outreach. The growth of evangelical churches in New York in recent years (up to one hundred church starts a year) has been fueled both by immigration (accounting for about half of these congregations since 1987) and by new church plants by leaders drawn to New York as a special mission field. Particularly since 2000, the influx of young professionals and the "creative class" to the city was followed by networks of church leaders and denominations seeking to plant churches for these lifestyle strata. (Carnes 2010).

Even in long-established congregations, denominational and nondenominational organizations, and seminaries (particularly in Manhattan), it is obvious that many professionals, leaders, students, and clergy regularly arrive from other parts of the United States and the world seeking to contribute to, as well as learn from, the life of this global city. In ecological terms this growth of religious organizations and professionals coming from outside the city can be seen as an invasion or incursion of transplanted elements into the natural religious soil of New York. A pattern of "insider" versus "outsider" has often marked the religious leadership of the city, which could lead to tensions as well as innovations. But whether invigorating or conflicting, the pattern of insiders and outsiders making and remaking New York religion has created a unique religious ecology, though one that may be increasingly common in an interconnected and pluralized urban landscape.[1]

The magnetism of New York in drawing high concentrations of religious elites and professionals has also created a resource base that has a significant effect on the religious ecology of the city. Whether in ecumenism, social action, theology, or liturgy, the numerous national and international organizations can deploy their personnel and expertise to congregations throughout the city. A congregation with its national or international headquarters nearby has greater access to resources than congregations at the periphery of the institution or movement, and this access likely affects its identity and mission. The exodus of several mainline Protestant denominational offices from New York in the last two decades to the South and Midwest (in the concern to connect with their rank-and-file constituents) has to a certain extent diminished this magnet effect, though many other denomination-based organizations remain (especially Jewish institutions) or have taken their place (such as immigrant and non-Christian religious groups).

ABOUT *ECOLOGIES OF FAITH*

In this book we seek to demonstrate the ways in which the religious ecology of New York is being reshaped in response to broader changes in the urban landscape. Using New York City as our laboratory, we examine three major sociological markers that reveal how the urban religious ecology is changing: gentrification, immigration, and entrepreneurialism. These markers represent important social, economic, and cultural changes in New York. Both gentrification and immigration are central to understanding the religious ecology, since these forces have transformed both the residential and commercial life of neighborhoods. Entrepreneurial activities among religious institutions, on the other hand, are the result of neighborhood changes and the pervasive influence of economic development. Social service provision, often in the form of mission work, is so greatly needed that new forms of adaptation and diversity are sought to support a neighborhood's needs. This support often comes in the form of property development, which yields the greatest revenue, especially in a development- and commerce-driven city like New York. These development-related activities may be business-oriented, but they are still mandated by a social justice perspective in which both the community and the institution benefit.

Each section of the book builds on and complements the other, and we believe this approach provides a unique contribution to the study of urban religion. Part 1, on gentrification, examines the basic theories of adaptation and niche formation. Part 2 builds on the first by examining immigrant incorporation and religious and ethnic succession. The third and last section focuses on adaption and innovation by religious institutions and ethnic groups through property development as a response to the changing urban environment.

While several works have been written on the role of religion in New York City, and on the theory of religious ecology, few have focused on the religious ecology of New York City. Nancy Ammerman (1997) explored the ways in which congregations adapt to their environments, drawing from a wide diversity of traditions and locales throughout the United States, while ours focuses on the dynamic nature of New York City. While she utilizes case studies, Ammerman's work differs from this one with respect to the practical applications of the theory. Her case studies serve to explain how the theory of religious ecology works, while our book focuses on the outworking of this theory in the three social, economic, and political spheres of urban America. Farnsley, Demerath, Diamond, Mapes, and Wedam (2004) use an ecological framework to examine the role of religion in the "de-centering" of Indianapolis, as social capital is generated and confined in various communities rather than directed toward the city center. The authors argue that this de-centering process is taking place in other cities, presumably including such global cities as New York and Los Angeles.

Orsi's collection of case studies (1999) is spread throughout the United States; the studies look at the way the "lived religion" of urban residents often extends beyond the walls of worshipping communities to create "sacred space" in the urban environment. In contrast, our book focuses on how religious institutions interact not only with each other and their immediate neighbors but with specific social, political, and economic forces and structures.

Nancy Eiesland (2000) examines the community of Dacula, Georgia, and focuses on the response of the religious community to larger urban structural changes in a small suburb. As she focuses on only one community, the case study does not reveal a replication of data, making it difficult to explore the theory and its implications further.

METHOD

Our base at the Ecologies of Learning Project (EOL) gave us a distinctive vantage point from which to study the interaction between religious institutions and communities in New York City. Lowell Livezey, founder and director of EOL, first began studying religion and the city during his tenure at the University of Illinois at Chicago's Religion in Urban America Program.

In Chicago, Livezey reviewed the history of religious and community research instigated and modified by Graham Taylor, who arrived in 1892 to teach at the Chicago Theological Seminary. Research methods for studying churches included "direct observation and social survey" (Livezey 2000, 16). Livezey's findings stressed that since World War II, social changes in American cities have been so fundamental as to be termed "urban restructuring." Livezey and his team identified the three processes of urban restructuring, religious restructuring, and social transformation in Chicago with which religious organizations must interact if they are to participate effectively in urban life today (Livezey 2000, 16–18).

At the Ecologies of Learning Project, we continued researching the relationship between the city and religious communities using the "grounded theory" approach employed by Livezey in Chicago. This approach moves inductively from data and observation to theory (Glaser and Strauss, 1967). Grounded theory respects the distinct identities of religious institutions and allows the researcher to remain open to questions that may not be apparent before work begins in the field. Cases were chosen based on our personal experience with the congregation, or through connections with the institution, and represent the socio-ethnic and religious diversity of congregations found in New York City. We studied both large and small congregations; some were from poor and working-class backgrounds, while others were middle-class. Immigrant and nonimmigrant communities were studied from Anglo, Latino, African, and Asian populations that spanned a spectrum of faiths – Christian, Hindu, and even new Asian religious movements, like the Falun Gong. The authors spent at least four months studying and deciphering each congregation and its issues. We used tools and resources provided by EOL to conduct interviews, observation, census track analysis, and historical data research to understand the impact of social, cultural, and economic factors on the relationship between a religious institution and the community. Using multiple forms of data collection, we created a triangulation of data that established the validity of our findings. Descriptive cases of congregations and their communities allowed patterns to emerge that substantiated and further expanded the theory of religious ecology. Through our research, we discovered particular constructs or issues through which our cases could then be organized and analyzed: gentrification, immigration, and entrepreneurial activities. Furthermore, we concluded that it was these three issues that are restructuring the urban landscape and religious communities in New York City.

PART I. RELIGIOUS INSTITUTIONS AND
GENTRIFICATION IN THE RELIGIOUS ECOLOGY

While "gentrification" has various meanings and expressions, for the purposes of this book, it can be defined as the process whereby new, upper-scale residents and businesses move into a neighborhood, challenging and replacing existing commercial and residential patterns. Part 1 of this book examines both how religious organizations are shaped by neighborhood transformation and how they seek to change this process. More specifically, we seek to address three questions: How are congregations and other religious institutions affected by gentrification? Can religious organizations change the course of gentrification in their neighborhoods, and if so, how? How do newer forms of gentrification affect the religious life of a community?

These questions highlight the interactive nature of gentrification and its place in the religious ecology. Congregations and other groups adapt in various ways to changes in their environment, often by drawing on their particular resources (for instance, theology and denominational connections) and by enacting new strategies (such as cooperating with neighboring congregations and community groups) that can themselves contribute to the neighborhood and the wider city.

These chapters are unique in that they capture the varieties of gentrification under way in New York. Thus the first chapter, "Disneyfication and Religion in Times Square," by Hans E. Tokke, looks at the understudied topic of commercial gentrification and the effects of such commodification on the theology and religious practices of two congregations in Times Square. Originally pioneered in the era of the economically devalued Times Square, these churches formulated ambitious missions for social justice and care for those in need living on their doorsteps. Tokke finds that they have attempted to adapt and assimilate to the middle-upper-income demographic and transient tourist populations surrounding them. Of broader interest in this study is the way religious groups attempt to reframe themselves to a new mission, while remaining faithful to their original mission, even when they are forced to evolve alongside urban ecologies driven by redevelopments intended to appeal to transient tourist consumers.

Chapter 2, "Filling Niches and Pews in Williamsburg and Greenpoint: The Religious Ecology of Gentrification," by Richard Cimino, examines the interaction between congregations and the process of gentrification in the sections of Williamsburg and Greenpoint, Brooklyn. The various waves of newcomers that have arrived in Williamsburg-Greenpoint and the subsequent relocation of the area's longtime residents during the past decade raises particular dilemmas that congregations seek to negotiate in various ways. For some of these congregations the dilemma revolves around the need to both minister to their existing members and make room for the new residents. Other congregations, because of their theology, organizational history, and structure, intentionally target the newcomers, or they maintain barriers that may actually exclude them. As Cimino suggests, there is not one path to adaptation, as each congregation seeks to fill a niche – some more successfully than others – that meets their own needs and strengthens their identity.

The last chapter in this section, Keun-Joo Christine Pae's "Korean American Churches and the Negotiation of Space in Flushing, Queens," examines how Korean American churches negotiated space in Flushing as they encountered commercial gentrification led by more recent immigrants. Similar to previous studies on immigrant religious organization, Pae's study finds that Korean churches have contributed to the formation of ethnic, racial, cultural, religious, and civic identities among Korean Americans. The ecological frame suggests that the process of Korean American Christian identity formation is interwoven with their congregations' local environment. In her fieldwork on St. Paul Chong Ha-Sang Roman Catholic Church and First United Method Church, Pae finds, first, that the two congregations did not consider expanding their facilities or moving to the suburbs, because of limited space for residency along with anti-Korean feelings in Flushing. Second, the regulations of these churches' denominations also limited their options. Both St. Paul and First UMC are attached to Flushing as a Korean space, although increasing real estate prices make it difficult for Korean churches to expand their facilities.

PART 2. IMMIGRATION, RELIGION
AND NEIGHBORHOOD CHANGE

The second section examines the responses of faith groups to increasing racial/ethnic and income diversity, as well as to demographic changes in their neighborhoods since 1965. Our research argues that these changes are the result of global processes of migration and immigration. Some key questions that we address are: To what extent do faith groups embrace or resist ethnic/racial diversity? To what extent do congregations challenge racial/ethnic boundaries in the community? When we consider religious ecology and immigration, we find that ethnic/religious diversity has not necessarily led to different ethnic groups and religious groups interacting with one another beyond their respective boundaries. In a global context, immigrant faith groups create transnational changes as they establish new connections between host and receiver countries.

Previous literature has suggested that neighborhood diversity may generate a decrease in social cohesion. In their chapters, Weishan Huang, Donizete Rodrigues, and Moses Biney look at the different forms of adaptation, competition, and conflict among religious groups, including mainline and evangelical Protestants, and a new religious movement, the Falun Gong, in diverse communities.

Weishan Huang's chapter, "Diversity and Competition: Politics and Conflict in New Immigrant Communities," aims to understand the religious reproduction of Falun Gong as a religious movement seeking to integrate itself within the economic and cultural life of the city. Huang finds that New York City has become the center of the group's resistance efforts on a global level. This study exposes the relationship between the wider city and the strategic practices of Falun Gong, such as its qi-gong exercises in public parks and its parades in Flushing and Chinatown in Manhattan. As for the conflict between Falun Gong and China's government, these tensions have translated to the streets of New York City, revealing the politics of immigrant communities as a reflection of domestic politics in their home country. Huang finds different strategic phases of Falun Gong's resistance, including a confrontational phase, a choice-of-lifestyle phase, and a path-of-cultivation phase. Her account of a dispute between the group and secular community organizations in Flushing and Chinatown illustrates territorial conflict in the immigrant community. Having suffered most from the Chinese government's "evil" propaganda, the Falun Gong practitioners felt they needed to clarify the truth to the community by fighting for participation and recognition. The practice of qi-gong in the park serves the purposes of "evangelical" recruiting and community building in this uninstitutionalized but highly mobilized faith group. The public display of qi-gong is a means of asserting that the group's religion belongs in New York just as much as yoga and other religious practices.

In chapter 5, "The Brazilianization of New York City: Brazilian Immigrants and Evangelical Churches in a Pluralized Urban Landscape," Donizete Rodrigues discusses the presence and spatial visibility of Brazilian immigrants and their evangelical churches throughout the New York Metropolitan Area. Brazilian congregations have concentrations in the Portuguese communities of Newark, Long Island, and New York City, and it is the common cultural and historical ties between these two immigrant groups that favor the religious strategies of cooperation rather than competition. The chapter focuses especially on the leadership, history, migration, and church-planting strategies of Brazilian evangelicals and Pentecostals, and it examines how these dynamics are manifested in the practices and worship of one congregation in Astoria, Queens.

According to Moses Biney, "Building and Expanding Communities: African Immigrant Congregations and the Challenge of Diversity," African immigrant congregations have to constantly deal with the paradox of homogeneity and diversity that exemplifies American society. These congregations seek to balance their mission to the often socially marginalized African immigrants, on one hand, with the needs of the larger neighborhoods within which they are located, on the other. Biney stresses that the challenge of diversity, particularly racial and ethnic diversity, must be seen against the backdrop of the larger American attitude toward diversity, especially in the context that America has been and continues to be a racialized country.

Biney's work examines four different congregations. In Day Spring Church (DSP), the pastor and African American members face the challenge of learning how much African culture that they can incorporate into their church life as DSP grows into a multicultural church. First Presbyterian Church also struggles between unity and diversity when church members try to establish their identity. St. Mary of Zion Ethiopian Orthodox Church faces linguistic challenges as most of the liturgical language and songs and *kidase* they use during service cannot easily be translated in order to reach out to the residents in the neighborhood. Redeemed Christian Church of God Chapel of Restoration encounters the major challenge of how it can become attractive to non-Africans or even non-Nigerians, and also how to worship in a way that satisfies both majority members and new African immigrants.

PART 3. ENTREPRENEURIAL INNOVATION
AND RELIGIOUS INSTITUTIONS

Part 3 examines religious institutions that are engaging in entrepreneurial activities as a response to their local religious ecology. Entrepreneurial activities can be defined as innovative, risky, but creative ventures that utilize land, labor, and capital to create new goods or services. The business created requires strong leadership and may not always be outwardly social in nature, but contributes to the welfare of the city and fulfills a community need. Through their involvement in entrepreneurial activities, religious institutions respond to local community needs and wider urban issues in innovative and creative ways that broaden the function of their organization, but still address the mission of their institution. In some cases, by creating not only social but monetary capital, entrepreneurial activities blur the definition of what it means to be a nonprofit institution. Through cooperation with secular and nonsecular groups, entrepreneurialism also creates new networks and partnerships. Engaging in such activity is a method of survival that benefits both the institution and the community.

In this section, we apply the term "entrepreneurial" to describe the involvement of religious institutions in different kinds of development, from building a community center to starting a small business. The chapters document three entrepreneurial-minded religious institutions from the Lower East Side, Upper West Side, and Queens, and address the following questions: Under what circumstances do religious institutions engage in entrepreneurship? What is the impact of these activities on the community? How does becoming an entrepreneur change the nature of the institution and local religious leaders? These questions highlight the process by which religious institutions incorporate secular and commodity-driven activities into their ministries.

In chapter 7, "Changing Lives One Scoop at a Time: The Creation of Alphabet Scoop on the Lower East Side," Sheila P. Johnson describes how The Father's Heart Ministries (FHM), a faith-based nonprofit organization, created Alphabet Scoop, a for-profit ice-cream parlor to provide at-risk youth with job training and employment. After conducting a community analysis, FHM realized that to survive on the Lower East Side, the church would have to change its mission to embrace a "prophetic social activism" that would address the high poverty and low education rates among residents, especially youth, through a social gospel that attempts to unite the sacred and the secular. Purchasing property to create an ice-cream parlor would provide mentorship and money to youth in- and outside the neighborhood, generate revenue for the church, and establish The Father's Heart Ministries as an asset to and leader within the community. This chapter finds that the creation of Alphabet Scoop addresses the social and distributive inequalities in the Lower East Side by mitigating the alienation and separation that arises between church and community.

Chapter 8, "Navigating Property Development through a Framework of Religious Ecology: The Case of Trinity Lutheran Church" by Nadia A. Mian, examines the decision-making process of Trinity Lutheran Church as it considers redeveloping its current property in order to survive. As property values rise, congregations diminish, and funds decrease in New York City, religious institutions are beginning to sell their air rights and property to developers to create multimillion-dollar development deals as a survival strategy. These new, mixed-use spaces generally reserve space for the church, and revenue from the development is set aside for the church. It has been argued that with these new projects, the function of churches is changing – they are becoming too entrepreneurial. Responding to the increasing gentrification of its Upper West Side neighborhood, as well as its own need for a new sanctuary, Trinity must decide whether or not property development would be the best method for serving not only the church but the community as well. Mian finds that religious institutions that create a process to understand their own religious ecology by examining their history, mission, and ministry – as well as cooperation, not competition, with civic and religious community members – are better able to ascertain the needs of their congregation and community. Although Trinity decided not to develop its property, and instead launched a capital campaign to save its building, the circumstances under which the members decided whether to engage in development is based strongly on an understanding of the church's local religious ecology.

The final chapter of the book, "Hinduism at Work in Queens," by Matthew Weiner, examines how the creation of the Hindu Cultural Center (HCC) stems from the secular civic participation of interfaith community religious leader Chan Jamoona. After surveying the needs of an increasingly aging population in Ozone Park, the Hindu Cultural Center was created to provide seniors with a space to engage in activities such as music, yoga, and spirituality. This chapter finds that the HCC, though religious in name, is an example of how civic activism can bridge the gap between faiths, as it has emerged to become a local community center – offering yoga classes and renting out banquet hall space for weddings and conventions.

Through these chapters we hope to elucidate how religious institutions respond to their external environment while mediating social, political, cultural, and economic issues. For the institutions cited in this book, these issues generally come in the form of gentrification, immigration, and entrepreneurialism. The chapters illustrate the complexity of relationships involved in a local religious ecology. Cooperation in the aid and use of resources between organizations can facilitate one's survival, migration can bring in new members, and adaptation can result in a new good or service to a neighborhood. The religious institutions of New York City are woven into an ecological framework that requires their participation to help not only themselves but also the communities they sustain.

NOTES

1. We would like to acknowledge Tony Carnes for this concept.

REFERENCES

Ammerman, Nancy Tatom. 1997. *Congregations and Community.* New Brunswick, NJ: Rutgers University Press.

Ammerman, Nancy T., Jackson Carroll, Carl Dudley, and William McKinney. 1998. *Studying Congregations: A New Handbook.* Nashville: Abingdon Press.

Balmer Randall. 2006. The Pluralist Imperative. In *Religion and Public Life in the Middle Atlantic Region,* eds. Randall Balmer and Mark Silk, 155–163. Walnut Creek, CA: AltaMira Books.

Blokland, Talja, and Mike Savage, eds. 2008. *Networked Urbanism.* Hampshire, UK: Ashgate.

Carnes, Tony. 2001. Religions in the City. In *New York Glory,* ed. Tony Carnes and Anna Karpathakis, 3–24. New York: New York University Press.

———. 2010. Manhattan, New York City – The Silicon Valley of Evangelical Church Planting. Unpublished paper presented at the meeting of the Society for the Scientific Study of Religion, Baltimore, October 29–31.

Carroll, Glenn R. 1984. Organizational Ecology. *Annual Review of Sociology* 10: 71–93.

Demerath, N. J., III, Peter Dobkin Hall, Terry Schmitt, and Rhys H. Williams, eds. 1998. *Sacred Companies: Organizational Aspects of Religion and Religious Aspects of Organizations.* New York: Oxford University Press.

DiMaggio, Paul. 1998. The Relevance of Organization Theory to the Study of Religion. In *Sacred Companies: Organizational Aspects of Religion and Religious Aspects of Organizations,* eds.

N. J. Demerath III, Peter Dobkin Hall, Terry Schmitt, and Rhys H. Williams, 7–23. New York: Oxford University Press.

Eiesland, Nancy L. 2000. *A Particular Place: Urban Restructuring and Religious Ecology in a Southern Exurb.* New Brunswick, NJ: Rutgers University Press.

Eiesland, Nancy, and R. Stephen Warner. 1998. Ecology: Seeing the Congregation in Context. In *Studying Congregations: A New Handbook,* ed. Nancy Ammerman, Jackson Carroll, Carl Dudley, and William McKinney, 40–77. Nashville: Abingdon Press.

Farnsley, Arthur E., II, N. J. Demerath III, Etan Diamond, Mary L. Mapes, and Elfriede Wedam. 2004. *Sacred Circles, Public Squares.* Bloomington: Indiana University Press.

Flanagan, William G. 1993. *Contemporary Urban Sociology.* Cambridge: Cambridge University Press.

Gamm, Gerald. 1999. *Urban Exodus: Why the Jews Left Boston and the Catholics Stayed.* Cambridge, MA: Harvard University Press.

Glaser, Barney, and Anselm Strauss. 1967. *The Discovery of Grounded Theory: Strategies for Qualitative Research.* Chicago: Aldine.

Hannan, Michael T., and John Freeman. 1989. *Organizational Ecology.* Cambridge, MA: Harvard University Press.

Hawley, Amos H. 1950. *Human Ecology: A Theory of Community Structure.* New York: Ronald Press Company.

Herberg, Will. 1983. Protestant, Catholic, Jew: An Essay in American Religious Sociology. Chicago: University of Chicago Press.

Klaff, Vivian Z. 2001. The Religious Demography of New York City. In *New York Glory,* ed. Tony Carnes and Anna Karpathakis, 26–37. New York: New York University Press.

Livezey, Lowell. 2000. *Public Religion and Urban Transformation: Faith in the City.* New York: New York University Press.

Livezey, Lowell W., and Mark Bouman. 2005. Religious Geography. In *Encyclopedia of Chicago,* ed. Janice L. Reiff, Ann Durkin Keating, and James R. Grossman. Chicago Historical Society. http://www.encyclopedia.chicago history.org/pages/1059.html (accessed June 24, 2009).

Lutters, Wayne G., and Mark S. Ackerman. 1996. *An Introduction to the Chicago School of Sociology.* Interval Research Proprietary. http://user pages.umbc.edu/~lutters/pubs/1996 _SWLNote96-1_Lutters,Ackerman .pdf (accessed November 15, 2008).

Martin, David. 2010. Inscribing the General Theory of Secularization and Its Basic Patterns in the Architectural Space/Time of the City. In *Exploring the Postsecular,* ed. Arie L. Molendijk, Justin Beaumont, and Christoph Jedan, 183–205. Leiden, The Netherlands: Brill.

McRoberts, Omar M. 2003. *Streets of Glory: Church and Community in a Black Urban Neighborhood.* Chicago: University of Chicago Press.

Mian, Nadia A. 2008. Profits-for-Prophets: Redevelopment and the Altering Urban Religious Landscape. *Urban Studies* 45(10): 2143–2161.

Park, Robert E., and Ernest W. Burgess. 1984. *The City: Suggestions for Investigation of Human Behavior in the Urban Environment.* Chicago: University of Chicago Press.

Singh, Jitendra V., and Charles J. Lumsden. 1990. Theory and Research in Organizational Ecology. *Annual Review of Sociology* 16: 161–195.

Stout, Harry S., and D. Scott Cormode. 1998. "Institutions and the Story of American Religion: A Sketch of a Synthesis." In *Sacred Companies:*

Organizational Aspects of Religion and Religious Aspects of Organizations, eds. N. J. Demerath III, Peter Dobkin Hall, Terry Schmitt, and Rhys H. Williams, 62–78. New York: Oxford University Press.

Vasishth, Ashwani, and David C. Sloane. 2002. Returning to Ecology: An Ecosystem Approach to Understanding the City. In *From Chicago to LA: Making Sense of Urban Theory*, ed. Michael Dear, 343–366. Thousand Oaks, CA: Sage.

Warner, R. Stephen. 1999. Changes in the Civic Role of Religion. In *Diversity and Its Discontents*, ed. Neil J. Smelser and Jeffrey C. Alexander. Princeton: Princeton University Press.

PART ONE

Religious Institutions and Gentrification in the Religious Ecology

Disneyfication and Religion
in Times Square

Hans E. Tokke

"Look, like it's all about consumerism, everywhere I see. There isn't much about the church here," said Alban Boucher, a member of our research team, as he stood amidst the flashing video screens, crowds of gawking tourists with cameras strobing away, and taxis aggressively jockeying for rides in the center of the global universe of media, technology, fashion, and advertising – Times Square.[1] Boucher grew up in New York City seeing the transformation of Times Square, but like many locals, he was unaware of the urban planning agenda behind the changes. An avid Christian, he was bothered that consumerism had ousted religion from Times Square, or so it seemed.

The influence of consumerism on hyperstimulating urban enclaves such as Times Square is a constant. Religious groups ministering within these environments must adapt and assimilate to these social and cultural changes in order to remain relevant. Often these transitions are predictable and measurable, with new residents replacing longtime tenants. The classic term of gentrification is often applied to the process of new, higher-income residents replacing the poor. However, a different type of gentrification takes place when urban planners deliberately reconfigure a neighborhood for the interest of tourism so as to increase economic activity at the expense of pricing local residents out of the neighborhood. Replacing neighborhood dwellers are transitory tourists staying in the hotels, eating in the restaurants, attending the shows and entertainment venues, and buying merchandise as iconic souvenirs of the trip. Cyclic tourist consumers like this add little in the sense of community ownership and vitality, resulting in the neighborhood becoming a themed environment (Gottdiener 2001) created by corporate interests for the purposes of enticing the consumption and self-intoxication of leisure and entertainment. Siegfried Kracauer, in "The Mass Ornament" ([1929] 2004), imagined this urban enclave of the tourist masses in characterizing "the Hotel Lobby" as a purposeless space, empty of aesthetic and community vitality or connectedness, but full of superfluous and contrived imagery. As Kracauer wrote: "A person can vanish into the undetermined void, helplessly reduced to a 'member of society as such' who stands superfluously off to the side and, when playing, intoxicates himself. This invalidation of togetherness, itself already unreal, thus does not lead up toward reality but is more of a sliding down into the doubly unreal mixture of undifferentiated atoms from which the world of appearance is constructed" (36).

This stands in stark contrast to "the House of God," where, according to Kracauer, "the congregation accomplishes the task of making connections," creating a "collective aesthetic," and constructing a "collective subjective." "In both places people appear there as guests. But whereas the House of God is dedicated to the service of the one whom people have gone there to encounter, the Hotel Lobby accommodates all who go there to meet no one" (36).

Significant problems for religious groups are encountered in this tourist entertainment environment. Churches, synagogues, mosques, temples, and other places of worship built on a social premise of accommodating believers with spiritual meaning and social purpose confront the exodus of congregants who have left the neighborhood. New people on the street visit the congregation as a part of their vacation plans, but have no future connectedness beyond being placed on the mailing list, receiving preaching tapes, sending in a periodic financial gift, and telling idealized stories of "the great church I went to" when they get back to their normal, mundane "church back home." In addition to what has been called the "zoo-tour tourist" congregation,[2] commuter congregants come to receive a boost of spiritual energy to strengthen them throughout the week.

With the value of congregations' real estate increasing due to the influx of hotel chains willing to accommodate tourists and buy out the congregations' facilities, as well as the shift from community to commuter congregants, church leadership is faced with the following choices: sell the property at a profit, relocate to another region of the city and engage a parish approach to mission, or continue on in the same location as a commuter tourist facility. The leaders must grapple with the extent to which compromises can be made in theology and praxis to accommodate commuters and tourists who still come and worship but are disengaged from the community mindset.

This chapter investigates these economic and social ecologies by looking at how two churches located in Times Square were confronted with tourist and consumer-driven gentrification and how they responded to the changes. Originally pioneered in the 1980s era of the economically depressed Times Square, Times Square Church and The Lamb's Manhattan Church of the Nazarene formulated ambitious missions for social justice and care for those in need living on their doorsteps. These churches were successful in their social mission while building middle-class multi-ethnic congregations to support the benevolent work among the poor, disenfranchised, and homeless.

A strong empirical question arises in this milieu. Knowing there was an agenda to change Times Square, what other options were available for the churches? What did the churches' decision-making process look like? In other words, what is the cognitive dimension of ecological adaptation in this case? Following a description of the changes wrought by the pressures of consumerism and commodification and the changes that result, this chapter shows how the two cases chose different cognitive paths though both were founded in an economic decision. These churches did retain their own sense of a theological core that affects their self-understanding of who they are to reach, yet they accommodated (Piaget [1936] 1963) and adapted differently to the changing environment (Ammerman 1997). The financial viability of staying in Times Square was the predominant decision-making factor that affected the response to the ecological changes; the move to Disneyfication wrought by the economic policies of the 42nd Street Improvement District forced the hand of both churches. The only alternative to conforming to the rapid change into a tourist space through renovating their buildings to abide by new heritage criteria demanded by the city was to move completely.

As the chapter reveals, once forced to make a decision based on economics, the churches varied in their response and built theological and sociological justifications in the new reality that would work to keep a connection with the past. One had the financial capability to renovate and stay, and chose to do so, whereas the other church was pushed out of the area so the owner of the building, the Manhattan Initiative, could lease the space for a significant sum and distribute the proceeds to various mission projects including The Lamb's Church. Partial motivators to reengage in another neighborhood were a promise of continuing support from the Manhattan Initiative and the desire for core church folk to continue their work in social justice.

The research method I used for this chapter was ethnographic and was primarily accomplished through participant-observation by the research team in both congregations at various times over a period of four years, combined with interviews of selected congregants and leaders. Several congregational services were attended at both churches. The researchers participated in small-group gatherings, Bible classes, and special events. Informal and formal interviews were completed with former and current congregants from both churches, visitors to Times Square, and both longtime New York residents and tourists.[3]

A BRIEF HISTORY OF NEW YORK AND THE
BATTLE FOR TIMES SQUARE

New York City has jockeyed for decades between being the glorious city or the notorious city. It has a cycle of boom and bust, often linked with fluctuations on Wall Street and their domino effect on the broader urban economy. During the near-bankruptcy of the mid-1970s, the city degraded into a haven for crime and urban decay. Times Square evolved from a center of cultural activity to one of half-empty theaters, drug dealing, the sex trades, and criminal activity. The poor and homeless were drawn to the area. Several social agencies came to Times Square in an effort to care for this new underclass. Religious organizations were part of this evolution, including Times Square Church and The Lamb's Manhattan Church of the Nazarene, featured in this chapter. To many, these were the bad days of Times Square.

New York City urban planners have a long history of redevelopment of neighborhood clusters into specialized economic zones. The Financial District, Fashion District, and Meatpacking District are all expressions of this mode of gentrifying neighborhoods in the interest of specialized industries. Among the recent, and perhaps most public, of these strategies is the redevelopment of Times Square into a tourist spectacle for middle-upper-income families. From an enclave of deteriorating theaters, markets for the drug and sex trade, and poverty-stricken residents, the new Times Square has emerged as a cacophony of consumer culture driven by media, retailing, entertainment, advertising, and marketing. Some have designated this transformation the Disneyfication of Times Square, the Disney Corporation being a foundational investor in creating this themed region formed around the adaptation of its films into live theater.

In 1984 the 42nd Street Development Project was approved by the city and state to create a plan to redevelop the area into a cluster zone for tourism, business, and entertainment. In a sense, this was an effort to bring Times Square back to its "glory years" of the 1920s and '30s, when it was primarily a hotel and entertainment zone for the upper classes. This was given impetus in the 1990s when Mayor Rudy Giuliani instituted a policing policy to obliterate petty street crime in New York City neighborhoods by engaging the broken windows theory (Wilson and Kelling 1982; Kelling and Coles 1996), which holds that where there are broken windows or graffiti there is petty crime, lower incomes, and an urban space in need of redevelopment. Accordingly, police presence was increased in these neighborhoods. The net result of this policy was crime moving underground and out of the city.[4] In the struggle for space, the poorer subcultures lost.

This led to an influx of young professionals into New York City and, simultaneously, mushrooming real estate values, particularly in Manhattan. In fact, the city planner's report on the redevelopment of Times Square promotes a sense that removing street people and homeless to subsidized housing, together with an increase in the number of fully uniformed Business Improvement District (BID) security guards working alongside the NYPD, is improving the neighborhood by providing a safe place for millions of tourists to mingle with businesspeople. More than 1.5 million people travel through Times Square on a given business day. Video screens and public spectacles entrance the masses. Along with this tourist mass, a concurrent immigration of about 15,000 upscale residents into Midtown condominiums have replaced the approximately 5,000 low-income residents who lived there prior to the renovations and rebuilding of the area, in addition to the homeless and other people who were forced out by policing actions. The use of mass media to promote this "positive growth" heightens the perception of the general public that the streets have been "cleaned up" and that the neighborhood is "much better now."

Today, Times Square is considered by city planners to be "the most exciting mixed-use district" in the city. The Department of City Planning (2009) boasts that "within its boundaries are 39 Broadway theaters, 35 hotels offering more than 15,000 rooms, movies showing on almost 40 screens, almost 300 restaurants, and more than 200,000 employees" (6). It is interesting to note that even city planners use entertainment industry and consumer language in their references to development, with little mention of where the poor have been relocated. Attracting a higher-income clientele means there are approximately 17,000 upscale residents who now live in the area, compared to a mere 2,000 who resided there in 1992. The researchers encountered many people whose perception of Times Square was that "it is much better now than before" but had never considered who it was better for or the negative effects on those displaced. This is certainly echoed in the city planner's own report: "Times Square is a unique mix of creativity, commerce, energy, and edge. The district is bustling and bursting with cutting-edge companies, exciting performances and attractions, chic innovative restaurants, and distinctive new retail destinations packed into 33 blocks" (Department of City Planning 2009, 7).

TOURIST GENTRIFICATION AND REDEVELOPMENT

Gentrification is often considered in terms of redevelopment of urban neighborhoods in the interest of increased real estate values, and the outmigration of lower-income residents to be replaced by wealthier socioeconomic classes. While the urban ecological approach is helpful in observing the evolution of such neighborhoods based on rental costs,[5] rental cost changes cannot answer questions about urban ecologies if the properties are converted to tourist zones like Times Square. Observing these changes requires a closer examination of consumer practices and theory.

Promoted by politicians, business leaders, and the upper-class residents accompanying the influx of tourists, gentrification for tourism is viewed as "improvement" and "positive development." There are various reasons provided for this claim. First, the crime rate is reduced with the exodus of lower classes. Second, retail business flourishes with the tourists' purchasing power, and property owners can increase the rental prices on retail business. Third, with wealthier residents moving in, there is a corresponding increase in taxes to fund municipal services. Fourth, renovations change the aesthetic from "dirty and despicable" to "desirable" – at least in the opinion of the newcomers. Legitimate or not, these are some of the public perceptions.

The success of neighborhood redevelopment is often measured in consumer activity and the increase in real estate values, not whether there is an increase in social capital, community activism, or neighborliness. Robert Putnam (2000) believes the latter three elements have been lost in American society, and perhaps this is due to the materialistic consumer culture. Neighborhood development for the purpose of increased consumerism becomes the primary goal and vision of civic leadership as it increases the "public good" of increased tax revenue. In this vein, a U.S. Supreme Court case that originated in New London, Connecticut, has rearranged the rules of how government can force lower-income people off their land in the interest of public benefit.[6] Eminent domain has now become a tool of government to forcibly purchase properties from residents in the interest of retail development. Public benefit is now interpreted as a means to support consumerism through building a shopping mall or other retail venue, not just its traditional meaning of improving public services such as schools, water treatment, or highways.

COMMODIFICATION AND THE DISNEYFICATION OF TIMES SQUARE

Modern American consumer society is driven by market segmentation, wherein each demographic group is defined based on its ability to purchase a particular brand identity or product type. The shopping mall developers recognized this in using Values and Life Styles (VALS) social research to determine the social identity of a suburban enclave that would be the most fruitful location for a mall.[7] Through demographic research of archetypes, the buying behavior of the neighborhood can be predicted and thus can be considered in the design of consumer spaces. The theming of America (Gottdiener 2001), then, is creating spaces that will entice consumption behaviors, or is redeveloping neighborhoods with themes that would tempt individuals and families with the financial means to move into the neighborhood, forcing out those with lower purchasing power. This form of gentrification is driven by the desire to shop.

Thorstein Veblen ([1899] 1992) was concerned that consumers were resorting to purchasing simply for the purpose of display. As Hine (2002, 157) elaborates: "For Veblen, emulation is the key mechanism by which this vicious consumption cycle is driven. One looks to the people at the top, more likely, or to those who slightly outrank you, and seeks to have the same things they do, and something more besides. Your taste in goods is thus determined entirely by people with power and wealth." In laymen's terms, everyone is trying to keep up with the Joneses. For Hannah Arendt, bourgeois society was "the relatively homogeneous community of educated and cultivated persons [who] had always treated culture as a commodity and had gained snob values from its exchange" (quoted in Bell 1976, 45). Consumerism was thus class-oriented behavior. Daniel Bell (1976) adds that consumer behavior evolved with a focus on entertainment. He cites Dwight McDonald, who wrote: "The trick is plain – to please the crowd by any means." "Mass society wants not culture," Bell argues, "but entertainment, and the wares offered by the entertainment industry are indeed consumed by society just as are any other consumer goods" (45). Walt Disney recognized that leisure could be translated into branded consumer behavior. The creation of exclusive theme parks aimed at middle- and upper-middle-class families – vacation venues promoted by the cross-marketing of Disney movies and products – stimulated families to empty their wallets for the cause of a social connection. He understood that by integrating the space with all things Disney and by packaging the family vacation around his films and products, he could entice the consumer to purchase the exclusive Disney brands.[8] Disneyland provided a venue for the family to enjoy its leisure time, enclosing the vacation experience in a confined, defined, and protected space that insured maximum saturation and sales. With an all-inclusive package that required ticketed entrance, the demographic would be limited to those consumers with expendable income. The vacation to the state park was replaced by the vacation to the theme park.

This principle of Disneyfication of space as themed zone is not lost on business improvement districts (BIDS) as they seek to define their market niche and attract targeted demographics. In the redevelopment of Times Square, the Disney Corporation was at the forefront of working alongside New York City urban planners in creating a targeted niche zone for middle- and upper-middle-class tourists. The adaptation of *The Lion King* movie created a new trend of branded productions for Broadway theater. The continued redevelopment of Times Square continues to gratify tourists' consumer tastes. Tucked into this Disneyfication are a few stalwart New York pizza shops, a deli, electronic stores, and the Times Square tourist office.

As mentioned earlier, the gentrification of Times Square was less a specific attempt to increase residential real estate prices as it was a move to increase tourism and corporate business. This makes it a unique instance of gentrification in that the displacement of the poor was based more on realignment of consumer behavior from subculture to mainstream middle and upper-middle class rather than residency migration. What was forced out by the Times Square BID was a subaltern market, to be replaced by a tourist and business market.

CONSUMERISM AND RELIGION

Religion has not been immune to the consumer society. Throughout history, Christianity has struggled to remain authentic in its pursuit of the righteous ideal of caring for the widow, orphan, and sojourner while facing pressures to live within the culture of the market. In modern American culture, individualization of consumerism and the creation of the single-family home has transformed the Christian communal life of faith into an evangelical belief in a "personal relationship with Christ" and individualized faith. Lyons (2000) pictures the postmodern American Christian as immersed in a theme of self. Using the analogy of a church day in Disneyland, he sees that many people function like tourists on a theme ride, investigating church life. They appear to choose their faith much as they choose their clothing labels. People in Times Square, it may be presumed, are affected by similar stimuli in their religious consumption. As researcher Alban Boucher observed: "In order to get some members and to evangelize, churches must use different methods. Some methods might be an imitation or a shadow of the Disneyfication effect. Examples can be videos, colorful tracts, tracts using current events, or sermons using real-life examples."

TWO CASE STUDIES: TIMES SQUARE CHURCH AND THE LAMB'S MANHATTAN CHURCH OF THE NAZARENE

Times Square has mirrored of New York's economy. In the 1980s, with New York City on the brink of bankruptcy and Broadway theater attendance at all-time lows, the neighborhood evolved into a haven for subalterns to live and be entertained. Prostitution, drug dealing, and homelessness were pervasive. The sex entertainment industry was superseding traditional Broadway theater with voyeurism, peep shows, strip clubs, and dance lounges. Within this subculture of poverty and social deviance, two evangelical churches were pioneered to minister to the needs of the people in the neighborhood.

In an interview for the *New York Times* in 1989, founder Rev. David Wilkerson said,

> I was doing evangelical work in Times Square, it was the summer of 1986, right after basketball star Len Bias died. I was walking down 42d Street and people were selling drugs saying, "I've got the stuff that killed Len Bias." It broke me down. Things had reached such a low. I felt something had to be done. . . . People told me no one would go to a church on one of the trashiest blocks in the city.[9]

The Lamb's Church was pioneered in 1975 by the Church of the Nazarene as an urban congregation with a mission to the broad spectrum of people living

FIGURE I.I. Times Square Church.
Photograph courtesy of author.

in Midtown Manhattan. With the goal of reaching both "saints and sinners," a small group of young professionals purchased the former Lamb's Club out of foreclosure.[10] In June 2006 the *New York Times* recalled the fascinating history. The facility housed a

> 140-seat theater on the ground floor and a 360-seat theater on the third floor, which it shares with the church. There are also 22 single-occupancy rooms and 5 apartments. The building was designed by Stanford White and built in 1905; the exterior and some interior portions are protected by landmark status. The six-story building originally housed a fraternal club of theater professionals called the Lamb's, after a similar club in England started by Charles Lamb. Members included Fred Astaire, Mark Twain and Douglas Fairbanks Jr., said Carolyn Rossi Copeland, the Lamb's Theater Company's founding producer. In the 1980's letters were still coming to the theater addressed to John Wayne.[11]

In the initial excitement, the congregation grew to more than eight hundred parishioners – a blend of young professionals, students, and the poor. The

FIGURE 1.2. The Lamb's Theater, where The Lamb's Church was
located, undergoing renovation into a high-end boutique hotel.
Photograph courtesy of author.

church quickly engaged programs that advocated for the poor while creating
a unique ministry of off-Broadway-style positive ethics and values theater.

A 1988 news report on Times Square Church described "its 1,200 seats
[holding] homeless people, prostitutes, AIDS victims and drug addicts all
exchanging handshakes of peace with young professionals and families from
Manhattan, Staten Island and New Jersey."[12] By 2008, its 2,000 seats held
a blend of upper-middle-class professionals, college students, and working-
class people, with a small number of street people. The demographics of the
church have changed coinciding with the gentrification of the neighborhood.
An interesting development over the years has been the increase in "first-
time visitors" to the church. About one hundred regularly come to the post-
worship-service newcomers' fellowship, where refreshments are served, a free
book and tape given out, and meeting of "New Yorkers" takes place. Some are
visitors from local areas, but there certainly are significant numbers of tourists who make a visit to Times Square Church a part of their vacation plans.

Often tour and church groups come en masse to the services. An interesting cultural diversion is seeing Amish visitors from Pennsylvania coming from time to time. The church has worked to adapt its presentation style to include this cultural mosaic.

Times Square Church is still committed to its social justice mission, but the constituency being served is not on its doorstep. The church supports a church-planting venture in impoverished East Harlem; congregants fund and volunteer for the Raven's Ministry, a mobile food kitchen serving the homeless; the Single Mother's Ministry is active in helping those in need; the benevolence ministry provides emergency help to people in crisis; and a variety of international mission groups travel to impoverished nations of the world. The church's website profiles its agenda as "giving aid to the poor, the hungry, the destitute and the addicted. This vision has grown beyond our borders." And Pastor David Wilkerson is quoted on the website as saying, "It is the Holy Ghost who has transformed Times Square Church into a missions-focused church, now taking the gospel to nations worldwide."[13]

Meanwhile, the social justice component of The Lamb's Church, so critical to its self-identity in the formative years in the 1970s and '80s, was lost with the exodus of the poor from the 42nd Street Improvement District. When visiting the facility for the first time in 1993, the researchers found a church actively engaged in a mission to people in need. One of its floors housed the national offices of Here's Life Inner City, the compassionate urban ministry of mega-evangelical parachurch organization Campus Crusade for Christ. The soup kitchen was revered as "one of the best places to eat a meal if you're poor."[14] The disabled were helped through a creative arts program. The homeless shelter next door served a steady stream of people in need. However, all that changed with the gentrification of Times Square into hotel and entertainment space.

Here's Life Inner City moved out in 1999. In the ensuing years the facility went into disrepair, made apparent by peeling paint, unkempt rooms, old furnishings, and unused space. The Lamb's Theater itself was well preserved thanks to renovations. However, with a shrinking congregation, and little hope of a resurgence in neighborhood residents coming to the church due to the influx of hotel space, the death of the church was imminent.[15] Writing in the Nazarene blog NazNet in October 2005, Dave McClung, board member of the Manhattan Initiative, which administered the leases of the building in Times Square, described for his constituency the situation at The Lamb's Church of the Nazarene: "Many people still think of the Lamb's Club as a soup kitchen. It really hasn't had that kind of ministry in a long time. If you haven't visited Times Square since the early days of the Lamb's, you will be surprised. That area has become affluent. There really hasn't been a need for the soup kitchen kind of ministry for some time." The Lamb's Church facility never had the significant outside funding sources that Times Square Church had, and it could not compete with the upsurge in renovations in Times Square. McClung further stated in 2005: "The building has reached the point that if the hotel deal doesn't go through, Nazarenes will be faced with raising a lot of money to upgrade the building. We basically own a very old, run-down building on a very valuable piece of property."[16]

Former pastor Rev. Dr. John Bowen, now executive director of the Manhattan Initiative, which manages the endowment funds from leasing the property to a hotel, stated the obvious: "The dynamics of poor people in this city have changed. We are going to be relevant. We are going where the need is." Ironically, with the moving of The Lamb's Church to the Lower East Side, the proceeds from the lease are actively funding social justice ministries in this neighborhood – true to the mission of the Church of the Nazarene generally, and to the new vision of Pastor Gabriel Salguero and The Lamb's Church specifically. However, the funds expected to be received from the Manhattan Initiative, which negotiated the deal to lease to the hotel, are not nearly what may have been expected and can in no way fully fund the operations of The Lamb's Church's new social justice mission. Much of the funding, it appears, goes to mission projects outside New York City and to the broader Nazarene mission.

THEATER CHURCHES

Times Square Church "was originally connected to the Town Hall of New York and later shifted its base to the Nederlander Theatre. However, since 1989, it has occupied the Mark Hellinger Theatre as its base, earlier known as the Hollywood Theatre."[17] After the facility was designated a landmark for both its interior and exterior qualities, city planning required restoration of the facility to much of its original 1930s glory. Upon entering the theater, one is struck by its beauty, the soaring lobby staircase, and neoclassical architectural details. In the circular lobby, festooned with classical lighting and brass fixtures, one can purchase books, CDs, and other consumer products created by the church. Following the services, there is often a long line up to the cashier as congregants supply themselves with their spiritual goods.

The auditorium is centered on an extravagant original crystal chandelier, with ceiling paintings of angels gazing down on those below. The deep cushioned theater seats are crimson velvet, with ornate wood finishes. The platform has been reconfigured into a somewhat typical church stage with pulpit, choir seating, space for musicians, and pastoral chairs, but retains its theater tradition with thick curtains that are drawn to the ceiling at the beginning of the service, and an array of theater lighting. Professional digital audio amplifies the music and preaching in pristine sound quality, and large video screens project both words and live pictures of the people on the stage. Although there are supplementary rooms in Times Square Church, the meetings held in the main auditorium are primary to the church's mission. The ushers wear noticeable chic gold-colored blazers to stand out from the crowd, evoking the theater theme.

Other elements of the church building include an office suite with pastor quarters resembling something between a corporate office and an upscale living room. A fellowship hall seating three hundred, wired with full digital audio and large-screen video, doubles as an overflow room during Sunday services. A Christian education wing has classrooms for children to go to during the services with secure and well-trained staff and volunteers. What is interesting is that children are not welcome to sit in the main auditorium during services. The researchers/participant observers were asked to take their children to the Christian education wing.

Yet even with this spectacular renovation of the largest theater on Broadway, Times Square Church did not host any theatrical events. Its conservative theological position put it at odds with the theater industry, suggesting that Broadway was the home of promiscuity and debauchery. This notion, of course, could no longer be supported as easily with the Disneyfication of Broadway and the displacement of racy shows by more family-friendly fare. In more recent years, Times Square Church has presented some drama and music productions, but not with the glitz, glamour, or production values of Disney Broadway.[18] During the renovation, urban developers and city officials pressured the church to sell the airspace above the auditorium for a hotel to be constructed while leaving the historic structure intact, along with giving up the baptismal tank because the space was needed for construction. It was announced from the pulpit during Sunday morning worship services that the church was resisting this pressure because construction projects would interrupt church operations. This is in contrast to The Lamb's Church, which embraced the real estate windfall.

MEDIA, MUSIC, AND SPECTACLE

The Times Square Church service is a spectacle of modern fundamentalist evangelicalism. The worship band is professional, and the choir is drawn from various New York communities. Several of the musicians are professionals. The preaching is always loud and charismatic with a strong appeal for congregants to redeem their lives and come to the altar at the front of the stage for special prayer by elders of the church. This has been a distinctive tradition of Times Square Church since its inception, as a fundamentalist charismatic nondenominational church. The lighting, sound, theater facility, music, media, and preaching blend into a concoction of evangelical spectacle that appeals to individual transcendence. It plays to a theme of contrived spectacle that is attractive to its adherents and to visitors. To attendees, there is great spiritual meaning to the style and rituals. It must be made clear that there was never a "seeker-sensitive" message to the unevangelized,[19] but rather a strong, almost hellfire-and-brimstone approach in which the church sets itself as against consumer society as it claims it is "not like the other churches."[20]

The Lamb's Manhattan Church of the Nazarene stood in contrast to the spectacle of Times Square Church. Where Times Square Church displayed megachurch Broadway, The Lamb's reflected Off Broadway aesthetics. Though held as well in a theater, The Lamb's Church's worship style was more sedate, and it's preaching more theological, bordering on intellectual. This was well accepted by the congregants, but there were few, if any, homeless people in the service during the period of this research. The congregation was a mix of middle-aged whites, college age or young professionals, some theater professionals and interns connected with the in-house theater outreach, and a growing group of Hispanics attracted to the young exuberant, charismatic, yet intellectual Pastor Gabriel Salguero. The biggest difference, of course, was in its size compared to that of Times Square Church around the corner. There were about 60 attendees on average in the service. This was down even from the time when the facility went into a partnership agreement in 1999 with a hotelier for redevelopment of the site. At that time 100 to 250 people attended the church. Although held in a former Broadway supper club/theater, the church services felt traditional. There was not the intentionally themed style that could be felt at Times Square Church. In fact, The Lamb's service was quaint and out of place in the spectacle of the new Times Square.

SALES AND MARKETING

Pastor David Wilkerson pioneered the Teen Challenge ministry in the 1960s to reach the gang members and street people of Brooklyn, and wrote a best-selling book, *The Cross and the Switchblade*, which detailed his work among the Mau Mau gang, and specifically the "saving" of leader Nicky Cruz. The book was subsequently turned into a movie popular among evangelicals in the 1970s. In this same vein, Times Square Church based its original mission on "saving New York" from the Babylon of urban decay. This commitment was evoked in sermons and in the narrative of Senior Pastor David Wilkerson's prophetic "call from God" to come back to New York to save it from degradation and destruction. With a significant financial support base from book sales and donors to his preaching ministry, Wilkerson was able to quickly draw congregants. Book sales, the pulpit series, and fund-raising from the international mailing list and other projects will keep Times Square Church well funded for years to come. From a church of social justice, it has become a consumer commuter church with associated ministries to the poor as attachments to its core agenda of preaching and worship music.

In contrast, The Lamb's Church did not make reasonable use of media, websites, radio programming book sales, or any of the consumerist attachments associated with many modern evangelical churches.

DISNEYFIED CHURCHES AND GOD'S HOUSE

Consumerism and Disneyfication have forced the churches in Times Square to revisit and revise their religious ideals. Lyons (2000), referring to the theories of Zygmunt Bauman and Manuel Castells, argues that in the postmodern era, religious practice is taking individualistic form. People choose what to believe and follow, rather than committing to a specific denominational or religious dogma inherited from family or social culture. Consumer society, with its powerful stimuli and vast choice, even in a hyperconsumerist environment like Times Square, may in fact encourage religious practice. People find, in the impersonality of choice, their own choice. As Lyons explains:

> Unlimited consumer choice and a variety of tastes integrate everyone into a
> spending utopia. . . . Bauman suggests that hyperconsumerism might be a
> cause of religious revival. In everyday life, people are obliged more and more
> to choose between alternatives, political and moral, as well as between com-

monalties at the mall. Yet at the same time they are deprived of the universal guidance that modern self-confidence once promised . . . fundamentalism is seen by Bauman not as an atavistic throwback but as a postmodern response to choice overload. (40)

Without doubt, Times Square Church is a Disneyesque themed religious space. Everything – book sales, music, preaching, media, mission projects, and environment – is focused on the Times Square Church theme and the ministry of Rev. David Wilkerson. There is little, if any, product placement of other ministries within the confines of the church's ministry. Whether there is a mistrust of other denominations is questionable, though there were periodic critiques from the pulpit of "other Christians" and the decline of "the rest of America."

The worship space evokes Kracauer's House of God, with people meeting for common purpose, though for many adherents and tourist visitors it remains an individualistic transcendent experience with little connection to other people in the church. The researchers did notice a significant number of attendees saving seats for the worship services, with several congregants arriving one to one and a half hours prior to reserve seats for themselves, friends, and family. This created a culture of in-groups and out-groups. Longtime attendees had devoted and intentional relationships with one another to the point of exclusivity. One researcher who deliberately sat in some of these sections to observe noticed several people conversing among themselves, not engaging others around them. Although there was a general greeting, even hugging, as a part of the church ritual during the service, this did not appear to lead to many further relationships following the service, as many people left immediately after the service ended.

In becoming a metro megachurch, Times Square Church has responded to urban mobility and anonymity. The church's investment in free parking for service attendees[21] and the youth ministry's evangelistic campaigns on the subway recognize the reality of urban mobility. From its founding a segment of attendees have commuted from the outer boroughs. As the neighborhood has gentrified into a tourist zone, a larger percentage of the congregation have become commuters. Observing the parking lot at the corner of 52nd Street and 8th Avenue on several Sunday mornings from approximately 12 to 1 PM from 2002 through 2005, the researchers met several congregants who commuted on Sunday from New Jersey and Long Island. In fact, a survey of license plates in the free parking areas after Sunday morning services revealed a large number of New Jersey plates. This makes Times Square a commuting and consumer church. With congregants filling all seats for most services, special seats in prime locations are held for visitors, first-timers, and tourists. They are demarcated with yellow cushion covers, with ushers dressed in uniform blazers escorting them to their seats. They are asked to stand during a service for a special greeting from the pastor and presented with a small gift packet. Following the service, visitors are invited to a special meet-and-greet reception with the pastors and their support staff. Guests are given a book and refreshments and are often entered on mailing lists for future correspondence and mailings.

Tourist churches host transient people who come for a momentary look at the spectacle, get on the mailing lists, and may become repeat visitors via podcasts, webcasts, or published sermons. Times Square Church made an effort to accommodate this reality through its media services and the Times Square Pulpit series, a member program for visitors to continue to receive recordings of the sermons "back home" and, it would seem the church hoped, send in a reciprocal donation. A tourist website claimed that "Times Square Church is among the most popular New York City tourist sites."[22] This statement was reflected in the attitude of some attendees. Many came to view the church or to attend a service because they had heard of David Wilkerson or had read his book *The Cross and the Switchblade*. Indeed, one researcher met many visitors over the four-year period of this project who came from out of town and "wanted to see Times Square Church" (note the tourist-oriented language). In an overstatement of what tourists may actually say, the church website claims, "Visitors are often led to exclaim, 'This is what heaven will be like!' when they see this great multitude of people worshiping together under one roof." Many may have come and enjoyed this diversity, but from the perspective of the visitors accompanying the researcher, most commented on the music, preaching, video screens, and beautiful theater – all Disneyfication elements in the themed space – not the "heavenlike" qualities of the congregation. But it could be said that the multicultural congregation supports this theme, with many people from many countries who are seen as visitors to America.

It is interesting that the success of Times Square Church lies partly in the distinctive fundamentalist-evangelical rhetoric that sets it apart from the world around it. The pulpit remains as the church's preeminent focal point. What is attractive about the church is not the intentional relationships people make – though some have noted that "their friends are there" – but the "prophetic Word from Pastor Dave" and the other pastors, as one congregant said in an informal lunch interview. Indeed, there was a sense that the pulpit minister had an insider view of what "God is saying" that must be listened to, revered, processed, and followed.[23] The ministers consistently evoked a mystical sense that they had a "special Word" from God that "came" when they were in prayer. This was a consistent pattern with Rev. Wilkerson, implying that he somehow had an insider perspective on the Bible that no one else had. One congregant said over dinner, "I believe Pastor Dave is a modern day prophet!" In a postmodern world in which mixed and confusing media messages attempt to make one product distinct from another, Times Square Church's method and themed environment is appealing and convincing to many.

Conversely, The Lamb's Church experience during the process of redevelopment was one of continued loss of spiritual and social significance in Times Square. In an interview on this era, Pastor Salguero said:

> There were multiple factors [that led to the change in location], and that decision was made before my arrival to the church. I know there were economic reasons. There were also changes in the context of Times Square. In the past Times Square was a very different place, and it was in this place The Lamb's was situated. Gentrification [happened] and the cost of living went up. Communities were pushed out; the context changed.

There was no significant means, or funds, to adapt the church's approach to appeal to the hyperconsumerism of Times Square, or even the desire to do so. The executive of the Manhattan Initiative recognized the opportunity to use the gentrification it could not combat to financial advantage to support The Lamb's Church and other Nazarene ministries and programs.[24] The property was leased at a high market value to hotel developer Vikram Chatwal for the development of a high-end boutique hotel. The Haute Living website states that: "The Chatwal will be a 7-Star hotel located on 44th Street. It is designed to salute the New York City 'baby grand' hotels of a bygone era. . . . This is a great, unique building,' Chatwal boasts. 'It's not to be found anywhere else on the island.'"[25] The Lamb's Church reacted to increasing real estate values by relocating to the Lower East Side, even though it was at the behest of the Manhattan Initiative. According to the church website, under new pastor Rev. Gabriel Salguero's re-envisioning, the new Lamb's Church is a "multicultural, multi-class, multi-generational urban congregation committed to developing Christian leadership and ministry that transforms individuals, culture, and communities through worship, education, compassionate ministry and community development."[26]

THE FUTURE AFTER GENTRIFICATION

The Lamb's Church continues to rediscover itself in its new location on Manhattan's Lower East Side. On the one hand, it has embraced the metro commuter model, with small groups meeting in several locations in the city during the week and then worshipping together as commuter Christians on Sunday. This recognizes the realities of urban mobility that people search for community and belonging in enclaves that cannot be forced into one location. Ethan Watters (2003) defines such communities as urban tribes, as the cosmopolitans embrace mobility and independence, but then find belonging with groups of friends. Retaining the sense of mobility in concert with community is critical to the ongoing success of the ministry. Whether consumerism appeals to theological values or not, it is here to stay and will continue to affect the postmodern congregation currently driving the replanting of the church downtown. The Lamb's Church continues, however, with its commitment to the local community. With retention of the Gifted Hands outreach and consistent preaching and teaching about social justice and compassionate ministry in its new location, The Lamb's will continue doing what it has always done as a Church of the Nazarene in the areas of social justice advocacy. By building a multicultural pastoral team, Salguero is drawing from the concept of incarnational mission (Perkins 1995), using a "plethora of sources" to address the evolving diversity and other urban changes in the city. In a formal interview with researcher Joseph Terry, he stated:

> The church intentionally meets the missional needs of being a church in
> lower Manhattan . . . with all the diversity it includes (cultural, generational,
> economic, language, etc.). "Diversity" is a big word for me. Our challenge is
> to transform culture. I think that every church must speak to every culture
> it is situated in, in its time. We practice incarnational and contextual minis-
> try/mission. This is one of our major motifs. We are living out [cosmopoli-
> tan] Christianity in the city – called to live in the city and the Kingdom: this
> dialectic tension is lived out.

Visits since the Times Square relocation affirmed this mission. There was numerical growth with a particular emphasis on college students, young adults, Hispanics, and Asian groups in nearby Chinatown. Pastor Salguero with the support of his congregation has been significantly engaged on the national scene advocating for immigration reform, placing The Lamb's Church in the unique position of being both local and national in its reach. These developments support the concept that congregations do change and adapt their methods according to the cultural changes that surround them. However, The Lamb's Church has not changed the core theological principles that drove it at the Times Square location, of being activists for social justice and a multicultural mission.

LIMITED OPTIONS

The question that remains with The Lamb's Church is what were its other options? The church could have been disbanded, leaving the fifty or so congregants who remained to find new church homes. A fund drive to renovate the building and support the theater program and an already functioning fine arts university center could have been established. Parts of the building could have been leased, while retaining the church in the current location and using proceeds from the individual leases to operate the church. The facility could have been sold outright, with the proceeds funding the building of a new facility in another location. This is similar to what took place with the long-term lease agreement. What is important to note is that remaining was not an option, since the church was forced by New York City planners to renovate the building to comply with new building codes. This practice of forced renovation continues in other regions of business improvement districts such as Harlem.[27]

According to Pastor Salguero, The Lamb's had to move for two major reasons. First, it was too expensive to continue, and the congregation had been dwindling since its heyday in the 1980s and early '90s. "We had to renovate" Salguero said. "The church could not support itself and was depending on rental fees from partners in the building such as The Lamb's Theater Group, Here's Life Inner City, among others." It had no significant outside funding to draw from, unlike the Times Square Church supported by David Wilkerson's financial support network. Second, the community had changed, and there was no way to continue with the compassionate mission, though the shelter remained next door.

COGNITIVE RESPONSE TO DISNEYFICATION

Jean Piaget, in his theories of assimilation and accommodation ([1936] 1963), argued that assimilation replaces previous cognitive responses with newly constructed responses. As environments change, people adapt and accept something new from their environment that changes their thinking about it.

Accommodation is accepting something from the environment. "Intelligence is an adaptation. . . . To say that intelligence is a particular instance of biological adaptation is thus to suppose that it is essentially an organization and that its function is to structure the universe just as the organism structures its immediate environment" (Piaget [1936] 1963, 3–4). People thus move from one view of thinking about the world to another. No one is inherently immune from the influences around them. "Assimilation can never be pure because by incorporating new elements into its earlier schemata the intelligence constantly modifies the latter in order to adjust them to new elements" (6–7).

This type of cognition is significant in the decision making that affected the way the churches reacted to the coercive actions of New York City planners in the push to change Times Square from what it was into an upper-middle-class family-friendly tourist zone. As Piaget explained, people change under altered environments. In this way, the leaders in the churches were forced into a new reality, irrespective of their previous views and desires to stay in Times Square, and accepted the fact of change. The independent variable was the coercion of the city planners in forcing change irrespective of the views and ministry of the churches already located there to do their work among the poor and disenfranchised. As Bronkema (2010) states:

> It seems to me a classic case of being driven to change by resources, and understanding how people see those situations and the changes they are forced to make in light of their religion and beliefs: How do they understand the situation they are placed in within the framework of their religious beliefs (is God acting through the BID policies?), and how did their religious thinking, or not, enter into informing the limits that are placed on them? How did the people in the different churches understand their position in terms of the resources available to them, and how did the access to, or lack of, resources, drive their thinking around the strategies they decided to adopt?

Thinking along these lines, in terms of resources being the independent variable that forced the decision-making process, the cognitive logic, then, may be:

1. Coercion
   New York City's 42nd Street Development District forces a change due to its BID policies that required the renovation of the churches' facilities to meet the new historical landmark building codes.
2. Reaction to compliance
   Both churches are compelled to react in order to comply with the orders.

3. Leadership assessment

   Both leadership groups assess their ability to react to the BID requirements based on financial capability to afford the renovations in order to comply with the order.

4. Cost analysis

   a. Times Square Church has money and people.

   b. The Lambs Church does not have these resources and the congregation is dwindling in numbers. The Manhattan Initiative, which owns the property, is to make the business decision on the property.

5. Investment and relocation

   a. Times Square Church invests in its facility in order to remain where it is as a voice in the district and to the world.

   b. The Lamb's does not have the money to renovate, and the Manhattan Initiative writes a lease contract to ensure the best possible financial outcome on behalf of the Church of the Nazarene denomination and The Lamb's Church.

6. Assimilation and accommodation

   Justification for the move is made by the churches in the way they assimilate and accommodate the new reality (Piaget [1936] 1963).

   a. Times Square Church adapts to the renovations with a pseudo-theater look. Though returning the Mark Hellinger Theater to its former glory, it remains firmly rooted as a fundamentalist charismatic multicultural church. The church remains committed to social justice and the poor through purchasing and maintaining food vans to travel to poorer neighborhoods to feed the homeless, and creating an international mission with a strong community development angle framed by evangelistic crusades. The external adaptation of the facility assimilates well into the new Times Square culture, and the church accommodates the tourist visitors. The church continues on with its fundamental charismatic evangelicalism, continuing its fire-and-brimstone message even in light of a media-savvy, secular world outside its doors. It remains true to founder David Wilkerson's theological interpretation of being in the midst of "Babylon," though the evil "New Babylon" has a different set of clothing in the form of media, Disneyfication, entertainment, and consumerism. It is

important to note that Times Square Church does not adopt a
seeker-sensitive consumer-driven mantra like that of other megachurches such as Willow Creek or Saddleback.

b. The Lamb's works through several choices, knowing none are really viable as the church cannot raise the funds to renovate the
building. Some untenable options (such as a small worship space
in the new hotel) are floated, but they would make it impossible
for The Lamb's to continue where it is. The leaders choose to
continue the congregation rather than disband, as they are committed to their church and the cause. The opportunity to move to
the Lower East Side and join forces with a Chinese and Hispanic
congregation, taking in their pastors, becomes the best model.
This is the accommodation of Piaget. The Manhattan Initiative
"justifies" forcing out The Lamb's through some ongoing support
for the Chinese congregation, though the support is nowhere
near the money being made for the broader Nazarene mission
or perhaps what The Lamb's old-timers expected. The justification for the Manhattan Initiative is that it is helping more people
around the world and in other places in the United States with
the $30,000 from the monthly lease than it would be by support-
ing the small work of The Lamb's.

7. Religious and Theological Justification

a. Times Square Church remains a voice within Times Square
consumer culture, speaking out against its evils while accommodating those coming from that environment through theatrical appearances. The church continues its international missions with social justice works to complement the evangelistic
crusades.

b. The Lamb's Church in the Lower East Side frames itself as a
cosmopolitan congregation defined by its crossover Chinese,
Hispanic, and white and inclusive class and age ministry for all
of God's people. It is active in neighborhood social justice. The
Manhattan Initiative frames itself as utilitarian in helping the
greater good of the Nazarene ministry outside of New York City
while continuing nominal support for The Lamb's to ensure it is
not seen as abandoning the original congregants who made their
income possible.

EPILOGUE

At this writing, the Manhattan Initiative continues to support The Lamb's Church by paying the salary of a half-time assistant pastor (the Chinese pastor) and some of the utility costs. This is out of a $30,000 per month lease fee it receives from the hotel tenant. Pastor Salguero did not know where the rest of the money was going but assumed it was to other Nazarene work nationally and possibly internationally. Nevertheless, there is very minimal ongoing support for The Lamb's. The expectation at the time of relocation that the former site would fund the newer site never materialized to the degree that was expected.

The current church has three pastors now under the lead pastor, Gabriel Salguero. In the church's new, more cosmopolitan self-definition, its leaders aim to be committed simultaneously to social justice and advocacy, multicultural and multi-ethnic ministry, and cross-socioeconomic and -age inclusivity. Salguero does not see The Lamb's as a melting pot, though it may appear that way to outsiders, but as a set of separate streams that work together to get along under the same spiritual umbrella. He has accepted the fact that the varied groups may not all weld themselves to one another but choose to culturally separate and define worship in unique ways. He says, "I could choose to bring in my Princeton University lingo, wear a cool jacket, and appeal to all the upper-middle-class college types who are moving into our neighborhood and are drawn to a church with an element of social justice, but it would be Christianity on their terms. But we are now in this neighborhood with a homeless shelter next door, low-income housing across the street, a high condo tower going up right nearby, and Chinatown on our doorstep." So The Lamb's Church remains strong and faithful to its social justice theme, but continues to work out a sociological context that is ever evolving and changing irrespective of the church's vision. Having brought in struggling ethnic congregations that had not worked at addressing the changes in the neighborhood, they may be stronger as a "salad bowl church" as Salguero describes them, but time will tell.

Alicia Wu, a congregation member, elaborates on the new Lamb's Church:

> For a church whose vision involves the words "multicultural," "multigeneration," and "multiclass," The Lamb's is certainly progressing in its venture to be a community that brings individuals and families together. Having the privilege and honor of being a part of this and watching it unfold in the past

year and a half has been tremendous and definitely impacted me in ways
I would have never imagined. To be a part of something that goes beyond
myself that is all about building bridges that are cultural, communal, and
societal, filling in gaps, and making a difference is so rewarding.

Reverend Wilkerson has since passed away,[28] and Reverend Carter
Conan has assumed the leadership of the church. This has not meant any
dramatic change at Times Square Church, as it continues on at this writing, successfully appealing to tourist churchgoers and city commuters alike.
Through its programming, the leadership continues to retain a commitment
to helping the poor, but with dwindling numbers of poor folk, the church will
most certainly evolve with the urban ecology of Times Square. It remains
committed to caring for the poor, but the compassionate ministries are pro-
gressively becoming international in scope through mission trips. Most recent
on-site visits to worship services bear this out. Global missions are more typically highlighted and promoted than local outreach. Times Square Church is
also evolving with the changes in New York as an immigrant city. The most
recent pastoral appointments are visible minorities (black and Hispanic). The
church is a magnet for minority populations, with many beginning to achieve
the elusive American Dream through middle-class incomes.

CONCLUSION

Both churches that originally ministered to residents in Times Square have
adapted to the broader influx of people in the city and to the changes in Times
Square, but with radically different outcomes. They recognized this transient
quality of urban life, magnified most by tourists, and are moving with cultural
changes rather than rejecting the mobility of consumer society that drives
them. This confirms Ammerman's earlier work (1997) showing that congregations do adapt to changing environments. However, it also demonstrates that
churches that adapt their cultural or social elements are not so keen to adapt
their message or theology to meet prevailing trends. Rather, they reframe
their social work within a consistent theological structure. Deeply engrained
religious rules are not simple to change or as adaptable as the external appearances or social application of the theology. Both churches have retained strong
segments of what they were prior to the push from New York City planners.
Thus, congregations such as these simultaneously adapt and retain elements
of what they claim to be – socially and theologically, as well as in their use of
physical space.

ACKNOWLEDGMENTS

The author wishes to thank Alban Boucher, Jerrel Burney, and Joseph Terry, who provided research observations, and Charles Bloch, and Jeff Beckmyer for editing and commentary. Partial funding for this research was provided through Noel and Phyllis Walker of the Alder Foundation.

NOTES

1. This was six months prior to the institution of traffic-calming measures in Times Square that changed Broadway from an arterial route into a European-style mall, pedestrian walkway, and café seating area. This further reconfigured Times Square into a tourist zone.

2. A colloquialism used by New York City urban tour guides when speaking about tourist groups coming to see the city sights, particularly in the inner city. One can buy a special bus tour to visit the church sites in black Harlem and its classic churches and gospel choirs. One congregant from Abyssinian Baptist Church, for example, noted that the congregation expects "tourist tithes" to enhance its budget.

3. A formal interview was given by Pastor Gabriel Salguero of The Lamb's Church, as well as a written presentation of the church's mission, vision, and future plans. No pastor or official from Times Square Church was formally interviewed, possibly due to the church's tightly controlled image. Much of the historical information on the church's development was gleaned from documents and conversations with longtime congregants and external sources.

4. Satellite cities received this influx of the poor. Yonkers, New Rochelle, Haverstraw, and Newburgh, New York – all within seventy-five miles of the city – have seen marked increases in depressed real estate values, criminal activity, and in-migration of poverty. Although difficult to document, continued poverty in nearby cities such as Bridgeport, Connecticut; Elizabeth and Camden, New Jersey; and Allentown and parts of southeastern Pennsylvania may be related to Giuliani policies.

5. For example, in an urban area like New York City where more people rent than own, the poor qualify for Section 8 subsidized housing based on income, whereas the wealthy can afford to rent in upscale neighborhoods. The working and middle classes are being forced out of the city due to housing costs. See Sassen (2002).

6. *Susette Kelo et al. v. City of New London, Connecticut, et al.* The governmental taking of property from one private owner to give to another in furtherance of economic development constitutes a permissible "public use" under the Fifth Amendment (affirmed by Supreme Court of Connecticut; argued before U.S. Supreme Court February 22, 2005; decided June 23, 2005).

7. Values and Life Styles (VALS) social research created nine archetypes of consumer behavior, including "Survivors" (no money), "Strivers" (middle-class individuals who want to appear wealthy), and "Innovators" (people at the top who can spend how they wish). Arnold Mitchell, *US Framework and VALS Types* (Innovators, Thinkers, Believers, Achievers, Strivers, Experiencers, Makers, Survivors), http://www.strategicbusinessinsights.com/vals/ustypes.shtml (accessed May 5, 2012).

8. James Farrell (2003) elucidates "lessons" of what made Disney so successful in generating consumerism: (1) positive effects and planning; (2) theming; (3) cineplexity (i.e., the visit plays out like a show with character actors, sets, and props); (4) imaginative fiction (the space inspires you imagine ideals that do not exist in reality); (5) sensual stimulation through sights, smells, and sounds; (6) family values and entertainment; (7) narrative of nostalgia and hope, looking at the past and the future; (8) infantilization (space for the inner child to be expressed for old and young alike); (9) value of vacation; (10) power of souvenirs to sustain positive memories of the vacation in the ordinary world; (11) brand identity and cross-promotion.

9. "A Times Square Church Gathers Rave Reviews," *New York Times*, Sunday, November 6, 1988.

10. Greg Sargent, "New Hotel Threatens Lovely Lambs Theater," *New York Observer*, http://www.observer.com/1999/10/new-hotel-threatens-lovely-lambs-theatre (accessed October 17, 1999).

11. Monte Williams, "Midtown Soup Kitchen Serves Its Last," *New York Times*, March 31, 2001, http://www.nytimes.com/2001/03/31/nyregion/midtown-soup-kitchen-serves-its-last.html (accessed April 29, 2012).

12. "A Times Square Church Gathers Rave Reviews."

13. http://www.tscnyc.org/our-mission.php.

14. Comment of a homeless person who came to eat at The Lamb's.

15. A *New York Times* article in 2001 described the closing of the infamous soup kitchen that had been a New York fixture since the founding of the church: "Despite colorful streamers and balloons, and simple white vases holding red and white flowers, this was hardly a celebration. The Lamb's Manhattan Church of the Nazarene was serving the last meal from its soup kitchen yesterday. About 70 men and women – all of them poor, many of them homeless and most of them forlorn – turned out for the last of what regulars called the best free meal in town. The neighborhood around the soup kitchen at 130 West 44th Street – once home to the disenfranchised, the sex industry and seedy bars – is now a precinct of entertainment Goliaths, publishing titans and trendy restaurants. The homeless have been pushed elsewhere – part of the city's effort to clean up Times Square." (Suzanne DeChillo, *New York Times*, March 31, 2001.

16. McClung went on to reflect on the policing policies post-9/11 that have significantly increased the pace of tourist gentrification in Times Square: "The building is full of activity every day. There are a wide variety of ministries; however, many of the activities that have been there in the past have had to leave because of restrictions by the city. Since 9/11, the building codes have been enforced at a higher level" (NAZ NET, accessed June 17, 2006).

17. "Times Square Church," Maps of World, http://www.mapsofworld.com/cities/usa/new-york-city/times-square-church.html.

18. In contrast to Times Square Church, throughout its history The Lamb's Church was a pioneer in the collaboration of theater and Christian mission. The Lamb's Club space was renovated into a cozy Off Broadway theater venue and was the home of several well-received Broadway shows.

19. "Seeker sensitive" is a term attributed to a movement of evangelical churches that deliberately incorporate popular cultural and social elements into their services with sermons and music that appeal to a general public and challenge nonbelievers to investigate Christian

faith. It is the antithesis of hard-line evangelistic approaches.

20. This tone of framing Times Square Church as an outsider to the Christian mainstream was a regular message from the pulpit, particularly when Rev. David Wilkerson preached. There was a regular sense that the pastors of Times Square Church had a "special message from God" that others may not have. An interview respondent ratified this tone in saying he believed there was a special prophetic message for him.

21. Sheller & Urry (2000) assert: "Urbanization and automobilization are together characteristic of modernity and of the culture of cities. Meeting places require that people get to them . . . the auto-freedom of movement is part of what can constitute democratic life." To gain free parking, deals were made with local parking garages within a few blocks of the church to provide reduced-fee parking at times when the lots would have down times. Following services, attendees can have their parking tickets stamped and receive parking rates from free to five dollars. Here Times Square Church has overcome the pressures of mobility that drive urbanites into dependence on their cars.

22. http://www.mapsofworld.com /cities/usa/new-york-city/times-square -church.html.

23. In a meeting, the researcher noted that Pastor Neil Rhodes could remember the general content and titles of Rev. Wilkerson's several sermons.

24. "The Lamb's Church has been re-located to another building owned by its denomination's district on the Lower East Side of Manhattan. The proceeds from the hotel transaction will be used to assist the Lamb's Church in its future development, as well as to establish new church plants in Metro New York." John Bowen, "Lamb's Manhattan Church of the Nazarene moves to Lower East Side," NCN (Nazarene Communications Network) News, February 2, 2007, http://www .ncnnews.com/nphweb/media/umedia /HQI/NCN/enews_archive/old/gnews0705 .html (accessed March 17, 2012).

25. Jeremy Lissek, "Sant Chatwel Is Hautel Living a Dream," *Haute Living Magazine*, September 9, 2008, http:// www.hauteliving.com/2008/09/sant -chatwel-is-hautel-living-a-dream/ (accessed April 29, 2012).

26. http://www.lambschurch.org /ministries.html.

27. The designation of West Park Presbyterian Church in Manhattan "as a historical landmark was upheld in May, preventing the church from tearing down part of the building to develop the site . . . it will cost [the] dwindling congregation $11 to $12 million to restore the building." *Christianity Today*, July 2010, http:// www.christianitytoday.com/ct/2010 /july/15.8.html?start=2, quoting Robin Pogrebin, "City Council Upholds Landmark Status of West Side Church," *New York Times*, May 12, 2010.

28. Margalit Fox, "Rev. David Wilkerson Dies at 79; Started Times Square Church," *New York Times*, April 28, 2011, http://www.nytimes.com/2011/04/29/ nyregion/rev-david-wilkerson-79-dies-in-crash.html (accessed May 5, 2012).

REFERENCES

Ammerman, Nancy Tatom. 1997. *Congregation and Community*. New Brunswick, NJ: Rutgers University Press.

Bell, Daniel. 1976. *The Cultural Contradictions of Capitalism*. New York: Basic Books.

Bronkema, David. 2010. Interview. St. David's, PA: Eastern University.

Crawford, Margaret. 2004. "The World in a Shopping Mall: Variations on a Theme Park." In *The City Cultures Reader*, ed. Malcolm Miles and Tim Hall, with Iain Borden, 125–140. London: Routledge.

Department of City Planning. 2009. "Amended District Plan for the Times Square Improvement District for the Times Square Business Improvement District in the City of New York." 2009. Borough of Manhattan, New York, March 3.

Farrell, James J. 2003. *One Nation Under Goods: Malls and the Seductions of American Shopping*. Washington, DC: Smithsonian Institution Press.

Gottdiener, Mark. 2001. *The Theming of America: American Dreams, Media Fantasies, and Themed Environments*. 2nd ed. Boulder, CO: Westview Press.

Hine, Thomas. 2002. *I Want That: How We All Became Shoppers*. New York: Harper Collins.

Kelling, George L., and Catherine M. Coles. 1996. *Fixing Broken Windows: Restoring Order and Reducing Crime in Our Communities*. New York: Touchstone Books.

Kracauer, Siegfried. (1929) 2004. "The Mass Ornament." In *The City Cultures Reader*, ed. Malcolm Miles and Tim

Hall, with Iain Borden. New York: Routledge.

Lyons, David. 2000. *Jesus in Disneyland: Religion in Postmodern Times*. Cambridge: Polity Press.

Perkins, John M., ed. 1995. *Restoring At-Risk Communities*. Grand Rapids, MI: Baker Books.

Piaget, J. (1936) 1963. *The Origins of Intelligence in Children*. New York: W. W. Norton.

Putnam, Robert. 2000. *Bowling Alone: The Collapse and Revival of American Community*. New York: Simon and Schuster.

Sassen, Saskia. 1991. *The Global City*. Princeton, NJ: Princeton University Press.

Sheller, Mimi, and John Urry. 2000. "The City and the Car." *International Journal of Urban and Regional Research* 24, no. 4: 737–57; reprinted in *The City Cultures Reader*, ed. Malcolm Miles and Tim Giles, with Ian Borden, 202–219. London: Routledge, 2004.

Veblen, Thorstein. (1899) 1992. *The Theory of the Leisure Class: An Economic Study in the Evolution of Institutions*. New York: Penguin Classics.

Watters, Ethan. 2003. *Urban Tribes*. New York: Bloomsbury.

Wilson, James Q., and George L. Kelling. 1982. "Broken Windows" *Atlantic Monthly*, March.

2

Filling Niches and Pews in Williamsburg and Greenpoint: The Religious Ecology of Gentrification

Richard Cimino

"Oh wow, wait a minute, this is weird," shouted a twenty-something spectator to a friend on his cell phone as he watched the float of a Marian statue and a procession of priests, pilgrims, and a small brass band pass him on Graham Avenue. "It's like a parade about our lady of caramel or something."

This brief encounter between the puzzled hipster and the Roman Catholic participants in the procession of Our Lady of Mt. Carmel in Williamsburg, Brooklyn, during the summer of 2008 illuminates the ongoing cultural disconnect between newcomers and old-time residents in this gentrifying neighborhood. As the procession winded its way through the side streets of what was once called Italian Williamsburg, the pilgrims handed out scapulars (necklaces with cloth images of the Virgin Mary) to neighbors while the priests greeted older parishioners as they stood waving by their doorways. The newer residents kept more of a distance from the spectacle. Sitting on the steps of her building, a thirty-seven-year-old woman who had recently moved to Williamsburg said, "I'm not religious, but it's good for the neighborhood . . . It keeps it safer."

While Williamsburg's longtime Catholic residents see the procession as enacting neighborhood memory and public devotion, newer residents view it as a public curiosity that can enhance the neighborhood's diversity and quality of life. These differing and sometimes clashing visions of the neighborhood become problematic for congregations charged with ministering to all people.

In many cases, new residents coming into a neighborhood through gentrification are viewed as potential members with identifiable needs that a congregation can meet, as well as talents that a congregation can use. An influx of young urban professional couples and families into a poor neighborhood may likely be seen as a mixed blessing – helping to raise the real estate values and driving many poorer residents out, but also bringing potential new members into struggling congregations.

However, the new people arriving in Williamsburg are largely young, single artists, creative professionals, students, and other residents with nontraditional lifestyles. This social stratum, often called the "creative class," is decidedly unchurched, if not secular (Florida 2002). How do religious congregations navigate such seemingly indifferent, if not hostile, conditions? This chapter looks at how congregations meet the needs of both newcomers and longtime residents in a period of drastic neighborhood change. I argue that gentrification challenges congregations to take up distinct roles and functions as they encounter a new pluralism in their neighborhoods. Rather than having a secularizing effect or rendering congregations as passive bystanders to larger structural forces, gentrification can activate communities of faith even as their neighborhood functions are drastically changed.

This study is based on ethnographic research of thirty congregations in the Williamsburg-Greenpoint sections of Brooklyn. From these thirty congregations, I selected fifteen for in-depth study between November 2007 and April 2009 (see table 1 and map 1 for a listing and locations of these congregations). My criteria for selecting these congregations were that they agree to provide researchers access to clergy and members for interviews and that they represent the denominational pluralism in Williamsburg-Greenpoint (including the internal divisions of mainline and evangelical Protestant) as well as the different organizational niches I observed in the area (discussed later in this chapter).[1]

THE ROLE OF RELIGION IN GENTRIFICATION

Religion has not figured highly in social science research concerning gentrification. Most social scientists who study gentrification tend to see religious groups and particularly congregations as largely marginal and passive bystanders in the larger structural processes of neighborhood change. The role and agency of religious institutions in much of the literature on gentrification is largely relegated to discussion of the faith-based social services and older

Table 2.1. Surveyed Congregations in Williamsburg (w) and Greenpoint (G), Brooklyn

	LIFESTYLE ENCLAVES	NEIGHBORHOOD SOCIAL CENTERS	ETHNIC AND RELIGIOUS ENCLAVES
Ascension Episcopal Church (G)		♦	
Calvary Spanish Baptist Church (w)			♦
Chabad Center (Lubavitch Hasidim) (w)	♦		
Charismatic Brotherhood Church (w)			♦
Devoe Street Baptist Church (w)			♦
Greenpoint Church of Christ (G)			♦
Greenpoint Reformed Church (G)		♦	
Holy Ghost Ukrainian Catholic Church (w)			♦
Holy Trinity Orthodox Cathedral (w)			♦
Lighthouse Church in the Loft (G)			♦
Messiah Lutheran Church (G)		♦	
Most Holy Trinity Catholic Church (w)			♦
North Brooklyn Vineyard (w)	♦		
Our Lady of Consolation Catholic Church (w)			♦
Our Lady of Mt. Carmel Catholic Church (w)		(In transition) ←	
Resurrection Polish National Catholic Church (G)			♦
Resurrection Presbyterian Church (w)	♦		
Revolution (w)	♦		
Sangha Yoga Shala (w)	♦		
St. Anthony and Alphonsus Catholic Church (G)		♦	
St. Cecilia's Catholic Church (G)		♦	
St. Cyril and Methodius Catholic Church (G)			♦
St. Francis Paola Catholic Church (w)			♦
St. John Lutheran Church (G)		♦	
St. John the Evangelist Lutheran Church (w)		(In transition) ←	
St. Peter and Paul Catholic Church (w)			♦
St. Stanislaus Kotska Catholic Church (G)			♦
Transfiguration Catholic Church (w)			♦
Transfiguration Orthodox Cathedral (w)			♦
Williamsburg Church (w)	♦		

Note: The arrows mean that the congregation is in transition from being an ethnic and religious enclave to being a neighborhood social center.

activist congregations working with the homeless and on housing issues (Marwell 2007; Abu-Laghod 1994; DeSena 2009). A 2007 Rutgers University study of gentrification in Williamsburg-Greenpoint also found that developers tend to ignore the importance of religious institutions and congregations in their real estate projects.

The process of gentrification has been implicitly and explicitly linked with secularization. A 1993 study that looked at major Canadian cities found that gentrified districts had the strongest correlation with religious disaffiliation. David Ley and R. Bruce Martin (1993) argue not only that the creative class moving into gentrified zones is secular to begin with, but also that the establishments (such as restaurants and entertainment venues) they bring into neighborhoods force congregations out of these areas. The researchers found that – as might be evident to anyone who spends an early Sunday afternoon in Williamsburg, Greenwich Village, or South Parkdale in Toronto – four times as many residents were at brunch in cafés and restaurants than in churches. Yet Ley and Martin admit that while conventional congregations may suffer losses and even shut their doors, alternative spiritual groups – from yoga studios to New Age shops – often replace them. In his research on the creative class, Florida argues that residents of cities (often in the most gentrified neighborhoods) and states catering to this class tend to embrace secular values or "opt to forgo church for less traditional methods of spiritual or religious practice" (Florida 2008, 171; 2010).

Richard Lloyd's ethnography of Wicker Park (2006), a gentrified section of Chicago with many similarities to Williamsburg, looks at how such areas form central nodes in the post-industrial urban and economic landscape of global cities, even as they are portrayed as bohemian and outside the mainstream. Lloyd notes that Wicker Park forms a "neo-Bohemia," serving as an enclave for artists and the creative class, while providing entertainment venues for cosmopolitan middle-class consumers. Since religion and art have often competed as meaning and symbol systems, it may be the case that congregations can play a similar role in such culture-making. This raises the question of not only how congregations adapt but also how they influence these gentrified zones and their residents.

The small yet growing amount of literature on religious ecology addresses – both directly and indirectly – the effects of gentrification on religious institutions as well as the agency through which congregations deal with these issues (Ammerman 1997; Eiesland 2000). Ecological theory has focused on the birth, death, and change of populations of organizations over a long period of time. (Carroll 1984, 74). But organizations – more specifically, congregations – can also fill niches and adapt to their environment to meet the needs of different groups rather than engaging in direct competition with one another. Niche theory distinguishes between specialist and generalist types of

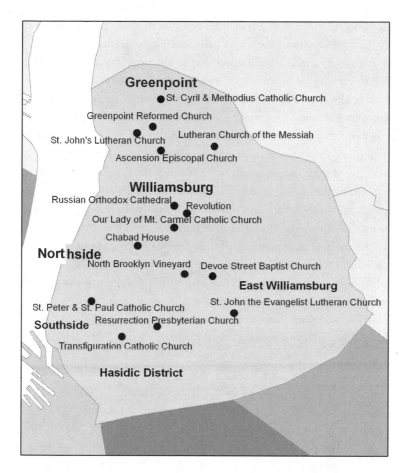

MAP 2.1. Congregations studied in Williamsburg-Greenpoint, Brooklyn.
Courtesy of Shirvahna Gobin.

organizations. According to DiMaggio (1998, 16), specialists are organizations that "intensively exploit very narrow niches, relatively small entities that do one thing very well. . . . Generalist organizations occupy broader niches, for example, offering several products in several markets." These niches can be defined as social spaces that can include geographic (such as city neighborhoods) as well as demographic dimensions. Important features of niches are their width, meaning how much space they occupy and draw resources from, and the degree of overlap between similar organizations (Scheitele 2007; Hannon, Carroll, and Pólos 2003).

Healy's overview of recent research on demographics and urban religion (2005) also addresses many of the issues surrounding congregations in gentrified areas. Healy cites research showing that in the post-industrial city and suburb, congregations are increasingly organizing themselves nongeographically and along the lines of social networks. Far more than belonging to the same neighborhood, congregations tend to attract those of particular age groups or generations as well as those with similar beliefs and worship styles, even eclipsing the importance of denomination (i.e., it is more important to have a born-again experience than to be Methodist, Baptist, etc.). Healy adds, "Because of the dependence of religious bodies on social networks, both religious subcultures and demographic uniformity have come to define congregations." Ammerman (1997) and others suggest that congregations respond to the challenges of gentrification in various ways according to their histories, denominational affiliations and theological resources, and patterns of interacting with their surrounding communities. Congregations do not merely adapt and passively respond to neighborhood change, but exercise agency as they apply their resources to social needs, encouraging the development of both civic skills and political action (Levitt 2007).

WILLIAMSBURG-GREENPOINT AND ITS
RELIGIOUS PAST AND PRESENT

Both the past and present religious ecology of Williamsburg and Greenpoint have been marked by prominent religious institutions with a distinctly public character. The early religious histories of Williamsburg and Greenpoint are closely related to the popular image of Brooklyn as a pastoral and suburban escape from Manhattan, though Williamsburg was an independent city until 1855 and displayed distinctly urban characteristics earlier than most other sections of the borough. The borough's reputation as the "city of churches" was reinforced by Dutch Reformed and New England Puritan influences and by the attempt to differentiate Brooklyn from more "worldly" Manhattan. In Williamsburg, as in the rest of Brooklyn, the old-line Dutch Reformed, Presbyterian, Congregational, and Methodist churches predominated up until the large influx of German and Irish immigrants in the mid-eighteenth century (Lederer and the Brooklyn Historical Society 2005).

The surrounding breweries, foundries, and factories employed thousands of workers and their families, who soon established and populated the area's many Lutheran and Catholic churches. The building of the Williamsburg

Bridge in 1903 led to an equally massive settlement of Jewish immigrants in the newly built tenements located in what is now considered the Southside of Williamsburg (or "old Williamsburg"). A religious landscape consisting of declining old-line Protestant, ethnic Lutheran and Catholic churches (and by then including Italian, Polish, and Hispanic immigrants), and synagogues defined these neighborhoods until the late 1940s. The industrial and economic fallout of the post–World War II period, including the closing of the Brooklyn Navy Yard and many factories and breweries, as well as the wider migration of many city dwellers to the suburbs, hit Williamsburg especially hard. Williamsburg's mainline Protestant base, declining since the 1920s due to overcrowding and deterioration in the area, was depleted by the 1960s, with most congregations shutting down. The construction of the Brooklyn-Queens Expressway in the 1950s cut through a swath of homes and even churches, further depopulating and depressing the area.

Between the 1960s and 1980s, the remaining Catholic and Lutheran churches faced neighborhoods dealing with significant poverty and crime. Since Williamsburg is a patchwork of neighborhoods, some churches formed the centers of ethnic enclaves, such as the Polish neighborhood in the northwest and the Italian section in the northeast of Williamsburg. Puerto Ricans took up residence along Graham Avenue in East Williamsburg in the 1950s and 1960s, forming the nucleus of what was to become the largely pan-Latino Southside in later decades. The Satmar Hasidic Jewish community, which established its presence before and after World War II around Bedford Avenue, likewise experienced little neighborhood decline, even showing a revival of community life and commerce starting in the 1980s (Lederer 2005).

The 1960–1980 period also saw the establishment of inner-city and social justice ministries that gained national reputations under the leadership of a younger generation of clergy-activists, such as Father Brian Karvalis of Transfiguration Catholic Church and Rev. Richard Neuhaus of the Lutheran Church of St. John the Evangelist. Such activism was unique in Brooklyn, if not New York City, and led to the formation of several church-neighborhood partnerships and faith-based organizations in Williamsburg, such as St. Nicholas and Transfiguration (Marwell 2007). Although Greenpoint faced demographic changes similar to those in Williamsburg, they were mitigated by a stronger working and middle class; most of Greenpoint's mainline Protestant churches have survived up to the present day, even if in drastically diminished form (Mader 1983). Greenpoint's industrial base declined at a slower pace, with a continuing influx of Polish immigrants that preserved a large working-class ethnic Catholic enclave much longer than in other areas of northern Brooklyn (DeSena 2009).

If there was a decisive point of neighborhood change in Williamsburg, it can be traced to the mid-1990s, though a pioneer artist wave of early or "pre-gentrification" was evident in the late 1980s. The rejuvenation of adjacent Manhattan neighborhoods such as the East Village and the rest of the Lower East Side in the 1990s made it only a matter of time before the streets of Williamsburg, just a subway stop away, would become a new urban magnet. There are indications that the artist-generated phase of gentrification has given way to an influx of urban professionals (seen in the construction of luxury apartments and condominiums), but the artistic and entertainment center of northern Brooklyn remains in Williamsburg.

A 2007 Rutgers University report on Williamsburg-Greenpoint (*Gentrification and Rezoning in Williamsburg-Greenpoint* 2007) documented the significant degree of gentrification that has taken place in these sections. The study found that the high demand for housing dwarfed the supply, with young professionals flooding the market. Average home values made the dramatic increase from $193,558 in 2000 to $582,700 in 2006. The Rutgers study found that 60 percent of the population has an income between $150,000 and $250,000. Whites represented 46.1 percent of the population in 1990 compared to 64 percent in 2006. Between 1990 and 2000, childless households had climbed to 72 percent of the population. Such a growth in the number of nontraditional families is partly tied to the young age of the newcomers – the median age of the new arrivals between 1990 and 2000 was thirty-five. The study found that older Italian, Hispanic, and Polish communities were in danger of being displaced.

In understanding the effects these changes have had on the religious life of Williamsburg-Greenpoint, it is tempting to view gentrification mainly as a secularizing agent, due either to intentional real estate efforts to exclude religious institutions from development or to the impact of unaffiliated and secularized newcomers. But such a position ignores the agency congregations exercise as they seek to meet the needs of newcomers and longtime residents in a changing neighborhood. In the case of Williamsburg-Greenpoint, I found gentrification to play both an invigorating and segmenting role in its religious institutions. As mentioned earlier, prior to 2002, religious institutions in Williamsburg and Greenpoint showed signs of decline and stagnation. Mainline Protestant churches in the area had either long since shut their doors (particularly in Williamsburg) or showed dwindling memberships with no steady leadership. Catholic and Orthodox churches remained, but, with the exception of the Polish and Latino Catholics, their members had been departing their neighborhoods for several decades – a trend that intensified as gentrification unfolded in the late 1990s. The Hasidic section in South Williamsburg remained relatively stable in size, though the members of this community felt new pressure to find adequate living space as gentrification proceeded.

Although no decisive event marked a turning point, the years since 2002 have shown a pattern of stabilization and growth amidst a new religious pluralism in Williamsburg and Greenpoint. Following the model of social ecology, these neighborhoods have experienced long-term organizational mortality and adaptations and, most noticeably, the birth of congregations. Full-time pastors have been appointed in the mainline congregations of Greenpoint – Evangelical Lutheran Church in America, Episcopal, and Reformed Church in America. St. John the Evangelist Lutheran Church, a historic Lutheran Church–Missouri Synod congregation in Williamsburg, also chose a full-time pastor – after a decade without one – who was selected partly for his ministry to "postmoderns," or the creative class. These congregations reported more new residents attending services than in the earlier period, even though the growth has been small to moderate. During this period, the Catholic parishes engaged in new efforts to minister to their members affected by gentrification, most notably in the area of housing. Churches United, a Catholic organization pressing for affordable housing in Greenpoint-Williamsburg, was founded in 2004.

Several new evangelical ministries to new residents started after 2002. As part of a loose network of recently planted Presbyterian Church in America congregations in New York, Resurrection Presbyterian, founded in 2005, draws an attendance of about two hundred to its Sunday evening services on Williamsburg's Southside. The Vineyard, a charismatic network of congregations, planted a church in 2006 and meets both in a Williamsburg bar on Sunday evenings and in a public school on Sunday mornings, drawing an attendance of more than one hundred members.

Jay Bakker, son of the televangelist Jim Bakker, moved to Williamsburg in 2006 and planted Revolution Church (a sister congregation to Revolution congregations in Atlanta and Charlotte, North Carolina) in Pete's Candy Store, a well-known Williamsburg bar and concert venue. Missionaries from a South Carolina conservative independent Bible church arrived in Brooklyn in 2006 and started Williamsburg Church, drawing about forty people to its services. In the same year, the Lubavitch Hasidim's outreach organization, known as Chabad, founded a North Brooklyn satellite right in the middle of trendy Bedford Avenue in Williamsburg, seeking to draw unaffiliated Jews to its Friday services and Kabbalah studies. Although not congregationally based, Eastern and New Age–based groups and services have also recently started in Williamsburg-Greenpoint, most notably yoga centers and holistic health stores, comprising a holistic and "detraditionalized" spirituality (Heelas and Woodhead 1998).

A TYPOLOGY OF NICHES IN THE RELIGIOUS ECOLOGY OF WILLIAMSBURG-GREENPOINT

All of these congregations have sought (some more self-consciously than others) to find their own niche in the religious ecology of Williamsburg and Greenpoint. These congregations have been categorized into three types based on how they relate to their own members and their immediate neighborhoods. As table 2 illustrates, I divide these congregations into lifestyle enclaves, neighborhood social-center congregations, and ethnic and religious enclaves. The thirty congregations are compared according to nine analytic dimensions: (1) primary identification, (2) neighborhood attachment, (3) membership composition, (4) neighborhood investment, (5) neighborhood activism, (6) prospects for growth, (7) tenure, (8) member proximity and commutation to congregation, and (9) sources of funding and other resources.

Lifestyle enclaves, representing six congregations, are the congregations or groups most obviously shaped by the process of gentrification; they were founded to minister to and evangelize the neighborhoods with a special focus on the new residents. They were intentionally planted "from outside" the neighborhood by networks and larger organizations often with a national, and in some cases, global reach. These congregations often view themselves as missionaries to "cultural creatives," stressing the values of intimacy, community, and authenticity. Although they seek to minister to their immediate neighborhoods, these congregations intentionally draw from a particular demographic and lifestyle stratum comprising mainly young (18–34), educated, white, middle-class or upper-class students and professionals, often

Table 2.2. Niches in the Religious Ecology of Gentrification

	LIFESTYLE ENCLAVE	NEIGHBORHOOD SOCIAL-CENTER CONGREGATION	RELIGIOUS AND ETHNIC ENCLAVE
1. Primary identification	Congregation as "missional" organization to reach individuals, particularly newcomers	Congregation as "social center" that ministers to social and religious needs of neighborhood residents, whether members or not	An enclave for preserving particular ethnic and religious traditions
2. Neighborhood attachment	Loosely tied to neighborhood (though may have strong appeal to new neighborhood residents); contact almost exclusively with newcomers	Close ties to neighborhood and local institutions; growth in membership from immediate area; contact with both newcomers and old-timers	Ministers to members in neighborhood and from other areas; minimal contact with newcomers
3. Membership composition	Functions along limited demographic and lifestyle lines, such as young adult, professional, and high educational strata	Moderate to wide range of ages, social classes	Moderate to wide range of demographics within same religious and ethnic community
4. Neighborhood investment	Tends not to own property or own building in neighborhood	Owns building, which is used as resource for broader neighborhood functions and relationships	Owns building but limits use to members
5. Neighborhood activism	Tends not to be active on neighborhood housing issues	Active on neighborhood housing issues	Active on neighborhood housing issues to the extent that they affect members in neighborhood
6. Prospects for growth	High or moderate membership increases	Membership stability; modest increase after period of decline	Decline, stability, or growth
7. Tenure	Recently established (since 2003)	Historic presence in community	Either longtime presence or more recently established
8. Member proximity and commutation to congregation	Few commuters, but proportion likely to grow due to rising housing costs	Decreasing proportion of commuters	Increasing proportion of commuters
9. Sources of funding and other resources	Funding and resources from local and national congregation-planting networks, denominations	Denominational and neighborhood-based funding and resources	Denominational, neighborhood-, and ethnic association-based funding and resources

considered the new "creative class" (Florida 2002). Because Williamsburg and increasingly Greenpoint draw many members of this class or lifestyle stratum, one might say these enclaves function as neighborhood congregations. Yet they maintain a low presence in their neighborhoods, often do not own property, and have few ties with longtime residents or neighborhood institutions and organizations. It is also the case that some members of these lifestyle enclave congregations who first attended services as neighborhood residents have since moved to other sections of Brooklyn (particularly in starting a family) and commute to the congregations. These congregations' support often comes from outside the neighborhood, at least initially, from denominations or church-planting networks.

Neighborhood social-center congregations, representing six cases, attempt to balance their outreach and ministry between newcomers and old-time members. These congregations have a greater mix of ages and social classes than the lifestyle enclaves, and have had a long historical presence in their neighborhoods. Their identities, usually based in mainline Protestantism and Catholicism, also provide resources and a background for social and neighborhood activism. Such functions can range from housing and other forms of activism to opening the doors of their buildings to nonmember artists and community groups. Clergy often cited these cultural functions, rather than adapting ministries (such as changes in liturgy) or providing services to newcomers, as the way their congregations are adapting to neighborhood change. These congregations tend to receive support from neighborhood and, to a lesser extent, denominational sources.

The ethnic and religious enclave congregations, including sixteen cases, focus on maintaining a particular religious or ethnic tradition. These congregations may show rapidly declining, stable, or even growing memberships, though gentrification, at least in Williamsburg-Greenpoint, tends to prevent the growth of particular ethnic concentrations. In such neighborhoods, high cost of living often breaks up ethnic solidarity as homeowners are tempted to sell their homes for the highest price or renters move to more affordable areas. As with neighborhood social-center congregations, ethnic and religious enclave congregations can have a fairly wide range of ages and social classes. Most important, neighborhood change has tended to split these congregations between resident and commuter members. Those who have left their original neighborhoods have settled in adjacent sections of the city or even the suburbs, but return to attend services, whether on a regular or occasional basis. Ethnic and religious enclave congregations receive both denominational and neighborhood resources, often from ethnic associations and events. I found the borders between neighborhood social-center and ethnic and religious enclave congregations to be relatively porous. As we will see in the case studies of the Shrine Church of Our Lady of Mt. Carmel and St. John the Evangelist Lutheran Church, the transition from the ethnic and religious enclave niche to a neighborhood social-center niche is difficult and uncertain.

LIFESTYLE ENCLAVES: RESURRECTION PRESBYTERIAN CHURCH

My first visit to Resurrection Presbyterian Church, a recently planted church affiliated with the Presbyterian Church in America (PCA) in Williamsburg's Southside, was enough to reveal that it is a highly networked place. At the conclusion of an evening service, congregants gathered in small groups of three or four engaging in genial conversation rather than filing out the door to greet the pastor. Most of the attendees were in their twenties or early thirties and had arrived at Resurrection through friendship and referral networks from college and their hometowns. Home fellowship groups have been established throughout Williamsburg and Greenpoint and now Bushwick and tend to serve as an entry point to congregational life.

Jerry, a twenty-five-year-old accountant, became involved with Resurrection in a typical fashion. He was referred to the church by a PCA pastor he knew in Atlanta. "I got involved in a home group and [through that] got a roommate instantly, and was plugged into the church." Although he now lived in Williamsburg, Jerry said, "the church is my main tie to the neighborhood. Williamsburg is not really my scene. I'm an accountant." Others interviewed said they valued the networking opportunities among artists in the church. Several were involved in social ministries and were strongly interested in the church becoming more diverse in age and ethnicity, though they also admitted that the youthful demographic initially attracted them to the church.

The church relies heavily on a network of New York churches affiliated with PCA, which refers members and visitors living or moving to Williamsburg to Resurrection. Most of the congregants I interviewed had come to the church or heard about it from the Village Church, a PCA church in Greenwich Village. These congregations draw their mission philosophy and strategies from Manhattan's large Redeemer Presbyterian Church and its pastor, Timothy Keller. Reaching "global cities" through Christian communities geared to an urban context has been a central feature of Keller's mission philosophy.

This is reflected in a 2007 brochure from the Brooklyn Church Project, a network of PCA churches in Brooklyn, which cites Williamsburg as a new center of arts and the indie music scene, as well as a "rich tapestry of ethnic communities," providing a "unique opportunity to declare the kingship of Jesus in a context where many people do not know him." The brochure adds that,

> While the growing population and swift development of Williamsburg has been positive in many ways, they have also brought questions about how these changes will affect the poor and the immigrants. Tensions have arisen between rich and poor, "old-timers" and newcomers, recently-arrived immigrants and those whose grandparents arrived here long ago. We see this as another way to declare the reign of the Lord who has broken down the dividing wall of hostility between all nations.

The youthfulness of the church, consisting largely of people in their early twenties to mid-thirties, was not planned, according to the pastor, Rev. Vito Aiuto. In fact, there is little in the church's outreach or programs that targets younger generations or hipsters, aside from a heavy if unofficial involvement in the arts among many members. The service, which meets in an old Lutheran church, blends the lyrics of classic hymns with jazz and more contemporary tunes, and communion is celebrated every week. Aiuto said that the church has not yet established a presence in the Southside neighborhood, especially among its largely Hispanic neighbors. But the network-based nature of Resurrection, with members coming into the church through the influence and referral of friends and like-minded congregations, suggests that it will be difficult to reach outside the church's demographic base. As Kevin, a founding member, commented, "There's a huge cultural element [to the church's growth]. People connect to each other and associate with other transplants from a specific area, with little interaction with locals. . . . It's kind of like a transplanted midwestern church inside Williamsburg. You won't see minorities [because] they're not socially tied to the early-twenties generation." The overwhelming majority of the church's members had been evangelical Christian – even if inactive – before coming into contact with Resurrection.

Another fast-growing lifestyle enclave congregation in Williamsburg, the Vineyard of North Brooklyn, has likewise grown through referrals and networks provided by other Vineyard churches in the area. The Vineyard name, associated with informal and expressive worship and relevant evangelical teaching usually based in gentrified neighborhoods, serves as a draw in itself, attracting visitors from around the world who are familiar with the name and the movement. In contrast, the Williamsburg Church, a start-up established in 2006 by a missionary couple from South Carolina with few ties to other congregations and social networks in New York, has shown little growth. As Healy (2005) noted, it is not only strict evangelical teachings and practices that drives evangelical growth in Williamsburg-Greenpoint but also the network ties that these churches draw on, a point I return to in the discussion section of this chapter.

GREENPOINT REFORMED CHURCH: A NEIGHBORHOOD-SOCIAL CENTER CONGREGATION

As with the other mainline Protestant churches in Greenpoint at the start of the new millennium, Greenpoint Reformed Church was in a state of serious decline. Once a prestigious congregation of the Reformed Church in America (RCA), with close to one thousand in attendance, the decline of industries in the area and the rush to the suburbs after World War II depleted most of its membership. The church, which is surrounded by historic brownstones and townhouses in the most gentrified part of Greenpoint, was without a pastor for several years until Revs. Jennifer Aul and Ann Kansfield became co-pastors in 2006. The pastors initially brought controversy to the church, making national headlines for their same-sex marriage in a denomination prohibiting gay pastors. However, with the arrival of these new leaders, the church has grown modestly and, more significantly, has reduced the number of commuters while showing an increase in the number of new members who live in the neighborhood. This change is in line with Kansfield's goal of the church "reflecting the whole community" and "building community roots." The establishment of a soup kitchen – the only one in the community – as well as an art gallery and a concert program are other new neighborhood functions that the congregation facilitates.

The newcomers who have joined Greenpoint Reformed Church and other neighborhood social-center churches show several differences from the members of the start-up lifestyle enclave congregations. They tend to belong to the earlier waves of gentrification (such as artists who first moved from Manhattan looking for space in the 1980s), rather than the more recent post-college newcomers who come straight to Williamsburg or Greenpoint. Kansfield finds that the more recent members tend to be social workers and teachers rather than those involved in the creative fields. The neighborhood social-center approach of Greenpoint Reformed is valued by new members for making them feel at home both in the church and in the neighborhood. Sarah, a twenty-eight-year-old social worker and musician, had actually attended Resurrection Presbyterian Church when she first moved to the area but left over its conservatism in theology and gender roles. She also said that the church did not seem to be part of the neighborhood and was "aiding gentrification, though they also provide spiritual support" to members. Sarah added that as a member of Greenpoint Reformed, particularly in working in its soup kitchen, she feels "supported by the church in living here. I feel very rooted in the neighborhood. The church has helped us stay here." She said she and her husband hope to serve as a "bridge between the old-timers in the church and the new people in the neighborhood."

ETHNIC AND RELIGIOUS ENCLAVES: TRANSFIGURATION RUSSIAN ORTHODOX CATHEDRAL AND TRANSFIGURATION CATHOLIC CHURCH

The Russian Orthodox Cathedral of the Transfiguration of Our Lord is surrounded by condominiums, art galleries, and bustling McCarren Park on Williamsburg's Northside. But the changes that have swept through Williamsburg and Greenpoint in the past ten years have had little noticeable impact on the church. The pastor, Fr. Wiaczeslaw Krawczuk, said that he is "very happy" with the neighborhood change that has taken place around the cathedral, as everything "looks nicer and cleaner." He added that the neighborhood is now safer but is not as quiet as it once was. His parishioners now complain mostly about parking problems when they commute in to the Sunday liturgy from neighboring parts of the city. The few who live in the neighborhood are elderly remnants of a once-larger Slavic neighborhood. The parish still draws around three hundred attendees to its Sunday liturgy, though that number and that for baptisms have declined since new Orthodox churches were built in Brooklyn and Queens to accommodate Orthodox immigrants arriving since the 1990s. Rather than trying to Americanize or adapt the cathedral to its predominantly non-Russian or Slavic neighbors, Fr. Krawczuk has maintained its ethnic identity. Although the liturgy has been bilingual for twenty years, the church is one of the few in the Orthodox Church in America to follow the traditionalist "old calendar" rite. The cathedral sees no need to draw in American converts (as have several Orthodox churches in Manhattan), with the exception of those who have intermarried into Orthodox families. Public concerts by the choir represent the few occasions when the cathedral opens its doors to the neighborhood.

The case of Transfiguration Catholic Church on the Southside of Williamsburg suggests that ethnic enclave congregations are capable of a strong neighborhood role in certain circumstances. The parish, bordering the Southside and the large Hasidic section, has served a historic neighborhood role, first for the Irish and German Catholics who settled there in the mid-nineteenth century and then for several waves of Latinos since the 1940s, and is rapidly shrinking due to the Hasidic community's expansion in the neighborhood. The parish and its several educational and social service buildings occupy the only street in the neighborhood without Hasidic residences and establishments. Like other Latino parishes, Transfiguration has been growing recently as it has become more open to celebrating the traditional observances of Mexican immigrants, many of whom come from outside Williamsburg. With a young American-born pastor, the parish is also seeing some young white newcomers at its Masses. Even though longtime Latino residents have been forced out of the neighborhood due to rising rents, gentrification is not seen as a major threat by members and priests. One member said that the influx of newcomers and the tensions they have with the Hasidim over housing could be "God's blessing because there is competition and it's good the [Hasidic Jews] have a little competition."[2]

CONGREGATIONS IN TRANSITION BETWEEN NICHES: OUR LADY OF MT. CARMEL AND ST. JOHN THE EVANGELIST LUTHERAN CHURCH

The largely Italian American Shrine Church of Our Lady of Mt. Carmel in the Northside of Williamsburg draws on the public nature of Catholicism as it tries to connect with the new residents and make the difficult transition from ethnic enclave to neighborhood social-center parish. For most of its 120 years, the church has been known for its "giglio feast," in which a towering statue is raised in honor of St. Paulinus by battalions of male parishioners, drawing thousands of New Yorkers every summer (Sciorra 1999; Primeggia and Varacalli 1996).

Today, many of the Italian residents have left the neighborhood surrounding the parish due to the rising cost of home ownership, but a fair number return for Mass on Sunday and especially for the feast. The parish may soon be facing a situation in which commuters will be running and attending the feasts and frequent processions in a neighborhood populated largely by unchurched and non-Italian residents. Tension has already arisen between newcomers and the parish, as seen in complaints about the bells rung daily to announce the morning Mass and about crowding conditions during the feast.

The pastor, Fr. Joseph Fonti, said his calling is to minister to the neighborhood, but he admits that the relationship has to run both ways, not only with making the church accessible to newcomers, but also with new residents recognizing the important and historic place the church has in the community, even if that "community" now extends beyond Williamsburg. With its new Montessori program, the parochial school is trying to meet the educational needs of the young families just beginning to populate the neighborhood. The parish also sponsors public classical concerts. Seeking to address concerns from the large gay community in Williamsburg, the parish hosted a seminar for gay Catholics and their loved ones. Yet the tightly knit quality of parish life is clearly reinforced by the feast – now the central event of the parish, which pays most of its bills. On one hand, there is an attempt to open the feast to outsiders, as seen by the attempt (largely unsuccessful) to enlist neighborhood artists in the effort. So far, only a small number of newcomers attend the festivities even as spectators. The pastor who has succeeded Fonti plans to distribute guide brochures to spectators that would explain the meaning and significance of the actions and rituals on display during the feast and procession. However, leaders and organizers of the feast admit the somewhat closed nature of volunteering for feast activities: participation is often a family matter passed on from one generation to another, with faith, ethnicity, and a sense of place closely entwined (Franco 2007).

St. John the Evangelist Lutheran Church in East Williamsburg faces dilemmas similar to that of Our Lady of Mt. Carmel. Rev. Jonathan Priest came to the church in 2002, after it had gone almost a decade without a full-time minister. His background in ministering to young adults (he plays in a Christian rock band) suggested that the congregation is interested in reaching beyond its African American ethnic base. The congregation's history reveals that it has effectively adapted to neighborhood change before. After serving as a stronghold of German Lutheranism in Williamsburg in the early twentieth century (claiming over 3,000 members), the church entered a period of decline as the ethnic composition of the neighborhood changed. At the time, the Lutheran churches had adopted a policy of "gathering-in" immigrants with a prior Lutheran background into active congregations and thereby leaving neighborhoods undergoing ethnic changes. (Of the fifteen Lutheran congregations in Williamsburg, Greenpoint, and neighboring Bushwick at the start of the twentieth century, only six continue to exist today). St. John the Evangelist challenged this practice, adapting to neighborhood change and eventually becoming one of the larger black Lutheran churches in the country. Under the pastorate of Richard Neuhaus in the 1960s and '70s, the parish became a center of "high church" liturgical innovation and social activism (Galchutt 2007). Priest notes that even today, the two pillars of social justice and worship remain priorities for members. But beyond that he thinks that the congregation is open to more informal services and might even consider tearing down its historic building in order to expand its ministry and create affordable housing. Congregation members interviewed acknowledged the effort to reach out to "progressives" (meaning white newcomers), but they also added that the church's longtime neighborhood and social activist role should be maintained. What such a neighborhood role may mean is in flux. For instance, Priest let an outside organization use the building, but when he learned that Buddhist services were being conducted, he asked the group to leave. He is also ambivalent about the whole idea of a hipster or "emergent" ministry. He does not like the way it stresses a homogeneity of culture (and generations) and ethnicity among people. He added that "being multicultural is my calling," and cited the church's social justice and multi-ethnic dimensions as showing that the "Gospel is for all people; it does not cater to homogeneity; it's not just about me."

NICHES AND NETWORKS IN THE NEIGHBORHOOD

The case studies described above suggest that congregations in gentrified neighborhoods encounter windows of opportunity but also "ceilings" that limit the directions in which they can move. These limitations were recognized by several congregations in my study that clearly staked out their niche and ruled out other possibilities. The different possibilities and limits set by occupying niches were shaped by the congregations' theological identities and social resources. The case of the lifestyle enclave congregations illustrates the importance of a theological fit with newcomers. These congregations have the most apparent success in a gentrified neighborhood because their function and form often bear an affinity with the mindsets and social patterns of new residents. Like the transient newcomers, these congregations, both in their teachings and in actuality (e.g., not owning a building), stress the importance of "journey" and spiritual practices over sacred places.

This can be seen most clearly in the Vineyard Church's stress on relevance, but also in Resurrection Presbyterian Church's blending of old and new (as heard in its music), and the stress on intimacy, authenticity, and community that strikes a powerful chord among young urban newcomers arriving on the current wave of gentrification (and among post–baby boomers in general; see Wuthnow 2007). Future research should look at whether the "spiritual authenticity" found in lifestyle enclaves is an extension of the quest for authenticity in architectural styles and cuisine that mark gentrified neighborhoods (Saracino-Brown 2007; Zukin 1998, 2010). Even members who were uncomfortable with a church full of their own peers admitted that the common interests among members drew them to these religious communities. The way in which new members (and often newcomers to the city) say these churches help them get "plugged in" (a phrase I heard more than once), whether in finding an apartment, roommates or a social circle, suggests that they are as much linchpins of social networks as sources of spiritual sustenance. Such friendship networks are intensified among young adults as they gravitate to cities and spend an increasing number of years in singlehood between leaving their families and starting new ones of their own. Watters (2003) suggests that these loose, flexible networks, which he calls "urban tribes," are connected through weak ties to other networks, helping young adults navigate the job search and other dimensions of urban life, including finding a suitable congregation. In contrast, ethnic and religious enclaves are composed of denser social ties, but those ties are limited to an in-group of residents that tend to be leaving rather than arriving in the neighborhood.

It is not only uniform social and demographic traits that make up lifestyle networks but also common values and beliefs. Market theory has posited that distinctive and usually demanding yet beneficial beliefs and practices are the main way that congregations grow and maintain themselves in a pluralistic environment (Stark and Finke 2000). The evangelical lifestyle enclave's demand that members hold to a common belief system lends itself to the formation of social networks of like-minded believers who define themselves against an unbelieving society. The social networks that form around common beliefs and practices may even advantage those networks based on similar demographic traits (and of course, they are related; mainline churches lack many of the network ties of evangelical congregations because of their lower birth and marriage rates). That may help explain the evangelical (in the broad sense of the term) nature of lifestyle enclaves. The lifestyle enclaves occupy a fairly narrow niche, serving a particular demographic group that does not overlap with the niches of other religious organizations (Scheitele 2007). As gentrification advances, it is likely that there will be niche overlap between competing lifestyle enclaves. We see this already in Williamsburg, where Jay Bakker's Revolution Church serves a "niche within a niche," drawing those from evangelical backgrounds seeking a more liberalized environment, especially on sexuality and gender roles (Bakker has become increasingly outspoken on gay rights).

The neighborhood social-center congregations draw on mainline Protestant and Catholic public traditions and theologies that value social justice and solidarity as much as, if not more than, personal evangelism. The concept of the neighborhood as parish (even as many Catholics choose their churches outside of parish boundaries) in the Catholic repertoire provides an opening to minister to newcomers and old-time members regardless of their faith. The mainline touchstones of social justice and cultural openness create similar opportunities.

The congregations' buildings and properties located in the center of gentrifying neighborhoods clearly constitute an important social resource sustaining their public role. But even the role of buildings was often a matter of conflict between longtime and new members. As Rev. Robert Pikken, the Episcopal priest in Greenpoint, said:

> Older members are connected to a spirituality of place. They grew up here and the events that took place are very important in shaping their lives. The newcomers have a spirituality of practice – the newer folks are not connected to the place as much as the practices of the faith. They won't respond to [pleas] to help save the building like the others. Some may not darken the door of the church, but they're involved in giving as a practice of faith, in working in the soup kitchen. That's what they do. There's a healthy tension between the two [spiritualities].

Location is an important factor, both for the neighborhood social center and ethnic and religious enclaves. Obviously, whether a congregation is near projects that are relatively unaffected by an influx of newcomers or is based in a prime real estate neighborhood greatly affects which niches will be filled. Interestingly, denominations and their leadership provided few tangible resources in sustaining either neighborhood social centers or religious and ethnic enclaves in their adaption to neighborhood change, a finding supported by other literature on congregational changes (Ammerman 1997). Most of the cultural resources that enhanced the public nature of these congregations were locally produced and supported (such as soup kitchens and art and concert spaces).

Mainline congregations seem best able to bridge the gap between old-timers and a segment of newcomers; their openness to the neighborhood and their liberal positions on women in leadership, gay rights, and other social issues seem a natural fit with new residents. But their broad, neighborhood-oriented niche ignores the dense demographic and lifestyle networks that bring new residents into these neighborhoods in the first place. The diversification of lifestyles and the dispersion of social capital and "participatory ties" (such as work, recreation, and even volunteering) outside one's neighborhood have become realities of urban life (Blokland and Rae 2008; Sampson 1999). As location and neighborhood become less important than demographic and lifestyle commonalities and network ties in congregations, the neighborhood center model may ironically appeal only to a small segment of residents in a gentrified neighborhood (Healy 2005).

In recognizing the difficulty involved in the broad neighborhood approach, the neighborhood center pastors often spoke of occupying other niches as well. The Episcopal priest cited his church as both "traditional (in worship) and progressive (on social matters)," while Greenpoint Reformed's pastor referred to her church's informal and questioning environment. Although the neighborhood social-center congregations showed signs of growth and stability, the growth was relatively modest and is complicated by the financial pressure on longtime residents and members to leave the neighborhood.

These clergy spoke of community values as extending beyond the congregation in a way that differed markedly from both the lifestyle and religious and ethnic enclaves. This was evident in the different ways in which these congregation members and clergy spoke of the role of artists and the arts in their congregations. Neighborhood social-center congregations opened their doors to secular artists and saw such cultural programs as enhancing and creating a greater sense of community in the neighborhood, as well as demonstrating the welcoming nature of their churches. In contrast, both the ethnic-religious and lifestyle enclaves saw the arts as a ministry or service by their own communities and members directed toward the neighborhood and beyond. The lifestyle enclaves provided artists with a strong support system and wide networking opportunities, but these were seen as building community within the congregation.

Rather than the neighborhood serving as a single entity and as a religious marketplace, gentrification and the network ties its new residents carry tend to fragment and even override neighborhood relations. In such a situation, we have seen that congregations increasingly function as niche congregations with distinct identities and purposes. Because of their various histories, missions, theologies, and membership traits, it is possible for congregations to fulfill only limited functions and purposes in an urban ecology undergoing gentrification. Of course, congregations can fill niches in environments of both neighborhood change and stability. But gentrification and the way it segments a neighborhood – at least in its early to middle stages – according to lifestyle, income, and ethnicity tend to force a congregation to define and thus limit its identity and ministry.

There was little apparent competition between the different kinds of congregations in the religious ecology of gentrified Williamsburg-Greenpoint. But as Scheitele (2007) notes, most competition takes place between those within a similar niche ("niche overlap") rather than between different niches. Niche congregations have often been viewed as specializing in a particular identity apart from the neighborhood as they draw members from throughout a metropolitan area (Ammerman 1997; Livezey 2000). But I have found that, especially under the segmenting effect of gentrification, different niches can exist within a single neighborhood. The same environment can encourage "niche-switching" (or attempts at switching) by congregations on a fairly regular basis. The presence of different niches existing side by side was most clearly seen among lifestyle enclaves and neighborhood social-center congregations, both of which sought to minister to the immediate community while having very different visions of their neighborhoods.

The rapid-fire changes that can reconfigure neighborhoods during gentrification (whether from rezoning laws or the closing of long-established retail outlets) makes transitions between niches both a problem and a possibility for congregations. It is obvious that ethnic congregations can play neighborhood social-center functions when their neighborhood is of the same ethnicity as their membership base. When their neighborhoods have changed, they usually have to switch niches to occupy that of an ethnic and religious enclave serving large commuter memberships. But an ethnic and religious enclave can theoretically move in the direction back toward the neighborhood social-center type. Denominational traditions and theological and social resources are especially important factors in determining the possibility of this transition. It will be interesting to see if lifestyle enclave congregations can switch to neighborhood social centers as a neighborhood enters the late stages of gentrification. But these congregations' reliance on mobile social networks and their missional approach may complicate such a transition.

Gentrification will play out differently in Williamsburg and Greenpoint than in other neighborhoods and cities. But the general process of neighborhood change entails a loss of urban cohesiveness and the growth of a new pluralism among residents that will compel congregations to reexamine their identities and play new roles.

NOTES

1. The thirty churches were selected by examining real estate and Yellow Page listings. In Williamsburg and Greenpoint, almost all of the congregations are Christian with the largest number being Catholic (15), followed by evangelical (10), mainline Protestant (6), and Eastern Orthodox (2). The Jewish groups were represented by the Chabad Center of the Lubavitch Hasidim. The research was conducted outside the district of the Satmar Hasidim, the predominant Hasidic group in Williamsburg, though a leader of the community was interviewed. A yoga center in Williamsburg was also included to represent Eastern/alternative spiritual groups. Preliminary research involved attending and observing congregational services and collecting literature from the congregations (including studying their presence on the internet). This survey provided a working "religious geography" of these neighborhoods, allowing me to initially classify the thirty congregations/organizations into a typology – of lifestyle enclaves, neighborhood social centers, and religious and ethnic enclaves – that is illustrated and defined in the text.

2. Lina Villegas conducted the research for the section on Transfiguration Catholic Church.

REFERENCES

Abu-Lughod, Janet, ed. 1994. *From Urban Village to East Village*. Cambridge: Blackwell.

Ammerman, Nancy Tatom. 1997. *Congregation and Community*. New Brunswick, NJ: Rutgers University Press.

Blokland, Talja, and Douglas Rae. 2008. "The End to Urbanism: How the Changing Spatial Structure of Cities Affected Its Social Capital Potentials." In *Networked Urbanism*, ed. Talja Blokland and Mike Savage, 23–39. Hampshire, UK: Ashgate.

Carroll, Glenn R. 1984. Organizational Ecology. *Annual Review of Sociology* 10: 71–93.

DeSena, Judith, 2009. *Gentrification and Inequality in Brooklyn*. Lanham, MD: Lexington Books.

DiMaggio, P. 1998. "The Relevance of Organizational Theory to the Study of Religion." In *Sacred Companies: Organizational Aspects of Religion and Religious Aspects of Organizations*, ed. N. J. Demrath, P. D. Hall, T. Schmidt, and R. H. Williams, 71–93. New York: Oxford University Press.

Eiesland, Nancy. 2000. *A Particular Place: Urban Restructuring and Religious Ecology in a Southern Exurb*. New Brunswick, NJ: Rutgers University Press.

Florida, Richard L. 2002. *Rise of the Creative Class, and How It's Transforming Work, Leisure, Community and Everyday Life*. New York: Basic Books.

———. 2008. *Who's Your City?* New York: Basic Books.

———. 2010. "It's Not the Economy, Stupid." The Creative Class: The Source on How We Live, Work and Play. October 26. http://www.creativeclass.com/creative_class/2010/10/26/it%E2%80%99s-not-the-economy-stupid/. Accessed March 18, 2012.

Franco, Philip A. 2007. "Educating Toward Communion: The Traditional Italian Feast as a Means of Christian Religious Education," unpublished paper presented at the Conference of the Society of Catholic Social Scientists,

October 27, Saint John's University, Jamaica, NY.

Galchutt, Kathryn M. 2007. "Lutherans in Brooklyn." Unpublished paper.

Gentrification and Rezoning in Williamsburg-Greenpoint. 2007. Edward Bloustein School of Planning and Public Policy, Rutgers University, Newark, NJ, Spring.

Hannan, M. T., G. R. Carroll, and L. Pólos. 2003. "The Organizational Niche." *Sociological Theory* 21: 309–40.

Healy, Anthony. 2005. *The Post-industrial Promise*. Washington, DC: Alban Institute.

Heelas, Paul, and Linda Woodhead. 2005. *The Spiritual Revolution*. Oxford: Blackwell.

Lederer, Victor, and the Brooklyn Historical Society. 2005. *Images of America: Williamsburg*. Charleston, SC: Arcadia.

Levitt, Peggy. 2007. *God Needs No Passports*. New York: The New Press.

Ley, David, and R. Bruce Martin. 1993. "Gentrification as Secularization." *Social Compass* 40, no. 2: 217–32.

Livezey, Lowell. 2000. *Public Religion and Urban Transformation*. New York: New York University Press.

Lloyd, Richard. 2006. *Neo-Bohemia*. New York: Routledge.

Mader, Donald. 1983. *A Witness in the City: Greenpoint Reformed Church*. New York: The Church.

Marwell, Nicole P. 2007. *Bargaining for Brooklyn*. Chicago: University of Chicago Press.

Primeggia, Salvatore, and Joseph A. Varacalli. 1996. "The Sacred and Profane among Italian American Catholics: The Giglio Feast." *International Journal of Politics, Culture, and Society* 9, no. 3: 423–49.

Sampson, Robert J. 1999. "What 'Community' Supplies." In *Urban Problems and Community Development*, ed.

Ronald Ferguson and William Dickens. Washington, DC: Brookings Institution Press.

Saracino-Brown, Japonica. 2007. "Virtuous Marginality: Social Preservationists and the Selection of the Old-Timer." *Theory & Society* 33: 437–68.

Scheitele, Christopher. 2007. "Organizational Niches and Religious Markets: Uniting Two Literatures. *Interdisciplinary Journal of Research on Religion* 3, no. 2. http://www.religjournal.com/pdf/ijro3002-pdf.

Sciorra, Joseph. 1999. "Go Where the Italians Live." In *Gods of the City*, ed.,

310–40. Robert A. Orsi. Bloomington: Indiana University Press.

Stark, Rodney, and Roger Finke. 2000. *Acts of Faith.* Princeton: Princeton University Press.

Watters, Ethan. 2003. *Urban Tribes.* New York: Bloomsbury.

Wuthnow, Robert. 2007. *After the Baby Boomers.* Princeton, NJ: Princeton University Press.

Zukin, Sharon. 1998. "Urban Lifestyles: Diversity and Standardization in Spaces of Consumption." *Urban Studies* 35, nos. 5–6: 825–39.

———. 2010. *The Naked City.* Chicago: University of Chicago Press.

3

Korean American Churches and the Negotiation of Space in Flushing, Queens

Keun-Joo Christine Pae

Eventually English will become a primary language at Korean Catholic
churches in the U.S. At St. Paul Church, however, Korean will be more
likely to remain an official language. The church will play the role of the
cathedral church in the Korean Catholic community in Greater New York
due to its location – Flushing. As long as Korean immigrants keep coming to
New York City, my church will be the Catholic community center for them.

FATHER LEE, ST. PAUL CHONG HA-SANG CATHOLIC CHURCH

Every day, New York City's No. 7 train, also known as the Oriental Express,
carries thousands of Asian Americans in and out of Flushing.[1] Stepping out
of Main Street Station, one faces a diversity of cultures and backgrounds,
including the largest Chinatown on the East Coast. An Indian teenage daughter and her mother in traditional attire walk by young Korean and Chinese
women dressed in the latest fashions. The smell of Chinese food and the scent
of Oriental herbs envelop historic St. George's Episcopal Church, which is
next door to the modern Sheraton Hotel. Downtown Flushing, where Main
Street, Roosevelt Avenue, College Point Boulevard, and 38th and 39th Streets
intersect on another, is filled with Chinese and Korean restaurants, clothing
stores, grocery markets, Korean Protestant churches, Indian-owned conve-
nient stores, and Korean snack stores, along with Starbucks coffee and Pink
Berry frozen yogurt. Queens Public Library stands against tall buildings
containing office space, shopping malls, and apartment complexes. Flushing,
the largest urban center in Queens, is known for its large Asian population,

which surpasses the number of Caucasian residents. Koreans are one of the main groups that have created Flushing's Asian culture and religiosity, as well as accelerated the area's gentrification.

For many Koreans living in Greater New York City, Flushing has special meaning.[2] The section represents "Little Seoul," a place where they can freely speak Korean without worrying about their imperfect and accented English, enjoy Korean food without being concerned about the smell of kimchi, meet other Koreans at various social and private events, go Korean grocery shopping, check out the most recent Korean movies and dramas, accidently encounter Korean celebrities, attend political campaigns organized by U.S. or Korean parties, and most important for this chapter, attend services at their respective religious organizations. Although Koreatowns are now found in Manhattan and in Fort Lee, New Jersey, Flushing still boasts the oldest and largest Koreatown on the East Coast.

Scholars from various academic disciplines, from sociology to theology, agree on two characteristics common to Korean Americans: most are post-1965 immigrants and their children, and Christianity, especially evangelical Protestantism, is a generally shared religious practice (Lee 1995, 23–25; Kwon, Kim, and Warner 2001).

To what extent have urban Korean churches been able to create and preserve Korean spaces in major U.S. cities where religiously, culturally, and ethnically diverse groups compete for limited space and cope with urban development? More specifically, what roles have Korean Christian churches played in formatting Korean spaces in Flushing? What challenges are Korean churches facing as Flushing experiences rapid urban development? How do Korean churches understand their spaces when they are forced to share limited space with other ethnic groups such as the Chinese, who also envision Flushing as their new home? This essay contemplates these questions within an ecological frame, which considers the mutual relationships and effects that take place between the local community and religious institutions (Eiesland and Warner 1998).

THE ECOLOGICAL FRAME AND NEGOTIATING SPACE

The ecological frame considers a congregation to be a social institution that forms and contributes to society – politically, economically, and culturally. Within this frame, "the congregation is analyzed as a unit interacting with other units in society: people, organizations, and cultures" (Eiesland and

Warner 1998, 40). The ecological frame challenges one to see Korean religious congregations as one among many social institutions that have constructed spaces in Flushing. Korean congregations consciously or unconsciously cooperate and compete with other institutions, as well as with local residents.

Korean churches have contributed to the ethnic, racial, cultural, religious, and civic identity formation of Korean Americans. The ecological frame suggests that the process of Korean American Christians' identity formation is interwoven with their congregations' local (and transnational) environment. In other words, a Korean religious congregation does not exist in a bubble but constantly interacts with its cultural, political, and economic environment based on the congregational perception of reality and the members' duties before God. If this is the case, we should not simply ignore the physical spaces of Korean congregations and the particular meanings attached to those spaces.

This article analyzes Korean churches' negotiation of urban space as it is "contested, negotiated, and expropriated by its different social groups, its minorities, and new arrivals" (Davey 2002, 22). Urban space, such as Flushing, is not a fixed entity but is socially and historically constructed and shared with various groups, including Koreans. This social construction happens on the basis of physical space – the foundation for cultural and religious formation.

This study argues that Korean churches have created their physical spaces and socially constructed Korean Christian identities in Flushing. As a result, many Koreans are socially and psychologically attached to the area. The hypothesis is that physical space has been the basis for the sociohistorical process of Korean space formation, and that threats to Korean churches' physical spaces from real estate development make these churches more self-interested, while they search for possibilities to harmoniously live with others beyond religious, cultural, and racial boundaries. Gentrification is referred to in this article as a process of urban redevelopment of commercial space that replaces previous businesses and housing.

METHOD

This chapter analyzes Korean churches' "negotiating spaces" through a study of two Korean congregations: St. Paul Chong Ha-Sang Roman Catholic Church and First United Methodist Church.[3] To understand how these two congregations have negotiated their spaces, first, the historical formation of Flushing, with a focus on religious, racial, and cultural diversity along with

urban development and gentrification, is explored. Second, the physical environments of these congregations and the formation of their religious and
cultural spaces is analyzed. Based on this analysis, I further inquire about
the manner in which these congregations understand physical, cultural, and
religious security in relation to the ownership of these spaces. Next, I study
how they have been attempting to negotiate their spaces for the next generation of Koreans in the midst of Flushing's urban development and growing
racial, ethnic, and religious diversity.

In spite of the growing amount of research focusing on Korean American
Christians and churches, most scholarly works have focused on the theological issues, identity politics, and cultural locations of these churches rather
than addressing regional differences among Korean churches. The relationship between urban development, especially the changes in the urban real
estate market, and Korean Christian institutions is a generally neglected
area. This chapter will contribute to the future scholarly discourse on Korean
churches, one of the most vital elements of our contemporary "U.S. civic
religiosity" (Ecklund 2006).

THE HISTORICAL FORMATION OF FLUSHING:
RELIGIOUS AND RACIAL/ETHNIC DIVERSITY

In an interview, Mrs. Lee, owner of a Korean cosmetic shop in Flushing, recounted:

> Koreans had increased a lot through the 1990s. Korean stores and restaurants
> sprang up everywhere just as Korean churches mushroomed. At that time, we
> ran our businesses on Main Street near the subway station. But soon Chinese
> took over Main Street. Obviously Koreatown in Flushing has been expanding
> because the Korean population has grown. I am not sure, however, whether
> our businesses have grown more. We are struggling. We had to move from
> Main Street to Northern Boulevard. More Korean businesses are moving
> eastward, all the way to Bayside. Who knows? In some years, all the Korean
> stores have to leave Flushing because of the Chinese influx.[4]

As many immigrants have found their new homes in Flushing over the
past four decades, their faith organizations – Christian churches, Buddhist
and Hindu temples, mosques, and Sikh gurdwaras – have also grown in number. Just as newcomers in Flushing struggle to adjust to the heterogeneity of
the neighborhood, their religious organizations have attempted to find their
place and create homogenous spaces. Perhaps it is not merely an accident that

Flushing has become home to a number of religions given that "two hundred different houses of worship are densely populated in a residential neighborhood and commercial district about two-point-five square miles" (Hanson forthcoming). One cannot understand the formation of Flushing without first considering religious freedom.

Flushing was founded in 1654 under Dutch Governor Peter Stuyvesant's official recognition of religious tolerance for English Quakers. The Flushing Remonstrance was the first official document that stipulated religious freedom in the United States (Jackson 1995). The Flushing Remonstrance was a theological and ethical document that spoke to the notion of "religious hospitality" (Eck 2002). Bowne Street is named after John Bowne, a Quaker leader at the time the Remonstrance was issued. Commemorating its legacy, the historic wooden Quaker Meeting House still stands at the intersection of Northern Boulevard and Union Street, across from Flushing Town Hall. The meetinghouse's signs, written in English, Spanish, and Korean, show Flushing's demographic diversity.[5]

Religious tolerance later attracted former African slaves in the eighteenth century. Richard Allen, first bishop of the African Methodist Episcopal Church, sent the first AME missionaries to expand the newly established church's mission in Flushing. The historically black Macedonia AME Church was founded in 1837 at Union and 39th Avenue, where it still stands. Macedonia has actively served the Flushing community ever since. Now Korean restaurants, bakeries, cafes, and hair salons surround Macedonia Church, as Union Street is the starting point of Flushing's Koreatown.

After the Civil War, Flushing grew rapidly. At the turn of the twentieth century, the electrification of the Long Island Railroad and full activation of the No. 7 line of the New York subway in the 1930s conveniently connected Flushing to Manhattan. Public railroad systems brought customers to the shopping district in Flushing. With the World's Fair of 1964–1965, Flushing was on its way to becoming a densely populated urban center (Jackson 1995).

In the 1970s, however, an exodus of people from the area began. Flushing residents and customers were lured to Long Island's better school districts, suburbs, and shopping malls. However, the decline of the commercial sector soon attracted new Asian immigrants because of the rock-bottom rental prices for housing and store space. With diverse religious backgrounds, Asian immigrants were also able to establish their respective religious institutions in Flushing. Diana Eck's celebratory approach to Flushing's exercise of religious hospitality notwithstanding (2002), it was not religious freedom that attracted religious Asian immigrants, but cheap real estate prices and easy access to Manhattan via public transportation.

Since the 1960s and '70s, the Asian population has sharply increased, bringing new economic development into Flushing. In 2006 more than 50 percent of Flushing residents (District 7) were identified as Asian. Fifty-seven percent of these were Chinese, while Koreans made up 27 percent of the population.[6]

FLUSHING'S RAPID URBAN DEVELOPMENT

Since the late 1980s, Flushing has experienced an economic boom that can be attributed to the flow of Asian money from Taiwan, Hong Kong, and South Korea. The real estate business grew as the Asian money market in Flushing expanded. Whereas mixed-use multifamily condominium buildings were characteristic of Flushing in the 1980s, in the 1990s, office and commercial buildings started occupying the downtown area. Flushing's skyline has changed seemingly every day. Three ongoing projects will make Flushing even bigger and more urbanized: transformation of the Municipal Parking Lot into a multi-entertainment complex with underground parking; development of the Flushing River for a shopping mall and a residential tower; and the new Mets stadium (Roleke 2005).

Since the late 1990s, Flushing real estate prices have climbed, raising concerns among longtime residents who feared they would be priced out of the market (Leduff 1997). As Flushing has become more densely populated, both longtime residents and newcomers have struggled to find affordable housing. For example, Katherine Williams of Macedonia AME Church, who has spent her seventy-some-year life in Flushing, told her fellow church members not to sell their houses to developers, because once their houses were sold, they would not be able to buy another house in Flushing due to the increase in housing prices.[7] During my interview with Ms. Williams, she repeatedly showed her frustration with development in Flushing – too many cars and people, increasing rental prices, and new expensive apartment complexes. "I am so lucky to own the house," said Williams. "Otherwise, I would have had to leave Flushing a long time ago. How can one afford to pay more than one thousand dollars for a one-bedroom apartment per month?"[8] She was happy with her church's new involvement with an affordable housing project; she showed me the blueprint of a tall apartment building, displayed in front of the sanctuary.

The huge influx of Asian immigrants, especially prosperous Chinese and Koreans, has increased demand for already scarce housing and office and parking space (Leduff 1997). In 2000, the median monthly rent in Flushing was $800, but since then, rents have risen (Ecologies of Learning Project [EOL], 2008). According to 2006 statistics, the rental price for a one-bedroom apartment ranged between $950 and $1,400 (Roleke 2005).

KOREAN SPACES IN FLUSHING

Where and how have Koreans formed their spaces, including churches, in Flushing? According to the Korean Council of Churches in Greater New York, in 2003, about two hundred Korean Protestant churches were in Flushing and its vicinity. The council, however, assumed the number would be approximately five hundred in Greater Flushing if non-council-member churches and nondenominational small-house churches were included.[9] It is well known that Korean churches have served as community centers for Korean immigrants in Flushing.

Next to Los Angeles, New York City is the second-largest U.S. entry point for Koreans. Approximately 60,000 Korean Americans currently live in Greater New York (EOL, 2006). If undocumented Korean immigrants and long-term visitors were included, this number would be much higher. The first Koreans in Flushing were nurses who worked at Flushing General Hospital in the late 1960s (Min and Song 1998), as well as those who attended the World's Fair. Since then, Flushing has been the symbolic home for Korean immigrants in the Tri-State area (New York, New Jersey, and Connecticut). With respect to the influx of Korean immigrants in Flushing, the area has become home to major Korean religious institutions, including Protestant churches affiliated with American and Korean denominations, the Catholic Church, Buddhist temples, the Latter-day Saints, Jehovah's Witnesses, the Won Buddhist temple, Jeung San Temple, and Shamans' houses, to name only a few.

Koreatown, the commercial hub, runs from Union Street eastward on Northern Boulevard to Bayside. Until the end of the 1990s, Flushing consisted of what Max Weber calls "clusters of different ethnic localities" (Weber [1921] 1968). Chinese, Korean, and South Asian areas surrounded the religious worship spaces of these groups and used to have somewhat visible boundaries. Chinatown, however, has outgrown other ethnic communities. Adjacent to downtown Flushing or Chinatown is Koreatown. Although the Korean commercial area of Union Street – "little Seoul," as Pyong Gap Min (1996) calls it – intersects with busy Main Street and Roosevelt Avenue, the eastern part of Northern Boulevard, where Korean stores have started moving from Main Street, looks less urbanized and quieter than downtown Flushing. Stores and apartment complexes spread out on Northern Boulevard, and most buildings are lower than five stories.

A few years ago, however, one might easily encounter Korean stores intermingled with Chinese stores in downtown. Although there are still small Korean stores such as a hair salon, a pharmacy, a couple of cafés, and a cosmetics store, the downtown core is predominantly a Chinese commercial area, known as Chinatown to Flushing residents and tourists. Reverend Kim, whose Reformed Church facility is located a couple of blocks away from downtown's busy streets, recalled that Main Street was formerly considered a Korean business sector. According to him, as Chinatown expanded, the building owners (mostly Caucasians) who rented their spaces to Koreans either sold their properties to the Chinese or rented spaces to Chinese residents instead because they offered better prices. Now his church building is located between the exclusively Chinese area and the edge of Koreatown. He believes that it was only by God's grace that his church bought the building twenty years ago.[10] Although many Koreans live and run their businesses in the neighborhood, they do not own these places, making them vulnerable to real estate development.

While longtime white residents are concerned about rapid community development fueled by the influx of Asian immigrants, Korean residents are worried about the expansion of Chinatown. In 2008 a Korean newspaper reported a newly opened Chinese grocery store on Northern Boulevard. According to the article, Koreans wondered whether this grocery store would be the beginning of Chinese expansion on Northern Boulevard, currently the center of the new Korean commercial area. Space that the Chinese grocery store inhabited had been empty for a while due to its rental price of $1 million per year.[11] Another small Chinese shopping mall is also located on Northern Boulevard, bisecting the line of Korean stores and increasing Chinese presence in the area.[12]

In constantly changing Flushing, where urban development is evident and Korean concern about the expansion of Chinese business is audible, it is worth examining the way in which Koreans have been negotiating their spaces. What changes and challenges do they see in Flushing, and how do their churches respond to these challenges?

ECOLOGIES OF ST. PAUL CHURCH AND FIRST
UNITED METHODIST CHURCH

Let us first examine St. Paul Church and First United Methodist Church in order to understand how these congregations negotiate their space and interact with urban change in Flushing. Both congregations are located in working-class neighborhoods near Northern Boulevard. St. Paul Church is one of the oldest Korean Catholic parishes on the East coast, with about 2,000 worshippers attending Sunday Mass. First United Methodist, which has approximately 1,600 worshippers on Sundays, is the largest congregation in the United Methodist New York Annual Conference and one of the five largest Korean United Methodist congregations nationally. South Korean leaders who emigrated with other Korean Christians after receiving seminary educations founded both churches.

First United Methodist is located in Koreatown's Food District (Muk-ja-gol-mok), two blocks away from the Murray Hill Station of the Long Island Railroad. It takes about twenty minutes to walk to First United Methodist from the Main Street subway station. Around the church one can easily find clusters of Korean restaurants, hair salons, and coffee shops. In contrast to First United Methodist, St. Paul Church is placed in the more culturally and religiously diverse area of Parsons Street, where a Conservative Jewish synagogue, a Sikh gurdwara, a Salvation Army church, a Jehovah's Witnesses kingdom hall, a Hindu temple, and a mosque are found.

OWNERSHIP OF THE WORSHIP SPACES:
SECURITY AND PROTECTION

Urban space is socially constructed. Korean churches have been constructed through Korean immigrants' social interactions, institutions, and understanding of space. The development of St. Paul Church and First United Methodist suggests that the congregants understand their church space in terms of social utility and property.

St. Paul Church first began as a small Bible study group in Rego Park, Queens, in the mid-1970s. The group used part of a local Catholic church building. Since most Korean immigrants are evangelical Protestants, Korean Catholics needed their own space for worship and social fellowship as they settled in the new country. In 1981, under the leadership of Father Chong from

South Korea, St. Paul Church purchased the land and building at its current location and thus secured its worship space. The Catholic Church of South Korea financially supported St. Paul's establishment. At the time of my field research at St. Paul (fall 2006 to summer 2007), three ordained priests served the church. The rector was a one-point-five-generation Korean, bilingual and bicultural, and had grown up in Brooklyn and received his seminary education in New York. Father Lee, the rector, was the first American-educated priest appointed to the parish. The other two priests had been sent from the Diocese of Busan in South Korea. While visiting New York City, many Korean Catholic visitors attend mass at St. Paul Church, as the church is well known even in South Korea.

First United Methodist was originally an all-white congregation. First established at Union and Main Streets in 1811, the church purchased land and the building at the current location of 149th Street between Roosevelt and 38th Avenue in 1951. In 1975 a Korean immigrant pastor was appointed to the Caucasian congregation. His presence attracted Korean Methodist immigrants, who would soon form a Korean congregation. In 1982 the Korean congregation joined the United Methodist New York Annual Conference as an independent church. Two racially different congregations thus cohabited in one building. In 1988 the two congregations decided to merge. More than twenty years later, First United Methodist is a Korean-only congregation.

For both congregations, as for other ethnic Korean churches, a physical worship space is important for religious practice. Most Asian religious organizations emphasize religion as doing – performing ritual, attending worship services, and doing charity work – rather than believing (Carnes and Yang 2004). In order to *do* religion, Korean Christians need physical spaces for their gatherings. Observing St. Paul Church's and First United Methodist's prayer meetings for young adults, I found that in spite of their different Christian traditions, both congregations expressed their gratitude to God for church buildings in a foreign country. In their prayers, Korean young adults confessed that thanks to God's grace, their churches could own the secured spaces, which enabled them to gather and spiritually grow.[13] Their church buildings were the spaces permitted by the dominant society where they could enter the sacred, as well as befriend Korean peers with whom they could intimately share life difficulties.

For these two Korean congregations, the security of the worship space is equated not only with the ownership of the space but also with protection of their Christian faith. If Koreatown in Flushing gives Korean immigrants a cultural sense of home, Korean churches located in the center of Flushing add a religious sense of home with an emphasis on doing. Cultural and religious diversity in Flushing often leads Korean Christians to articulate their religious and ethnic identities, which differentiates them from religious and racial others.

Both St. Paul Church and First United Methodist define themselves primarily as a community of worship. In spite of their different Christian traditions, both churches see Korean Christians as spiritually enthusiastic and loyal to their congregations. Korean church spaces become the nurturing ground for spiritual enthusiasm. In these spaces Korean Christians build a relationship with God, "the invisible significant other" and experience "therapeutic spirituality" (Carnes and Yang 2004). Father Lee commented that the "younger Korean American generation should emulate their parents' spiritual enthusiasm and sincere service for the church."[14] Pastor Park of the First United Methodist also emphasized this point: "Korean American youth and children should learn the core of Korean Christianity – dedication to God and spiritual growth."[15] While I observed St. Paul Church's young adult Healing Service and First United Methodist's young adults prayer meeting, in spite of the different forms of rituals, both services emphasized one's spiritual purification, healing, and dedication to God. Both services consisted of contemporary gospel songs, accompanied by drums and a synthesizer, which seemed to provoke enthusiastic participation among attendees.

Although the secured church space is important for Korean Christians to practice their faith, they are not necessarily self-enclosed, nor do they try to find their Christian identity only through the religious service. For example, the pastoral leaders of First United Methodist seek to establish the church's identity in Flushing through involvement in social services there. First UMC identifies itself as a "flagship church."[16] As such, the church emphasizes its civic responsibility beyond the Korean community. First United Methodist runs several scholarship programs for youth and college students in Greater Flushing and actively participates in local cultural festivals. According to Reverend Kim, the senior pastor of First United Methodist at the time of my research, the flagship church is a theologically cultivated identity. Christians should take responsibility to lead human society under the guidance of God's love and justice. To be a community leader for a good cause is not only a Christian responsibility but also enables First United Methodist to be spiritually and physically sustainable in New York City.[17]

THE CHURCH AS A CULTURAL AND EDUCATIONAL
SPACE IN A POOR URBAN NEIGHBORHOOD

Although both St. Paul Church and First United Methodist Church seem to place Christian identity over Korean ethnic identity, it still may be questioned whether these two congregations separate the two dimensions. Korean Christian identity, marked by enthusiasm and dedication, is normalized among Korean Christians in Flushing. These days both St. Paul and First United Methodist attempt to make their churches culturally Korean-Christian spaces, especially for Korean children and youth. The security of the space is important not only for passing down Korean Christian culture to children and youth, but also for protecting them from urban problems.

Aiming to nurture Korean children and youth's Christian faith, Korean megachurches, including St. Paul and First United Methodist, have organized various after-school programs for children, such as a Korean language school, an English-learning center, and vacation Bible school. These faith-based after-school programs are important for Korean youth and children in Flushing, where resources for healthy entertainment for youth and children are limited. Angie Chung's research (2000) on Los Angeles's Koreatown youth is especially relevant to those in Flushing's Koreatown. Chung argues that Koreatown youth face the structural disadvantages of low-income status, lack of parental guidance, the absence of neighborhood recreational spaces, and the poor quality of the local school system.

As Manuel Castells notes, urbanized Flushing is experiencing injustices such as poverty and the marginalization of immigrants, and city dwellers have mobilized to change the political and economic structures of the city (Castells 2002). Various Korean faith-based organizations, such as the Korean Youth Council, are aware of the social disadvantages that Korean youth and children are facing in Flushing and try to organize cultural programs and healthy recreation for them. Korean churches' after-school programs cannot be understood merely through the lens of preservation of Korean culture. Rather, these programs aim at protecting youth and children from crime, violence, drug addiction, early sexual involvement, and most important, identity problems, all of which can lead to dropping out of school. Pastor Park, the youth minister of First Methodist Church, said, "There is a class issue between youths in Flushing and those on Long Island. The youths from Long Island are middle- to upper-middle-class kids, who are provided with financial and cultural resources by their parents. The Flushing youths are the children of single parents or working-class families. They do not have enough resources. So the church tries to provide various programs, such as lock-ins, sports games, movie nights, and cooking schools, especially during the spring break and summer vacation." In this sense, the Korean church becomes a socio-economic service center. While Flushing does not offer enough recreational spaces, Korean church buildings become public spaces for disadvantaged Koreans.

During my field research, however, I failed to find that Korean churches connected urban issues (poverty, drug addiction, crime, etc.) to the larger social system. Most leaders of the Korean faith-based organizations emphasized individual changes through Jesus Christ so that Korean American youths and children would not mess up their lives with "bad, secular" culture.[18] Elaine Ecklund's research on Korean American evangelicals (2006) has yielded similar findings.

PHYSICAL SPACES IN THE MIDST OF URBAN DEVELOPMENT

As we consider the important roles that Korean churches play as social institutions, we can see why physical spaces are crucial for them. Korean churches' efforts to secure their worship spaces have been challenged by urban development and by the increasing population in Flushing. Outdated city zoning laws have helped Korean churches flourish in the neighborhood. Laws adopted in 1961 allow the establishment of community facilities, including religious centers, in residential sections. If a church decides to take over a house, the action does not require community board approval so long as no additions are made (Kuriakos 2001). In fact, ten years ago, Salvation Army Church, across the street from St. Paul, bought houses around the church building and turned them into a parking lot. The Flushing community wondered whether this would happen more often. Currently a Korean congregation shares the Salvation Army Church building with a Caucasian congregation. Instead of expanding its space, St. Paul Church occasionally uses the Salvation Army's parking spaces and playground. Father Lee considers the use of Salvation Army's facilities as a form of interdenominational interaction.

When the zoning laws were written, the legislators envisioned a religious facility with fixed seats like pews and mandated a certain quota of parking spots accordingly. But more Korean churches have found a loophole by using folding chairs and valet parking (Kuriakos 2001). The expansion of Korean churches has raised further housing issues in Flushing. Real estate companies aggressively buy small houses and turn them into apartment complexes. Urban development exacerbates scarcity of parking spaces, lack of playgrounds for children, traffic jams, and population density. As long as many people live in a limited number of spaces, Korean churches saturating Flushing can hardly be welcome. Moreover, most Korean churches in Flushing do not engage in community concerns like housing and urban development. However, Korean community activists, such as YKASEC/Empowering the Korean American Community, urge Korean churches to participate in community issues of political economy beyond their evangelical boundaries.[19] Otherwise, these activists predict, anti-immigrant feelings will increase in Flushing.

For the last three decades, the physical expansion of Korean churches in Flushing has increased anti-Korean sentiment among longtime residents and home owners. White residents whose houses are surrounded by many Korean churches complain of feeling alienated in their hometown and of losing privacy (Kuriakos 2001). It is not unusual to encounter more than five Korean churches within one block. For example, on Union Street between 35th and Northern, ten Korean churches neighbor one another, with seven of the ten occupying one building.

In April 2008 the Ecologies of Learning Project organized a Flushing Forum in order to listen to diverse congregational voices in the neighborhood. Chinese, African American, Korean, Indian, and Caucasian religious leaders gathered and shared their congregational concerns related to urban development. These leaders all unequivocally said that the increasing population and the restless urban development project in Flushing exacerbated urban problems such as traffic jams, pollution, poverty, lack of affordable housing, and lack of parking spaces. Moreover, since Flushing is easily accessible to New York City public transportation, many immigrants and longtime residents want to remain in the area despite the deteriorating environment. The rising price of rental housing has become burdensome to many people, as well as religious institutions. Urban development has caused conflicts between longtime residents and newcomers, between residents and merchants, and among diverse ethnic groups. In addition, many of Flushing's religious institutions serve members who live on the outskirts of the community; therefore the lack of parking spaces and large number of traffic jams cause difficulties for these institutions in organizing their worship activities.

Every Sunday the streets around First United Methodist and St. Paul Churches are filled with people, cars, and noise. Their neighbors frequently complain about these congregations' domination of the spaces, while some of the congregants wonder why the churches do not expand their facilities or move to the suburbs. As their congregations grow, Korean churches usually move their facilities into suburbs or cheaper areas in Queens where larger buildings and parking spaces are available. Otherwise, a local Korean church may purchase and demolish small houses around the church facilities in order to expand its space, just as the Salvation Army did.

Although neither St. Paul Church nor First United Methodist Church has enough space for their activities, the two congregations have not considered expanding their church facilities or moving into suburbs. Presumably, the limited space for residency along with anti-Korean feelings in Flushing do not allow the church simply to buy land or houses. In addition, the Roman Catholic hierarchy and the United Methodist episcopacy do not allow their local churches to move out of their diocesan or district boundaries.

Both St. Paul and First United Methodist attempt to accommodate their activities to the current church facilities. The major reason that neither of these congregations considers moving out of its facilities from Flushing is that it feels attached to the area, as a Korean space. Reverend Kim of First United Methodist said, "More than 50 percent of our members rent apartments around the church. They built up the church and have maintained the church ministries. If we move the church building to somewhere in Long Island, these people will have a hard time attending the church services, because of lack of public transportation. We should be loyal to the Flushing residents."[20]

Similarly, Mr. Yim, a lay leader of St. Paul Church, said that the church's identity was interwoven with Flushing. According to Yim, Flushing gave a sense of comfort to Korean Catholics. Even after many of them had moved out of Flushing, they continued to attend St. Paul Church, though other Korean Catholic churches were available in their new neighborhoods. This sense of home eventually led those who left to return to the church after they married and were looking for a community for their families.[21]

Increasing prices in the real estate market in Flushing make it difficult for Korean churches to expand their facilities. At the same time, it becomes a new task for Korean churches to secure their worship spaces for the next generation of Koreans. Due to high rental prices, small Korean churches undergo financial difficulties and are forced to close their ministries. Reverend Kim of First United Methodist criticized many Korean churches for investing large portions of their funds into church buildings that can be a financial burden on the next generation.[22] To avert this, First United Methodist tries to secure financial resources for the younger generation, which will eventually take over the church.

The instability in the housing market and the increasing density of population in Flushing increase economic injustice, such as poverty. While struggling to maintain their congregational facilities, Flushing's religious institutions attempt to serve the poor and open their spaces for community activities, as with the aforementioned after-school programs for youth. First United Methodist's merit-based scholarship programs focus on working-class teenagers, regardless of their racial/ethnic identities. Elderly Korean immigrants are common guests at Macedonia African Methodist Episcopal Church's food pantry and soup kitchen. H Korean Presbyterian Church is the only Korean congregation in Flushing that runs a soup kitchen for local residents.

Although I did not witness St. Paul Church's active involvement in economic issues in Flushing, church leaders were fully aware of the presence of low-income members in their congregations. Meanwhile, First United Methodist communicates with non-Koreans and demonstrates its presence in Flushing by distributing social services. First United Methodist spends a significant amount of money on community service, such as donations to the Rainbow Center, which helps poor Korean women immigrants. Every Saturday morning First United Methodist members distribute free doughnuts and coffee to the mostly Latino day laborers on Northern Boulevard near the church building who look for jobs. First United Methodist thus tries to demonstrate its leadership in the Flushing community through involvement in social activism.

CONCLUSION: NEGOTIATING SPACES IN FLUSHING'S URBAN DEVELOPMENT

Even though technological advances allow first-generation Korean immigrants in New York City to keep in daily contact with South Korea, they still need a physical place where they can touch, smell, see, hear, and feel Korea. American-born Koreans also need a physical location to help ground their identity as both American and Korean. The Korean church leaders whom I interviewed envisioned Flushing as the physical place or substitute home for Korean immigrants.

At the same time, Korean churches face the question: What does it mean to be a good neighbor to religiously, racially, and culturally diverse others who are also coping with urban development and seeking to secure Flushing as their home? Perhaps this sort of question will become more relevant to Korean churches in Flushing as urban development continues to reshape the area. If Korean churches as social institutions have shaped Korean Americans' identity (Cha 2001) and their understanding of civic responsibility and participation in society and politics (Ecklund 2006), the ecological frame suggests that Flushing's Korean churches will continue to serve these roles in correspondence to Flushing's social, political, and economic environment. This chapter argues that a permanent physical space is the foundation for all these roles that Korean churches play as social institutions.

Korean churches have been havens for Korean immigrants in the United States. The construction of Koreatown in Flushing first became possible because of the affordability of real estate. Korean churches moved into Flushing with Korean immigrants and turned Flushing into a home for Korean Christians. Religious and cultural diversity in Flushing leads Korean churches to be defensive of their Korean-Christian faith. Cultural, religious, and ethnic diversity in Flushing does not necessarily lead different groups to interact with one another beyond comfortable boundaries. Although different groups are aware of others' presence in Flushing, as Lowell Livezey argues based on his research in Chicago's Rogers Park (2000), the diversity of a particular neighborhood may result in the active creation of enclaves and boundaries, the articulation of rationales for separation, and competition for social benefits. Korean churches' survival strategies have depended on separation from others and even from political and social justice concerns. In response to current urban development in Flushing, Korean churches have tried to secure their physical worship spaces so that they will be able to hand down "Korean Christianity" to the next generation of Koreans. Korean Christians understand physical space as providing an opportunity for practicing their enthusiastic Christian faith and feeling a sense of home, as well as enabling their children to continue their legacy of faith.

Since their arrival in Flushing, Koreans have continuously negotiated their own spaces with others. The established church properties of both St. Paul Church and First United Methodist Church are negotiated spaces. Based on these negotiated spaces (physicality), the two congregations have built up "intimate connections" among their members, who also feel emotionally attached to their particular spaces.

As socially diverse people are located in a densely populated and limited space, competition for those spaces seems inevitable. Due to the scarcity of residential space, Korean churches cannot avoid social interaction with other ethnic groups. Urban development and dense population lead Korean religious institutions to negotiate their physical as well as social spaces. Their physical spaces become more difficult to secure as developers aggressively purchase properties and as urban development projects use up more of Flushing's real estate. Nadia Mian's research (2008) on religious institutions in the Greater New York City area shows that urban changes such as immigration and gentrification lead religious institutions to sell or redevelop their properties to create either commercial facilities or market-rate and affordable housing. Sooner or later, Korean religious institutions in Flushing may join this trend as described by Mian. Korean religious institutions cannot simply stay inside their negotiated spaces. They must continue to renegotiate those spaces with others to survive in the city.

Although many Korean churches are indifferent to economic issues in Flushing, First United Methodist shows that a Korean congregation can move outside its religious and cultural comfort zone in order to live with others in the limited space. St. Paul Church also demonstrates an effort to adapt to changing circumstances. Perhaps these two congregations are strong enough to do so because of their secured physical spaces and church memberships. The examples of these two congregations suggest that churches do not live in a bubble, but consciously or unconsciously interact with their social and physical environment (Mian 2008). The ecological frame highlights that churches are always negotiat*ing* their spaces rather than existing within negotiat*ed* spaces. St. Paul Church and First United Methodist congregations' interactions with their environments are the result of their consistent efforts to negotiate their spaces for physical, social, cultural, and spiritual security, not only for the current members but also for future generations.

NOTES

Epigraph: Fr. Gabriel Lee, interview with the author, Flushing, Queens, New York City (December 2006).

1. The term "Asian American" is used loosely in this article to include Asian immigrants, American-born Asians, and Asian short- or long-term residents.

2. This essay uses the term "Koreans" in an inclusive way in order to take diverse people culturally and ethnically rooted in Korea into consideration. There is much diversity among so-called Koreans in the view of their non-Korean counterparts in the United States. Second- or third-generation Korean Americans, who were born in the United States, share cultural identities different from those of their parents – first-generation Korean Americans. One-point-five-generation Koreans emigrated into

the United States when they were young, and therefore their immigration was somewhat forced by their parents. There are also a significant number of Korean international students, businessmen, visitors, long-term residents, and un-documented immigrants, as well as bira-cial Koreans. Although first-generation Korean Americans and their children have become the most vital members of ethnic Korean churches, all the Koreans mentioned above compose the bodies of the churches. This article also uses "Korean American" to specify those whose academic and religious work is based on U.S. contexts.

3. As a research and teaching fellow with the Ecologies of Learning project, I spent approximately eighteen months (fall 2006–spring 2008) researching Korean churches in Flushing, including Catholic, Methodist, Presbyterian, and Reformed congregations. The main research method was a qualitative ethnographic approach. Data for this article was collected mostly from my two-year field research involving participant observation in the churches' worship and community services, numerous site visits, and in-depth interviews with twenty local Flushing residents, including Korean clergy and lay leaders, non-Korean religious leaders, police authorities, and small-business owners.

4. Interview with the author in Korean, Flushing, Queens (April 2007).

5. Personally I never met Quakers or saw their church while growing up in South Korea. It was a surprise for me to encounter the Korean Quakers' meeting-house in a foreign country.

6. Data based on 2000 U.S. Census and 2005 Queens Borough Census.

7. Williams, interview with the author, Flushing (December 2007 and April 2008).

8. Ibid.

9. Reverend Cho and Reverend Lee, interview with the author, Flushing (May 2007).

10. Reverend Kim, interview with the author, Flushing (January 2006).

11. Jong Hoon Kim, "A Northern Building Taken over by Chinese," USA Joong Ang News, August 20, 2008, http://www.koreadaily.com/news/read.asp?art_id=676179 (accessed March 19, 2012).

12. Since my research focused on Korean religious institutions in Flushing, it does not address the expansion of the Chinese market. Through conversations with my fellow researcher Weishan Huang, whose research interests include Chinese religiosity in Flushing, I discovered that Taiwanese American corporations and real estate companies have purchased land and properties in Flushing and developed Chinatown. These companies had a blueprint for urban development when Chinatown started forming in Flushing. Strictly speaking, Taiwanese, not mainland Chinese, were the first Asian settlers in downtown Flushing and were major dealers in its real estate market. Recently, mainland Chinese, especially the Fuzhounese, have moved to Flushing for jobs. Kenneth Guest's *God in Chinatown* (2003) is a relevant resource on Chinese migration into Flushing, though his research focuses on Manhattan's Chinatown.

13. St. Paul Church, Young Adults' Healing Service, participant observation by the author, Flushing (October 2006). First United Methodist Church, Young Adults' Bible Study and Prayer Meeting, participant observation by the author, Flushing (February 2007).

14. Father Lee, interview with author.

15. Pastor Woo Young Park, interview with the author, Flushing (November 2007).

16. This term was uniquely developed by First UMC's senior pastor, Reverend

Kim. Reverend Kim, interview with author, Flushing (February 2007).

17. Ibid.

18. For example, during my interviews with the staff and the youth members of the Korean Youth Council, all of them unequivocally said that Flushing did not have a good environment for Korean American youth. The positive changes for Korean American youth would not come from the social changes but through Jesus Christ. If they met Jesus Christ, they would step away from the bad environment. Interviews by the author, Flushing (January, May, and June 2007).

19. This information was obtained through informal interviews with the activists from YKASEC and Rainbow Center.

20. Reverend Kim, interview with the author.

21. S. Yim, phone interview with the author (October 2006).

22. Reverend Kim, interview with author.

REFERENCES

Carnes, Tony, and Fenggang Yang, eds. 2004. *Asian American Religions: The Making and Remaking of Borders and Boundaries.* New York: New York University Press.

Castells, Manuel. 2002. *The Castells Reader on Cities and Social Theory.* Malden, MA: Blackwell.

Cha, Peter. 2001. "Ethnic Identity Formation and Participation in Immigrant Churches: Second-Generation Korean American Experiences." In *Korean Americans and Their Religions: Pilgrims and Missionaries from a Different Shore,* ed. Ho-Youn Kwon, Kwang Chung Kim, and R. Stephen Warner, 141–56. University Park: Pennsylvania State University Press.

Chung, Angie. 2000. "Korean American Youth in Koreatown: The Impact of Neighborhood Structures." In "The Korean Diaspora in the USA: Challenges and Evolution." Special issue, *Korean and Korean American Studies Bulletin* 11, no. 2: U21–U35.

Davey, Andrew. 2002. *Urban Christianity and Global Order: Theological Resources for an Urban Future.* Peabody, MA: Hendrickson.

Eck, Diana. 2002. *A New Religious America: How a "Christian Country" Has Become the World's Most Religiously Diverse Nation.* New York: Harper One.

Ecklund, Elaine Howard. 2006. *Korean American Evangelicals: New Models for Civic Life.* New York: Oxford University Press.

Eiesland, Nancy, and R. Stephen Warner. 1998. "Ecology: Seeing the Congregation in Context." In *Studying Congregations,* ed. Nancy Ammerman, Jackson Carroll, Carl Dudley, and William McKinney, 40–77. Nashville: Abingdon Press.

Guest, Kenneth. 2003. *God in Chinatown: Religion and Survival in New York's Evolving Immigrant Community.* 2003. New York: New York University Press.

Hanson, Scott. Forthcoming. *City of Gods: Religious Freedom, Immigration, and Pluralism in Flushing, Queens, New York City, 1945–2001.* New York: Oxford University Press.

Harvey, David. 1996. *Justice, Nature, and the Geographies of Difference.* Malden, MA: Blackwell.

Jackson, Kenneth. 1995. *The Encyclopedia of New York City*. New Haven, CT: Yale University Press.

Kuriakos, Sajan P. 2001. "Holy Land: The Growth of Korean Churches in Flushing Sparks Community Tensions." *Village Voice*, February 13. http://www.villagevoice.com/2001-02-13/news/holy-land/ (accessed April 23, 2012).

Kwon, Ho-Youn, Kwang Chung Kim, and R. Stephen Warner, eds. 2001. *Korean Americans and Their Religions: Pilgrims and Missionaries from a Different Shore*. University Park: Pennsylvania State University Press.

Leduff, Charlie. 1997. "Neighborhood Report: Flushing; For Asian-Americans in Flushing, Boom and Maybe Bust: Housing Prices Rise with Immigration." *New York Times*, December 7.

Lee, Jung Young. *Marginality: The Key to Multicultural Theology*. Minneapolis: Augsburg Fortress Press, 1995.

Livezey, Lowell. 2000. "Communities and Enclaves: Where Jews, Christians, Hindus, and Muslims Share the Neighborhoods." *Public Religion and Urban Transformation: Faith in the City*, edited by Lowell Livezey, 133–62. New York: New York University Press, 2000.

Mian, Nadia. 2008. "Prophets-for-Profits: Redevelopment and the Altering Urban Religious Landscape." *Urban Studies* 45, no. 10 (September): 2143–61.

Min, Pyong Gap. 1996. *Caught in the Middle: Korean Communities in the New York and Los Angeles*. Berkeley: University California Press, 1996.

Min, Pyong Gap, and Young I. Song. 1998. "Demographic Characteristics and Trends of Post-1965 Korean Immigrant Women and Men." In *Korean American Women: From Tradition to Modern World*, ed. Young I. Song and Ailee Moon. Westport, CT: Praeger.

Roleke, John. "Flushing: Queens Neighborhood Profile." In "Queens, NY." About.com. http://queens.about.com/od/neighborhoods/p/flushing.htm (accessed April 2, 2009).

Weber, Max. (1921) 1968. *The City*. Glencoe, IL: Free Press.

PART TWO

Immigration, Religion, and
Neighborhood Change

4

Diversity and Competition: Politics and Conflict in New Immigrant Communities

Weishan Huang

Falun Gong (FLG) stepped onto the world stage with its sit-in demonstration in Beijing on April 25, 1999 – with more than 10,000 participants, the largest public protest in China since the Tiananmen Square incident in 1989. Since then, New York City has become the center of the group's resistance efforts. Established by its charismatic leader, Master Li Hongzhi, Falun Gong is an interesting case study of a modern Buddhist-Taoist–qi-gong faith group with a highly mobilized group of followers.

This chapter seeks, first, to understand the changing ecology of Chinese immigrant communities in New York and to discuss the gentrification of Flushing, which is triggered by transnational capital. Second, the chapter introduces the practices of Falun Gong and focuses on the strategic campaigns of the movement in New York, particularly its parades in immigrant communities. The research has discovered that, to understand the politics of diversity within ethnic Chinese politics, we have to locate the immigrant community in a global milieu. The conflict between Falun Gong and China's government has been translated onto the streets of New York City, a development that reveals the politics of immigrant communities as a reflection of domestic politics in their home countries.

Working within the framework of religious ecology, I examine Falun Gong in New York as a network "unit" that interacts with other units in society: people, organizations, and cultures. The group's practices in public parks and community parades are examined in terms of the purposes of "evangeli-cal" mission and community building in this noninstitutionalized but highly mobilized faith group.

A MULTILAYERED RELIGIOUS ECOLOGY

As conceived by Nancy L. Eiesland, Nancy Ammerman, and R. Stephen Warner, the ecological frame recognizes that a congregation is one among many, each having its own functions, membership, vision, and influence. Ei-esland and Warner (1998) introduced the concept of the open-ended character of the congregation's environment: its extension from the local neighborhood to the global community, and from the immediate present to the past and future. A congregation is linked to networks and events across geographic and temporal space. Not only are communities discrete localities with stable boundaries and fixed constituencies, but they are also characterized by shared conversations, common practices, and structures that promote cooperation and exchange. These conversations, practices, and structures often connect communities and congregations in what some have called the "global village" (Eiesland and Warner 1998, 40–41). Eiesland and Warner also offer the con-cept of a "multi-layered religious ecology":

> To speak of several layers refers to the fact that the interconnection between a congregation, or any institution, and its environment occurs at different levels. We will use a three-layer conceptualization from the discipline of sociology to speak of the social fabric of any community as a complex web of people, meanings, and relationships, alterations in any one of which can result in social ramifications elsewhere. The first layer is *demography*, or the characteristics of the people in the community, described in terms of numbers, age, and sex distribution; ethnic and racial profile; and changes in these data over time. The second layer is *culture*, or the systems of mean-ing, values, and practices shared by members of the community and groups within the community. The third layer is *organization*, or the systems of roles and relationships that structure the interaction of people in the community. (1998, 41–42)

Eiesland and Warner thus recognize the variety of religious voices just as the ecological perspective on the natural world leads us to see ourselves as one of several billion individuals within a species that is itself one among millions (1998, 40–41). What does it mean to say a congregation exists in relation to an environment? The religious ecological perspective identifies a congregation with a wide-scope view, made up of layers and elements both relatively invisible and visible. Although the group I studied for this chapter is not a conventional "congregational" organization, the theory of ecology is still valuable in terms of examining the relations between the group and the community and the interactions between in-group and out-group relationships in that community.

As may be seen with the parades I describe in the second part of this chapter, the defined cultural or changing values shared by members of the community and groups within the community emerge through the interactions of Falun Gong and others in Flushing, Queens. This chapter examines Falun Gong's network in New York and how these relationships structure the interactions of people in the Chinese immigrant community.

NEIGHBORHOOD AND RELIGIOUS CHANGES IN FLUSHING, QUEENS

In examining immigrant religions in New York, one has to pay attention to the characteristics of the people in the immigrant community – the first layer of the religious ecology. Throughout its history, New York has been a city of immigrants and one of the gateway cities to the United States. The flow of immigrants has not only changed the demographics of New York but also revitalized the practices of faith groups. From 1990 to 2000, the Chinese population in New York City rose from 232,908 to 374,321 – an increase of 61 percent: far more than the city's overall 9 percent increase, but less than the 71 percent expansion of the city's total Asian population. Asians comprised nearly a quarter of the city's post-1964 foreign-born population. By 1998, the number of foreign-born Chinese (China, Hong Kong, and Taiwan) living in New York City was more than twice that of any other Asian immigrant group. In fact, in 1990, New York had the largest Chinese population among American cities (Foner 2000). The 2000 United States Census ranked Queens as the ninth–most populous county in the United States with over 2.2 million residents.[1] According to the Census Bureau, Queens has experienced over a 14 percent increase in population since the 1990 census. The 2000 Census also reflected the growth of the Asian population in Queens, with over 391,500 people identifying themselves as Asian Americans. More than half of Flushing's population is Asian American, and many of the neighborhoods around Flushing have an increasing number of Asian American residents. It is also claimed that Flushing has the largest ethnic Chinese community in the New

York metropolitan area, surpassing the number in Manhattan's Chinatown. Today, Flushing has the second-largest ethnic Chinese population of any urban area in the United States.[2]

The characteristics of the people in Flushing have likewise changed over the years. Newcomers have brought in new beliefs and ways of worshiping that speak to their experiences with international migration. Flushing has a long history of religious diversity. Historian Scott Hanson refers to Flushing as "the most religiously diverse community in America. There are over 200 places of worship in a small urban neighborhood of about 2.5 square miles" (Hanson 2008) Today, the Quaker Meeting House, St. George Episcopal Church, the Free Synagogue of Flushing, St. Andrew Avellino Roman Catholic Church, and St. Nicholas Greek Orthodox Church exist side by side with immigrant churches and Buddhist, Hindu, and Sikh temples in Flushing.

The second layer of religious ecology is culture, which is generated by changes in demography produced by international migration and the effects of an "economic cluster" of immigrants. In previous research using the case study of Flushing, I have discussed how culture and economics intertwined in urban restructuring before and after the 1990 recession in New York City. The early-1990s recession was a turning point for gentrification in New York, but this transition has still not been satisfactorily explained. My research demonstrated a cultural dimension that contributes to an understanding of gentrification as an economic, social, and cultural restructuring under the impact of international immigration (Huang 2010).

Since the 1980s, Flushing and nearby Elmhurst in Queens have both become diverse communities that mainly accommodate newcomers, as well as serving as the sites of new and revived commercial zones. Elmhurst was the first settlement choice for many Taiwanese immigrants before 1980. The changes in Flushing were dramatic enough to create an immigrant-developed commerce zone. Thus "gentrification" was driven by a new minority group, the Taiwanese Americans, though Korean immigrants were also involved in this hot market (Chen 1992; Huang 2008). In the eyes of Taiwanese immigrant developers, Flushing could serve as an important transportation hub in Queens, a location with great potential for enabling them to realize their dream in the United States of a promised land for economic and social well-being.

As mentioned earlier, the flow of immigrants has not only altered the demographics of New York but also revitalized some declining neighborhoods. Flushing's prosperity reflects both the successful investment of Taiwanese and Korean merchants and the formation of a new Asian community with a unique kind of religious pluralism. Community business leaders in Flushing also find ways to promote ethnic enclaves as tourist attractions, such as with the Lunar New Year Parade.

The initial transfiguration of Flushing took place in early 1981, before the financial recession in the late 1980s, and was triggered by Taiwanese American immigrants. The initiative that prompted this transformation was started by a single Taiwanese immigrant, Tommy Huang. One might expect to see the involvement of the state in fostering this transformation, but, interestingly, the state was not present in this case. The Flushing Business Improvement District (BID) was not established until September 2003, disregarding protests from small merchants afraid of being marginalized by this transition. The local government aid arrived after the transformation of the neighborhood. Finally, the anti-gentrification movements were initiated by older white residents who had been marginalized and who eventually moved out of the neighborhood by selling their properties. This varies somewhat from standard patterns of gentrification (Hackworth 2002).

CULTIVATION AND SPIRITUAL MOVEMENTS

What is Falun Gong? Falun Dafa or Falun Gong, which can be translated as a "Practice of the Dharma Wheel," is a type of qi-gong, a central element of traditional Chinese medicine. According to the book *Zhuan Falun*, Falun Gong is an advanced cultivation system of the Buddhist School but is not limited to Buddhist teaching.[3] Falun Gong's teaching of Buddha Law can be summarized in three words: Zhen-Shan-Ren (truthfulness, benevolence, and forbearance). The process of cultivation is thought to be one in which the practitioner assimilates himself or herself to a higher level, Zhen-Shan-Ren, which is the essence of the universe.[4]

Practitioners believe that cultivation of *gong* is guided by this supreme nature, and based on the principles of the universe's evolution. Founder Master Hongzhi Li's teaching states, "Falun Buddha Fa also includes cultivation of the body, which is accomplished by performing the exercise movements of the Great Consummation Way – a great high-level practice of the Buddha School." In the end, the purpose of exercise and cultivation is to achieve consummation. Li Hongzhi also stated in his "Falun Buddha Fa" lecture in Europe the reason for practicing Falun Gong. "It's because our Fa can truly enable people to consummate, truly save people, and allow you to truly ascend to high levels in the process of cultivation. Whether it's your realm of mind or the physical quality of your body, the Fa truly enables you to reach the standards of different levels" (Li 1998).

Falun Gong is a practice focusing not only on the spiritual mind but also on attempts to transcend the profane body. An inner logic connects a human being's mind and body. One can gain virtue (De) from one's benevolent behavior when one has honorable thoughts. This De can materialize and be part of one's physical body. Qi-gong practice is not a new phenomenon, and it has been popularly practiced in both private and public sects in Asia; nevertheless, this is one of the rare cases in which a spiritual group has developed the practice into a mass movement.

Some informants have reported developing supernormal abilities since they have been practicing Falun Dafa. Master Li defines supernormal abilities as "a being's innate abilities. The higher a being's level, the more fully his innate abilities can take effect; conversely, the lower a being's level, the more difficult it is for his innate abilities to take effect, or to take full effect."[5]

The qi-gong practice itself produces a mystical and religious experience in human bodies. Many practitioners report healing miracles, and some experience feelings that go beyond their knowledge. Both miracles and "holy" emotions bring practitioners into a sacred experience. The power of healing is an important aspect of this religious movement. Much of the time, religion is associated with healing and suffering. The ultimate goal of all schools of Buddhism remains the same: to liberate one from suffering. Master Li claims that Falun Gong is a complex combination of Buddhism and Taoism. The discourse of a co-relationship between illness and karma in Falun Gong is not new. We can find similar sources on the "meaning of illness" and the "sense of healing" in conventional Buddhist teachings and in folk practices. The primary source of human existence and the force that maintains and controls it are perceived in motivated action (karma). Positive and negative actions can be neutralized by each other or accumulated, and that brings a self-made result of a good or bad life in this world or the next life. Intentional actions always lead to retribution and consequently perpetuate existence, but they never bring complete freedom from suffering.

The healing power of Falun Gong contains two senses: the restoration of health and the restoration of peace. FLG faith groups have functioned much like other religious groups in society. I discovered that this qi-gong faith group with its stress on healing power also functions like a conventional religion. It is concerned with human destiny and welfare, and it provides support, consolation, and reconciliation. Falun Gong also offers the emotional ground for a new security and firmer identity (Odea 1966, 15).

State-run TV in China has shown footage of FLG practices causing suicides and the deaths of sick followers because of their refusal to seek proper medical treatment. Not taking medicine is a rule strongly advised by FLG teaching, but it is not a commandment related to Falun Gong's philosophy of cosmology. This recommendation, however, is the exact issue taken up by the state of China and used to show the illegitimacy of the healing belief of Falun Gong. Just as the Chinese state has outlawed the healing system of FLG, many nonpractitioners also consider this teaching very controversial. Yet it should be noted that qi-gong promotion was a national project in China before 1999 and that the widespread practice of Falun Gong accompanied the fashion of qi-gong fever before the crackdown on the practice.

PARKS AND CULTIVATION

Like many other qi-gong groups, FLG followers practice in public areas, such as local parks. But unlike other qi-gong groups, FLG requires followers to read its books as well as practice its teachings within a group. Master Li also encourages new practitioners to practice together in addition to practicing privately at home. A conventional group practice takes place at an assistant's household and in local parks. This routine conventional meeting develops members' sense of fellowship and community. It is also the key element in helping Falun Gong grow as a collective force in the first place. Each site functions as a nucleus. There are more than forty practice sites in New York City. In addition, each site provides either weekday or weekend free lessons or practice schedules (some offered seven days a week), which means, on a weekly basis, that there are more than a hundred Falun Gong activities taking place citywide. Practitioners are more than just a large mass of followers; they are qi-gong practitioners with a collective faith and worldview. They are members of a cultivation group with a clear sense of community, calling themselves Falun Dafa "disciples."

I researched the citywide practice sites online and visited some of them. On one morning in Flushing, I witnessed a practice routine at a park site. Neighborhood residents could easily spot this qi-gong group because they not only practice as a group but also called attention to themselves by their bright yellow sweatshirts or T-shirts. Their slow movements followed the rhythm of music. Most practitioners closed their eyes during the exercise. After the thirty minutes of meditation at the end of five movements, they started reading the sutra Zhuan Falun together in Mandarin for one hour.

Until 2001 the majority of practitioners were Chinese or Chinese Americans, with one Hispanic group meeting in Queens and a Russian-American group meeting in Brooklyn. A few Caucasians and a few Taiwanese could be found in all groups. During the 2001 annual New York conference, there were practitioners from all over the world, including Asia, Europe, and other areas.

Becoming a disciple of Falun Dafa (Falun Gong) does not mean that the new member can just start another group. Informal approval from other groups and senior disciples is necessary to start a new chapter. The person who leads the group, called a "supporter or assistant" (Fudaoyuan), cannot have his or her personal interpretation of the Falun Gong sutra. Her or his task is to play music at the park, bring display signs to the site, and assist the new practitioners by teaching them movements of gong and helping them to find sutra books and the literature online.

WALKING DOWN OUR STREET: PARADES
WITHIN THE IMMIGRANT COMMUNITY

The study of public events offers a way to understand the relationship between the observed group and other groups in the community. During my interviews and while chatting with some faith-based groups, I sensed a reservation and hesitation among participants about expressing their thoughts on this "new faith group," which has been labeled an evil cult by China's government. As for secular organizations, such as Chinese hometown-based associations, the leaders of these groups tend to express their animosity toward FLG. The following events reveal the relationship between FLG and other groups in the community.

In 2001 the organizers of the Lunar New Year Parade in Flushing had a heated dispute over whether they should allow FLG to join the parade. That was the first year that some Chinese groups (from the People's Republic of China, or PRC) intended to join the activities in Flushing, and they strongly protested FLG's involvement in the parade. The Taiwanese community insisted on letting FLG participate. First, the Taiwanese argued that this is a free country, and therefore, any group should be welcome to join and to celebrate the New Year. Secondly, the Taiwanese groups understood that the dispute was connected to a territorial conflict with Chinese mainlanders; therefore, they wanted to support FLG as a means of adopting their own radical stance against

FIGURE 4.1. An FLG practitioner teaches gong to followers in the park.
Photograph courtesy of author.

the invasion of Taiwan. Finally, after these multi-ethnic community leaders reached an agreement by voting, the resolution was passed that FLG should be invited to join but could not demonstrate their gong during the parade march. The FLG practitioners agreed, as they are always seeking opportunities to let the community gain a better understanding of the practice. For the first time, practitioners decided to walk down the street with balloons and without a qi-gong demonstration.

One year later, the 2002 parade was organized by the Flushing Lunar New Year Parade Committee (FLNYPC), which was staffed by pro-KMT (Kou Min Dang), pro-PFP (People First Party, Ching-Min Dang), and pro-NP (New Party, Xin Dang) people and Chinese from Taiwan (immigrants from Taiwan who identify themselves as Chinese). One week before the parade, the People's Republic of China Consulate in New York released a statement condemning FLNYPC for allowing FLG to be part of the parade. On February 7, two days before the parade, for the first time FLNYPC held a closed-door meeting and, also for the first time, voted against allowing FLG to be part of the parade. FLG practitioner Hanru Chu, an "assistant" in Flushing who has been in charge of the FLG parade in Queens for years,[6] told me over the phone that he had delivered FLG's clear message to the committee right before they voted. "I told them not to give up the right principles only because of pressure from the PRC Consulate. I understood they used the vote to exclude us because they couldn't give us a reason why we, Falun Gong, couldn't join the parade." I told him that the Taiwanese Association of America–New York (TAA-NY; migrants from Taiwan who identify themselves as Taiwanese) was very angry about the voting outcome and intended to invite FLG into the TAA-NY parade groups. That same night, TAA-NY and FLG held a brief meeting.

FLG sent a Taiwanese practitioner and met with the vice president of TAA-NY, Borcheng Hsu; Patrick Huang, from DPP-AE (Democratic Progressive Party–American East, a political party based in Taiwan); and Cary Hung, chair of Asia Democracy. The Taiwanese team offered the following terms: (1) The Taiwanese team would be the FLG guardian if it decide to march with the T team.[7] (2) The T team would carry protest banners if FLG requests them to do so. The very next day, at 8:30 AM, some practitioners arrived to help the Taiwanese volunteers with parade preparations. This was the very first occasion that I noticed FLG trying to work in partnership with another group. Yuan Feng, a spokesperson for Falun Gong, along with some practitioners, also held a press conference before the parade to clarify the truth about the parade committee's attempt to deny FLG practitioners participation in the parade.

Despite the guardianship of the T team, FLG still faced opposition from one of the FLNYPC's committee members, M. W., the director of the Chinese-American Planning Council, who insisted on removing FLG from the lineup. However, the Flushing Police Department sided with FLG. The police spokesperson told FLNYPC, "I know how you voted. But it doesn't count. It's unconstitutional." Therefore, FLG was able to march down Main Street with its own banners and its own delegation.

Because of the parade committee's attempt to bar the FLG group from participation in the parade, it was forced to wait a long time and walked as the last group in the parade. Practitioners held their heads high and sang the song "Falun Dafa Is Good" several times during the march. When they eventually arrived at the central stage, the master of ceremonies suddenly announced that the parade had come to an end, purposely omitting the FLG group. Even the sanitation trucks, which trailed the parade and cleaned up the streets after the march, were announced in order to insult the FLG group.

The FLG group decided to change the plan as well. They stopped right in front of the central stage, played the Pudu music loudly, and performed

Exercise Number One in front of all the VIPS. This unexpected action lasted for a few minutes and forced the master of ceremonies to broadcast "Falun Dafa Happy New Year" in order to fill the silence and embarrassment of the command stage.

How can we unpack this community dispute within the framework of a religious ecology that acknowledges the reality of Asian geopolitics? The Flushing Lunar New Year Parade had clearly become an arena of Asian geopolitics. In 2001, a Korean group refused to speak with another Korean group because the two could not agree with each other's representatives for community leadership. Similarly, a Chinese group was angry with a Taiwanese group because the Flushing Police Department granted the latter the official permit to hold the Flushing Lunar New Year Parade, which was considered a sign of leadership in the Asian community in Flushing. Among the Taiwanese American groups, a pro–Taiwan independence group has had a very tense relationship with a pro-KMT group (it has been divided into pro-KMT, pro-PFP, and pro-NP groups) for years.

The Chinese immigrant newcomers in Flushing have created new political power in this Asian community. The attitudes of different groups and how they reacted to the FLG incident can help us to understand the spectrum and transition of the groups' political orientations. Up until 2001, FLG was just one of the parade groups. Although there were some extra rules binding this religious group, sensitivity to FLG's background of political persecution in China did not create strong objections among other community groups. However, objections from the Chinese Consulate in New York have increased since FLG's march in Manhattan's Chinatown in April 2001. It was the first time FLG had encountered public opposition overseas. The dispute over the 2002 Flushing Lunar New Year Parade was settled with the police verdict, but the precedent set by this incident makes certain that there will be future conflicts in this ethnic community.

PRACTICING IN PUBLIC AS A NEW YORK FAITH

In the conflict between China's government and Falun Gong practitioners and scholars, defining the religiosity of Falun Gong often involves the "politics of naming," touching on contested questions of politics and identity. Due to its political impact and its social implications for China, Falun Gong, as a "faith" group newly rising within the last two decades, has become a popular subject for many journalists. Falun Gong's campaign has become a global public phenomenon, rather than just a private spiritual practice, due to the impact of governmental persecution in China.

Since their persecution by Chinese authorities began, FLG practitioners have struggled with the impact of the politics of identity. For FLG practitioners, putting themselves out in public is a way of resistance, denying that they are followers of an evil cult or practitioners of mysterious rituals. They demonstrate with their bodies and qi-gong movements in the parks and parades as a strategy of resistance, a strategy that not only rejects the power of labeling but also proclaims the practice of Falun Gong to be a lifestyle choice.

There are various layers of meaning in FLG's public practice of resistance. Despite all of the tensions with parade committees and restrictions on how they can represent themselves, Falun Gong practitioners insist on walking down main streets with community groups holding their heads high. When I interviewed one of the Falun Gong representatives, Hanru Chu, during the negotiation meeting with the Lunar New York Parade Committee, she clearly stated, "We just want to participate in the parade." Having suffered greatly from the Chinese government's propaganda, the Falun Gong practitioners felt they needed to "clarify the truth" to this group of people by fighting for participation and recognition. "We reject [refuse] to accept this kind of evil arrangement," one practitioner said. "We have to clarify the truth and the *fa* [Buddhist law]." By successfully participating in the community parade, they have successfully rejected the power and influence of China's government and the Chinese consulate in New York. They rejected the power by rejecting the labels applied to them by their oppressors.

Regarding the non-Chinese nonbelievers, FLG hopes to demonstrate a positive image of their lifestyle choice by practicing qi-gong in public spaces and outside of immigrant communities. The purpose is to show the public who they are and to eliminate public misunderstandings. FLG has established practice sites in public and private spaces throughout the entire city in order to fight the power of negative labeling. They now not only practice in public spaces, such as parks or community centers, but everywhere. They are, in effect, stating: "We are part of New Yorkers' life routine. Qi-gong practice should be understood as a healthy exercise such as yoga, which is practiced indoors and outdoors."

Of course, Falun Gong is not just a qi-gong practice. In all of the sites, qi-gong is a way to attract the attention of nonbelievers. FLG is a group promoting cultivation. All new practitioners are carefully and clearly instructed about the cultivation of Xin-Xing, which is how Falun Gong differentiates itself from other qi-gong groups. In pursuing cultivation, practitioners are part of other moral communities in New York City. As mentioned earlier, Master Li clearly instructs participants to practice in a group, not individually. This environment creates group pressure to encourage new practitioners to continue their practice. The groups I observed are not just social groups dedicating their time and energy to health issues, but rather are involved in political actions based on their belief in cultivation.

Previous research has also discovered a tendency toward ethnic diversification within Chinese immigrant communities in New York. Two waves of diversification took place in Flushing, the first wave caused by post-1965 migration and the second by post–Cold War migration (Huang 2010). The changed demographics of the Chinese population in Flushing has altered the political dynamics within the community. The Taiwanese came to the United States after 1965, and Taiwanese American groups had a more relaxed relationship with Falun Gong. Yet the Chinese Taiwanese had ambiguous attitudes toward the movement. More and more Chinese arriving after 1990 were hostile toward Falun Gong due to their strong bonds with the Chinese government.

The road to being embraced by the ethnic Chinese community will not be easy for Falun Gong. The group has gained support from anti-communist groups, such as the Taiwanese American Association of New York, the Democratic Progressive Party–American East, and Asia Democracy. Those pro-Taiwan groups offered to guard Falun Gong and invited it to march down the street based on the standard of human rights, which is a rare instance of friendship for practitioners who keenly felt the attack from China's general consulate in New York.

CONCLUSION

In studying Falun Gong, I view the unconventional practice of this group as an entity strategizing its interactions with other entities inside and outside the immigrant communities – including interactions with people, organizations, and cultures – in order to claim its own identity and resist the labels of others. The high-profile practices of Falun Gong acknowledge that New York City has become the center of the group's global resistance efforts.

This study discloses the relationship between the wider city and the strategic practices of Falun Gong, such as its qi-gong exercises in public parks citywide and its parades in the immigrant community of Flushing. The tension between Falun Gong and China's government has been translated to the streets of New York City in conflicts that reveal the politics of immigrant communities as a reflection or extension of domestic politics in their home countries. Falun Gong's campaign has become a global public phenomenon, rather than just a private spiritual practice, due to the impact of governmental persecution in China. The public exhibitions and cultural parades on the city's streets have served the function of "outing" participants so they can find a place in New York's and America's religious landscape.

NOTES

1. U.S Census Bureau, 2000, http://www.census.gov/.

2. U.S. Census Bureau, http://www.census.gov/fastfacts/. These data are based on U.S. Bureau of the Census, 1900 and March 1998.

3. FLG is a method for the cultivation of Xin-Xing (mind or character).

4. Hongzhi Li, "Falun Gong" (4th translation ed., updated April 2001), http://www.falundafa.org/book/eng

/flg.htm (accessed April 2, 2007).

5. Hongzhi Li, "What Are Supernormal Abilities[?]" (lecture/sutra), Falun Dafa Clearwisdom.net, June 14, 2001, http://www.clearwisdom.net/emh/articles/2001/6/15/11481.html (accessed April 2, 2007).

6. In Falun Gong's terminology, an "assistant" is an organizer.

7. Parade under the English alphabet letter T, for "Taiwan."

REFERENCES

Ammerman, Nancy T., Jackson Carroll, Carl S. Dudley, and William McKinney, eds. 1998. *Studying Congregations: A New Handbook*. Nashville: Abingdon Press.

Chen, Hsiang-Shui. 1992. *Chinatown No More*. Ithaca, NY: Cornell University Press.

Eiesland, Nancy. 2000. *A Particular Place: Urban Restructuring and Religious Ecology in a Southern Exurb*. New Brunswick, NJ: Rutgers University Press.

Eiesland, Nancy, and R. Stephen Warner. 1998. "Ecology: Seeing the Congregation in Context." In *Studying Congregations: A New Handbook*, ed. Nancy Ammerman, Jackson Carroll, Carl Dudley, and William McKinney, 40–77. Nashville: Abingdon Press.

Foner, Nancy. 2000. *From Ellis Island to JFK: New York's Two Great Waves of Immigration*. New Haven, CT: Yale University Press.

Hackworth, J. 2002. "Postrecession Gentrification in New York City." *Urban Affairs Review* 3, no. 6: 815–43.

Hanson, R. Scott. 2008. "Historian Scott Hanson Discusses Religious Diversity in America." America.gov Archive. Ask America web chat transcript, August 19. http://www.america.gov/st/texttrans-english/2008/August/20080819162731xjsnommiso.5391199.html (accessed March 2009).

Huang, Weishan. 2008. "The Making of a Promised Land: Religious Responses to Gentrification and Ethnic Diversity in Flushing, Queens." *CrossCurrents* 58, no. 3 (Fall): 441–55.

———. 2010. "Immigration and Gentrification: A Case Study of Cultural Restructuring in Flushing, Queens." *Diversities* (UNESCO) 12, no. 1: 56–69.

Kivell, Jonathan. 2002. "The Birthplace of Religious Freedom: Continuing to Welcome the World's Faith. *Queens Tribune.* http://www.queenstribune .com/anniversary2002/religion.htm (accessed January 2009).

Li, Hongzhi. 1997. *Zhou Falun.* Hong Kong: Falun Dafa Press.

———. 1998 "Teaching the Fa at the Conference in Europe" (lecture presented in Frankfurt, Germany, May 30, 1998). *Falun Buddha Fa.* http:// www.falundafa.org/book/eng/europe 1998a.htm (accessed April 2, 2007).

New York Department of City Planning. "North Flushing Rezoning – Approved!." NYC.gov. April 22, 2009. http://www.nyc.gov/html/dcp/html /north_flushing/index.shtml (accessed June 20, 2009).

Odea, Thomas F. 1966. *The Sociology of Religion.* Upper Saddle River, NJ: Prentice Hall.

Tseng, Yen-Fen. 1997. "Commodification of Residency: An Analysis of Taiwan's Business Immigration Market." *Taiwan: A Radical Quarterly in Social Studies* 27: 37–67.

5

The Brazilianization of New York City: Brazilian Immigrants and Evangelical Churches in a Pluralized Urban Landscape

Donizete Rodrigues

In the last two decades, Brazilian immigrants and their evangelical churches have become more visible in the New York Metropolitan Area. Their congregations and small businesses have provoked important changes in several neighborhoods and in the larger pluralized ethnic and religious landscape. As Tony Carnes and Anna Karpathakis (2001) point out, "New York . . . is attracting one of the most diverse concentrations of religions that the world has ever seen . . . and is increasingly being transformed into a city of faiths" (3).

Given this context of religious pluralism, the main theme and purpose of this chapter is to discuss the process of Brazilianization caused by the increasingly significant presence of Brazilian immigrants and their evangelical churches in the New York Metropolitan Area (Rodrigues 2010). By "Brazilianization" I mean the increasingly visible and expressive presence of Brazilian immigrants (and also tourists) in New York City. A significant influence of Brazilian culture also pervades multicultural American society, including music, books, movies, soap operas, food (açai), drink (guarana, coconut juice), and clothing (Havaianas flip-flops). Events like the Brazilian Day Celebration, which has taken place since 1984 in the first week of September in Midtown Manhattan, attracts more than a million people and heightens the visibility of Brazilian culture. "Brazilianization" further refers to the strong presence of Brazilian evangelical churches, whose congregations are in prominent locations and are adorned with cultural names and the country's flag, contributing to ethnic succession and the subsequent creation of Brazilian religious ethnic enclaves.

To illustrate this phenomenon, first, I focus on the increasing presence of Brazilian immigrant churches and their interactions with the urban environment. I then specifically examine the organizational structure and religious ecology of a particular congregation, the Igreja Pentecostal Missionária de Língua Portuguesa (Pentecostal Missionary Church of the Portuguese Language, or PMCPL). The Brazilians' cooperative relationship with the Portuguese community, based on their similar sociocultural history, further allows their immigrant churches to grow and become more innovative as they engage in church-planting strategies.

BRAZILIAN IMMIGRATION AND RELIGION IN THE UNITED STATES

With more than 450 million followers around the world, Pentecostalism is the most rapidly growing religious movement. Mostly immigrants and people from the lower socio-economic strata have joined this religious movement. By offering strong spiritual, emotional, and social support, Pentecostalism, it is said, suits the needs of many poor people; for this reason it is often considered the "church *of* the poor" rather than a "church *for* the poor people," like the Catholic Church (Rodrigues 2002).

Religion frequently becomes more important when people or groups migrate. The diaspora's circumstances may strengthen the needs of fellowship amongst them and revitalize their religious traditions. In the context of migration, it is important to re-establish a sense of belonging to the ethnic group, and religion plays an important role in the attempts of the group to maintain its cultural and linguistic identities (Haddad, Smith, and Esposito 2003; Pluss 2009).

Pluss (2009) notes that "often, religious organizations are the first associations that immigrants set up in a new place of residence. These organizations serve as networks from which the migrants can gain multiple forms of support and provide symbols of unification . . . by providing symbols of unification and support, immigrant religion also works as a conceptual and emotional resource to generate solidarity among co-religionists" (495). Along these lines, McClymer (2006) writes that "religion was, and remains, a central dimension of the immigrant experience . . . it supplied a frame through which immigrants and their descendants made sense of their new world, it spoke to their need to find hope and solace . . . it assisted their efforts to become citizens and to rise economically."

As Vásquez and Marquardt (2003) have suggested, "part of Pentecostalism's success can be attributed to the fact that it offers believers resources to relocalize themselves, to renew broken selves, and build tight affective communities in a world that has become increasingly baffling" (55). And as Diana Eck (2001) has noted, religious affiliation enables immigrants to maintain their sense of identity and also gain acceptance in the wider society (see also Vásquez and Marquardt 2003). André Droogers and others (2006) have argued that Pentecostalism is often seen as a form of popular religion and, therefore, it has little social prestige. Though often socially marginal before the conversion, afterward the evangelized people perceive themselves as a spiritual elite. As "chosen people," they feel a certain pride and even superiority vis-à-vis the rest of society.

In the specific case of Brazilian immigration, evangelical churches play an important role in helping immigrants maintain their ethno-religious identity, while they adapt to the new culture and society where they are now living (Ebaugh 2003). The migration process has been extremely important in the creation, expansion, dispersion, and globalization of religions and new religious movements, and this has been especially so for Pentecostal churches. According to Pluss (2009), "Migrants, including missionaries, engage in a process of globalization of their religious beliefs and practices when they express these beliefs and practices in cultural, social, political, or economic arenas that span several geographical regions" (491).

Protestantism was introduced in Brazil in the nineteenth century through the immigration of settler families from Europe and the United States, mainly in the south of the country. In the early twentieth century, Pentecostalism was imported to Brazil from the United States and grew rapidly in large urban centers (such as Rio de Janeiro and São Paulo) during the 1960s (Martin 1990; Chesnut 1997). Nowadays the process of religious transformation in Brazil is marked by a strong institutional pluralism characterized by two principal tendencies: the proliferation of neo-Pentecostalism and the Catholic charismatic renewal movement, the latter of which was introduced to Brazil from the United States in 1969 but gained more importance after the 1990s (Freston 1997; Rodrigues 2002, 2003, 2006).

Since the introduction of Protestant neo-Pentecostalism and the Catholic charismatic renewal movement in Brazil, the situation has now inverted: the emigration of Brazilians to the United States and Europe has been accompanied by a massive exportation of Brazilian neo-Pentecostal churches. Following Brazilian migration flows, pastors of the Brazilian Pentecostal churches migrated to Australia, Japan, Western Europe (particularly Portugal and England), Canada, and the United States (particularly the New York Metropolitan Area), both to accompany their already converted compatriots and to evangelize Brazilian immigrants, as well as other immigrant groups.

The large-scale migration from Brazil to the United States is a relatively new phenomenon. The first wave of emigration was in the second half of the 1980s (Margolis 1994, 2009; Jouët-Pastré and Braga 2008), especially because of the Brazilian economic crises. Brazilian immigrants came predominantly from such regions as Minas Gerais, Goiás, Rio de Janeiro, São Paulo, Parana, Santa Catarina, and Espírito Santo, and the great majority of these immigrants were of European heritage and came from the lower and middle classes of Brazilian society (Levitt 2007). As Portes (1995) points out, people with some resources are more likely to migrate than are the poor.

The most common way for Brazilians to illegally enter in the United States is with tourist visas. However, a substantial number enter via the Mexican border, but this way is extremely dangerous and more expensive, as was portrayed in the soap opera *America*, broadcast in 2005 by the Globo Television Network. Quantifying this particular form of emigration is very difficult, if not impossible. Because the great majority have entered without documents as illegal immigrants, it is estimated that between 1.2 and 1.5 million undocumented Brazilians are presently living in the United States (Levitt 2007), with most concentrated in New York Metropolitan Area (which includes northern New Jersey), Boston, Miami, Washington, D.C., and Los Angeles (Beserra 2003; Jouët-Pastré and Braga 2008).

Although there is a long tradition in the United States of studying immigrants and their religions (Eck 2001; Haddad, Smith, and Esposito 2003), a search for anthropological case studies on immigration and religion turns up little such research. A major issue is the role of religion in the formation, maintenance, and reproduction of ethnic and cultural identities in succeeding generations (Warner, and Wittner 1998). While there are many studies of economic strategies, ethnicity, and identity among Brazilian immigrants (Badgley 1994; Marrow 2003; Martes 2007), until the past decade, there have been very few studies about the relationship between religion and Brazilian immigration (Levitt 2007). With the exception of Freston (2008), scholars have treated religion as a secondary issue (see, for example, Margolis 1994, 2009; Sales 2003; Martes and Rodrigues 2004; Martes 2011). Considering the relationship between religion and immigration, a very conservative estimate (2006) is that there are around eight hundred Brazilian Protestant churches (with approximately 48,000 members) in the United States (Freston 2008). Therefore, there is a potentially significant field for sociological and anthropological research on this topic. As a recent survey revealed (Pew Forum on Religion and Public Life 2008), half of all Latinos (included Brazilians) who have joined Pentecostal denominations were raised as Catholics. Conversions are a key ingredient in the development of evangelicalism among Brazilians.

THE RELIGIOUS ECOLOGY OF BRAZILIANIZATION

My ethnographic fieldwork took place largely in Astoria, Queens, an area with a large concentration of Brazilian immigrants. Brazilians, like most other immigrants in the United States, tend to cluster. Following Portes (1995), I define an enclave as a spatially clustered network of businesses owned by members of the same ethnic minority that emerges in the same areas where they reside. Their emergence is signaled by the transformation of the urban area, which displays distinct ethnic characteristics, languages, and religious places. For an immigrant group to establish an enclave, a process of ethnic succession usually takes place. "Ethnic succession" refers to the process of one ethnic or racial group replacing another racial/ethnic group from an established residential, occupational, or political niche (Herman 2007). The ethnic succession model has often been portrayed as one of conflict between newcomers and established groups occupying a particular niche in the urban ecology. As Herman notes, however, natives and newcomers have in some cases established common ground as members of religious organizations or through overlapping civic ties based in interethnic business associations or other voluntary organizations. As noted above, in the case of Brazilians, their settlement in small and often shrinking Portuguese neighborhoods has caused little conflict, because of common language and cultural ties. Such common ties have led to a spirit of cooperation between the already-small Portuguese Protestant community and their burgeoning Brazilian co-religionists.

During my initial fieldwork in 2008, I spent several hours a day walking through the streets, looking and asking for restaurants, shops, and Brazilian evangelical churches. I found three such churches and conversed with some of the Brazilian population. One of the focal points for the Brazilians in Astoria is a Brazilian restaurant where immigrants regularly go to eat, meet friends, make conversation, exchange information on employment and rental housing, and try to start small businesses.

Near the restaurant is the Rio Bonito Supermarket, a mini–shopping center with various types of commercial activities: a grocery store specializing in Brazilian food and drink, newspapers and magazines, DVDs and CDs; a travel agency offering dollar remittance service to Brazil; and a cafeteria. There is also an evangelical bookshop. These commercial places and other Brazilian small businesses in the neighborhood well illustrate the interactions between immigrants and their surrounding environment, and corroborate Suro's point (1999) that immigrants and religious organizations provoke renewed, replacement, and urban changes. It was at the restaurant (close to three Brazilian churches) where I first met Pastor Zeny Tinouco, the founder and leader of a Pentecostal missionary movement in Brazil, and the Igreja Pentecostal Missionária de Língua Portuguesa (PMCPL), who was to become my principal gatekeeper for gaining access to the evangelicals in the neighborhood.

My first week of ethnographic research in New York City coincided with Brazilian Day (September 6), the celebration of Brazil's independence from Portugal. It was a good opportunity to see the large and much-dispersed Brazilian population concentrated in a small area of Midtown Manhattan. This event, which began in 1984, is held annually in "Little Brazil" (46th Street between Fifth Avenue and Avenue of the Americas). This all-day street party attracts almost two million people; participants wear green and yellow, dance to Brazilian music, and enjoy Brazilian food and drink. Although Brazilian Day is a secular festival, some pastors and evangelical churches had rented stalls and were preaching and distributing pamphlets and other literature about their churches. Two churches present were the Brazilian Church of Manhattan and Metro Brazilian Baptist Church. During the next week, I visited those churches, both in Manhattan, and noticed that they shared their space with other churches; in fact, due to the high rent, they had sublet arrangements with other Protestant churches.

In my ethnographic research, I located 213 Brazilian churches, most of them concentrated in Queens and Newark. In Queens alone, there are 86 congregations, with 30 in Astoria and Long Island City. These neighborhoods are undergoing Brazilianization, the increasing visual presence of Brazilian culture with a significant impact on the religious ecology. The great majority of Brazilians live in Astoria, Queens, for various reasons, including close proximity to Manhattan (where most of them have jobs), cheap rent, and easy access to public transportation.

There are also 83 Brazilian congregations in northern New Jersey, with a large concentration in Newark (51). This city has a long-established Portuguese community, but is being succeeded by Brazilian immigrants (Ramos-Zayas 2008). Well known as "Little Portugal," though now with an increasing Brazilian population, Newark shows enormous urban changes, especially in the Ironbound neighborhood. Brazilian immigrants, when they first began arriving in the New York Metropolitan Area, sought refuge in places where there was an established Portuguese community, because of the shared language (Portuguese). Considering that the vast majority of these Brazilian immigrants spoke little or no English, being part of a Portuguese community helped them find places to live and jobs. These two immigrant groups – the older Portuguese and the more recent Brazilian – have historical ties, share many cultural similarities (such a common language), and have kinship and friendship relations. In terms of religion, however, the Portuguese people are traditionally Catholic, so there are very few Portuguese Protestant churches in the New York Metropolitan Area. Cooperation between Brazilian and Portuguese churches occurs only in very specific cases, for certain religious events. Despite the different religious backgrounds, the shared culture and history have allowed ethnic succession and socio-ethnic cooperation to take place that still aided Brazilian immigrants in adaptation strategies such as church planting.

On Long Island, I found 22 Brazilian congregations, concentrated in Mineola and particularly Garden City (14). Besides Brazilian evangelical churches, I also located the Portuguese Assembly of God Emanuel. This church, founded in 1979, has three congregations, in Brentwood, Farmingville, and Mineola. Living, working, and praying in the same neighborhoods, Brazilian and Portuguese immigrants through their churches participate together in some religious activities, such as special worship services and vigils, but do not share houses of worship, resources, or finances.

Like northern New Jersey, Long Island has had a traditional Portuguese immigrant community, creating a similar religious ecology marked by church planting and socio-ethnic camaraderie. Cooperation with other evangelicals is not limited to the Portuguese. Various ethnic evangelical churches have participated in the annual "March for Christ" in Newark. Many younger, second-generation Brazilian evangelicals have also discovered an affinity with the young cohort of Hispanic evangelicals, possibly forming an emerging "pan-Latino" evangelical identity.

Upon completion of my survey I decided to conduct research on the Pentecostal Missionary Church of the Portuguese Language in Astoria. Having already made contact with Pastor Zeny in October 2008, I assumed I would be easily accepted in his church. Methodologically, if I had not been accepted, it would not have been possible to carry out insider anthropological fieldwork. This religious movement was originally founded in Brazil, but it now has five congregations in the New York area and one in Connecticut and is expanding rapidly to Europe, particularly Portugal. My anthropological research on Brazilian immigration and Pentecostalism precisely involves this Brazil-USA-Europe triangle. My focus on the pastor and this congregation also shows how "outsider" religious innovators target New York as a special mission field and introduce new organizational growth into its religious ecology that can lead to further transplants, even on a transnational basis.

PLANTING SEEDS

One of the important aspects of ecological theory is the history of an organization and the changes taking place within it. Since I am describing a transnational movement, this account begins in Brazil. Zeny Tinouco was born into a poor black family in the state of Espírito Santo, Brazil, in 1945. From an early age he was very religious; Zeny was a practicing Catholic and an altar boy. In 1974, he had his first contact with the Protestant movement. In August of that year, the famous American evangelist Billy Graham brought his evangelistic crusade, organized by the Baptist World Alliance, to Rio de Janeiro. Two hundred thousand people filled the Maracanã Stadium, and thousands of them were converted, including Zeny Tinouco. After this evangelical meeting, he remained close to the Billy Graham organization and to the evangelist himself.

After this deep religious experience, he decided to be baptized in the Methodist church. He rose within that church extraordinarily fast; a short time after his baptism, he briefly attended a theological seminary, believing he had a signal from the Holy Spirit that it was "the time to be a pastor." In 1975 the young and single pastor Zeny moved alone to Brasilia. There he began a life of sacrifice, in both economic and religious terms. Without the support of any evangelical church, he began a small prayer group. After a year in Brasilia, he met a young evangelical named Maria do Socorro, a white woman. After a year of dating they married, soon had three children, and found a small evangelical congregation.

Slowly the congregation grew, and pastor Zeny rented a small room – an important step in transforming the congregation into a new church. After

FIGURE 5.1. The building of the Pentecostal Missionary Church
of the Portuguese Language (PMCPL) in Astoria, Queens.
Photograph courtesy of author.

some years in Brasilia, in 1991 he founded the Pentecostal missionary movement Comunidade Cristã Ministério da Fé (Christian Community Ministry
of Faith). Zeny Tinouco had strong theological and preaching influences
from the Rev. Billy Graham. In 1988 the famous evangelist invited him for a
gathering of pastors in Los Angeles, a city with enormous importance in the
expansion of Pentecostalism.

   The establishment and development of PMCPL was a function of transnational evangelical networks. In addition to his meeting with Reverend
Graham in L.A., Pastor Zeny made contact with Brazilian immigrants and
realized that he would have plenty of opportunity to expand his religious
movement internationally. During one of our interviews, Pastor Zeny said,
"In that time, praying with Billy Graham, in a moment of profound spirituality, God spoke to me, saying that I had an important task of evangelization
to do in the United States, especially New York, the sinner city." Three years
later, with the religious movement already well established in Brazil, he de-

cided to emigrate to the United States. This decision was linked to a time of deep prayer, when he said Jesus Christ spoke to him and asked him to open the Bible and read Mark 16:15: "Go into the entire world and preach the good news to all creation." In 1991, with this "great commission from God," Pastor Zeny emigrated illegally with his family to the United States. They arrived in New York in March and promptly began a religious mission in New York City, with a small group of people who gathered in the pastor's house on 44th Street in Astoria, Queens. The group later met in a room of a Chinese restaurant on 21st Street. In 1992, with a significance increase in worshippers, he rented a place of worship at 36-11 33rd Street, with seating capacity for two hundred people, for $4,000 a month. This was the official founding of the Igreja Pentecostal Missionária de Língua Portuguesa, or Pentecostal Missionary Church of the Portuguese Language.

The strategy of almost all neo-Pentecostal churches is to grow and expand rapidly, and Zeny Tinouco and his congregation was no exception. "God commanded and has guided me and helped me to convert thousands of sinners," Pastor Zeny believes. "Glory to His name. Nowadays, not only in Brazil, but in many parts of the world, in Europe, and here in United States. I am a soldier of Jesus Christ, my sword is the word of the Scripture, and the Holy Spirit is my guide."

The second congregation of the PMCPL was founded in East Harlem in 1995. Zeny's son Pastor Fabio is responsible for this congregation. The church sublets the space from the Hispanic Macedonia Church of the Assemblies of God. The building was originally home to the Presbyterian Church of the Ascension, organized in 1909 by Italian immigrants, who were later displaced by a Hispanic population. Two years later Pastor Zeny moved with his family to Newark to evangelize Portuguese-speaking immigrants in New Jersey. After having great success in New Jersey, Pastor Zeny purchased a six-hundred-seat building (previously operated by a black Baptist church) and formally changed the headquarters of the PMCPL from Astoria to Newark.

The PMCPL had considerable success in Newark; it converted and baptized hundreds of Brazilian and dozens of Portuguese. Pastor Zeny, with the aim of attracting even more Portuguese people, brought in two Portuguese women pastors. The implantation of this religious movement among the Portuguese community in Newark brought many benefits to PMCPL. Firmly implanted in Brazil (the Christian Community Ministry of Faith), and with three congregations of the Pentecostal Missionary Church of the Portuguese Language, Bishop Zeny used New York as a pivotal point and base from which to develop his religious movement transnationally; he then began the "conquest" of Europe. Following the example of dozens of other Brazilian churches, he chose Portugal as a gateway to Europe, with the aim of converting Brazilian immigrants. In 1999, with the cooperation of wealthy Portuguese followers who are businessmen in Newark, Bishop Zeny went to Portugal and founded the Igreja Pentecostal Missionária Cristã (Pentecostal Missionary Christian Church), with three congregations. This church has a branch congregation in Switzerland and is trying to open a new one in England. Attracted by a large concentration of Portuguese immigrants and their descendants in Mineola, Long Island, the third congregation in New York was founded in 2005, subletting space from a Baptist church in nearby Garden City. On June 6, 2005, when Billy Graham was in New York for his Revival Crusade, held in Flushing Meadows, Queens, Bishop Zeny was one of his special guests. They appeared together in a photograph published in the newspaper *Newsday*.

In 2006, trying to expand the Pentecostal Missionary Church of the Portuguese Language beyond the northeastern United States, Bishop Zeny founded the Pentecostal Missionary Church Florida, in Boca Raton. Nevertheless, it was not as successful as he had anticipated and closed its doors in 2009. Additional congregations have been founded in Fort Lee, New Jersey, and Bridgeport, Connecticut. In March 2006 Bishop Zeny, as the leader of the expanding Pentecostal missionary movement, already present in Brazil, the United States, and Europe, founded a New York–based seminary for training leaders of its different branches.

The relationship between religion and entrepreneurship in the PMCPL has also taken on more overtly financial forms.[1] Pentecostal churches defend the so-called "prosperity theology" (Coleman 2000), and Bishop Zeny and his church teach that God's wishes believers to be prosperous and successful in the present life. As a Protestant church, the PMCPL encourages an ethic of hard work, teaching that Christians have to be diligent and hardworking in all aspects of their lives. Coupled with the immigrants' own strategy of making money and improving their economic situation, the evangelical churches encourage the economic success and social mobility of their members as a religious belief. As Max Weber well explained the matter ([1922] 1965), prosperity is justified as a form of divine recognition of the effort and merits of the believer. In fact, the church exhorts hard work and encourages its members to earn more money, thus seeking to ensure and increase the volume of contributions through tithes and offerings (Martes 2011).

WE ARE THE CHURCH

As discussed in the above history of PMCPL, Zeny Tinouco claims to have received from God through the Holy Spirit not only the task of being a pastor but also the role of founder and leader of a new religious movement. He is thus the bishop, senior member, founder, and head of the general administration (political, financial, and religious) of PMCPL and is responsible in ensuring theological and spiritual order. Besides the position of bishop, the church also includes "workers," a group of believers who devote part of their time to church, carrying out many different secular tasks such as maintenance and cleaning of the building and collection of tithes and offerings during worship services. "Missionaries" are charged with evangelizing and nurturing new members and expanding the church. They seek to convert people, whether on the streets or in schools. Under the supervision and at the request of the pastor, they visit congregants to pray in their homes and visit the sick at home and in the hospital. With regard to activities inside the congregation, missionaries may organize worship and prayer groups and start the service with the first prayer. The church musicians usually are missionaries.

Other roles in the church include "deacons" and "deaconesses," who often are still studying in the church's seminary and are responsible for running worship and prayer groups, preaching, and assisting the pastor or bishop in the Holy Supper. "Presbyters" are ministers of the second order, allowed to preach in their own congregation but not given the autonomy to manage their congregations as a pastor. Finally, "missionary-pastors" (usually males) are in charge of missions and are sent by Bishop Zeny to propagate the Word of God and speak about the work of the church, as well as to open and expand new congregations.

In the words of Bishop Zeny, the church's "mission is to welcome the immigrant and be his guide and his support." In fact, these immigrant religious communities offer many kinds of support to their believers: legal counseling and documentation for immigrants (the majority of whom are illegal), English-language classes, day care and activities for children, women's groups, information about jobs and housing, collection and distribution of food and clothing, health services, and recreational activities.

In addition to its spiritual character, the church is a place where immigrants meet one another, discuss their needs, and share information about resources available in the community. It "provides social and physical space and social networks that help the immigrants reproduce and maintain the values, traditions, and customs in the midst of an often alienating and strange American society" (Ebaugh 2003, 230).

First-generation immigrants feel comfortable in the Brazilian evangelical churches because they offer a Brazilian environment where they can speak Portuguese (many speak little or no English) and can share experiences with people from the same country, the same culture. This contact acts as a form of support and comfort, on both a psychological and a spiritual level. Religious messages that they hear in the church are of encouragement, giving them hope for a better future.

The Brazilian evangelical immigrants share a dual identity – ethnic and religious (Ebaugh 2003): the ethnic-cultural identity as their Brazilianness (*Brasilidade*), and the "spiritual identity" as evangelical. They express their ties to Brazil at church. Being part of the "evangelical family," the believer shares a specific sense of self-identification as a distinct group of elected representatives of people chosen by God for salvation. These views reinforce the construction and reproduction of a distinct "community ethos" (Martes 2011).

Almost all members participate regularly in community religious and leisure activities. But each member must also take responsibility for the maintenance of the church, contributing to it with money and volunteer work. Each local congregation is responsible for the upkeep of its building. Members of the local congregation pay all expenses, including the salary of the local pastor.

The church members tend to socialize only with other evangelical people, especially Brazilians. In fact, for participants in church activities, there is little time left over to socialize with non-evangelical people. Therefore, the PMCPL becomes the center of members' social lives. As with other neo-Pentecostal churches, the great majority of PMCPL members are women (approximately 80 percent), though they are not in leadership positions except for the pastorate (in many cases because they are pastors' wives). The great majority are white people, though they are considered Latinos in the American ethnic classification system (see Marrow 2003; Martes 2007); they are overwhelmingly from the Brazilian lower-middle and middle classes; they tend not to have university degrees. They are also a rather young population; the majority are married and in their thirties, forties, or fifties, with not many who are over sixty. What do the Brazilian evangelicals do for a living? The evangelical males take jobs mainly in civil construction in small companies and as gardeners. Some have small businesses that employ their evangelical brothers and sisters. Females take low-wage jobs, working especially in domestic service, office cleaning, beauty salons, and day care services, usually for private households.

TEMPLE, ALTAR, AND RITUAL

I chose to study the congregation in Astoria for several reasons. Although this congregation is currently not the church headquarters, it was the first congregation founded by Bishop Zeny in New York. Furthermore, it is the congregation frequently visited by believers and ministers of other PMCPL congregations and even by other Brazilian evangelical churches. Astoria is not the administrative center (that is in Newark), but it is the PMCPL's religious center. Taking a closer look at the rituals of this congregation allows us to understand the internal dynamics that create the Brazilian evangelical enclave within the broader ethnic enclave of Brazilians in the New York metropolitan region.

The congregation meets on the second floor of the building on 33rd Street in a commercial section of Astoria. No structural alterations have been made, and passersby can identify it as a religious place only because of the plaque with the name of the church and a picture of the Brazilian flag near the top of the building. The congregation is partly a house of worship and partly a community center, though these two functions are separated only by a wall. A missionary is devoted to the Astoria congregation: she has the key to the church and takes care of cleaning, cooking, and buying the goods consumed there. She also oversees the women workers. She knows all the believers of the congregation and monitors members' frequency of attendance at all worship services. If someone misses many services, she calls or may even visit the believer to find out why he or she has become distant from the church and seek to bring them back into fellowship.

As one enters the church, there is wall space ("Cantinho Comunitário") set aside to publicize important church and community news and information: dates of anniversaries, jobs, babysitter services, and ads for apartments, cars, and furniture. Such mutual assistance defines much of the congregation's life. In the Astoria congregation the pulpit is framed by three flags: American, Brazilian, and Israeli. The Brazilian flag represents the origin of the church; the Israeli flag, the historical and theological (Jewish and Christian) origin of this religious movement; and the American flag, the host country where the church operates. At the beginning of the worship service, the pastors bow their heads toward the floor and pray. The floor of the altar is considered even more sacred than the room's space. After I participated in more than one hundred services in different congregations of PMCPL and other evangelical churches, it was possible to perceive a pattern, a worship ritual typical for

FIGURE 5.2. Worship Room of the PMCPL building.
Photograph courtesy of author.

this church. What is the significance of the worship service of this evangelical church? It is the seeking and worshiping of God through prayer, hymns, and Holy Communion (the Sunday Holy Supper).

Actually, participation in the worship ritual begins before the believers come to church – the sacred place. It begins while they are at home – the domestic place. They must prepare their bodies and souls before going to the "temple." The believer' body is the temple of God, the Holy Spirit (I Corinthians 6:19–20). God makes no separation between physical and spiritual, body and soul; both are part of the same life. The believers must honor God with their bodies. Because of this, the believers must clean their (impure) bodies before worship. After cleaning the body of impurities (i.e., by taking a bath), God expects a believer to spend some time in meditation and prayer (spiritual purification), preparing the soul for worship before coming into the house of God.

The ritual of the PMCPL (and of all neo-Pentecostal churches) can be characterized by a trinity of attributes – *open, happy,* and *varied* – traits that make these churches very attractive, especially to the poorest and the migrants in society (Rodrigues 2002, 2010). It is *open* due to these congregations' easy access. As mentioned previously, they are found in central locations of urban areas close to where members live and work. It is also open in an inclusive sense, through its policy of receiving everyone, regardless of his or her ethnic group, social class, religion, or gender.

It is *happy* for many reasons: because of the music played, usually popular; the great number and diversity of the hymns sung (accompanied by the clapping of hands) and the collective prayers; and the informality of the pastor-actor while preaching, thus establishing direct communication with the worshippers and encouraging their active participation. The ritual is *varied* by virtue of the diversity of activities. The audience is encouraged to move and gesticulate. There is a dialogue between the congregation/audience and the preacher on stage (though the responses are simple and patterned) during the high points of the service and during the collective exorcisms, which are always dramatized by numerous symbolic actions.

Prayer in the ritual of the PMCPL merits special attention for many reasons. First, it fulfills an important psychological function in that the congregation finds in these special and spiritual moments a prime opportunity to manifest (and act out) their deepest feelings. Prayer is also the special channel of communication between members and God. Prayers can be repeated various times during the worship service, but those at the beginning, which are generally longer, are used to identify the specific problems and issues of those present – unemployment, lack of money, illness, or marital and family troubles.

The pastor takes special advantage of the moment of prayer (purported to be spontaneous) to emotionally steer concerns in certain directions. This is done with the aid of music and by dimming the lights and asking the people present to close their eyes, place their hands on their hearts, and converse with the Holy Spirit about their problems. The pastor-actor, with his or her words and gestures, works at integrating all of those present into the process of a collective exteriorization-interiorization of the faith.

Music contributes significantly to the ritual atmosphere. Apart from supporting the preacher's management of emotional expression, music also provides a vehicle for the expression of collective unity (Lehmann 1996). As Bloch-Hoell (1964) notes, "The Pentecostal sermons, hymns, meetings, and music, as well as the conduct of the preacher and the followers, encourage the development of strong, primitive emotions, and the release of these feelings."

In the sermon the pastor often uses the Bible to discuss day-to-day issues and problems. The sermon is delivered in simple language so that everyone will understand it; it is important to always remember the humble origins of the neo-Pentecostal churches' followers, as may be seen in PMCPL. The pastor asks the congregation many questions, the answers to which are already known. The followers need only say "yes" or "no." "Amen" is also repeatedly used to elicit a response from the flock. It helps guarantee lively participation among the people present.

The sermons are strongly influenced by the language of television evangelism. The constant pacing back and forth on the altar-stage (scenery) by the pastor-actor, with microphone always in hand, is an apropos visual image. Added to this is the pastor's remarkable expressive vocal ability (especially its emotional capacities) to keep the congregation's undivided attention and full participation. The sermon's message, when analyzed, can be reduced to various patterns, techniques, and strategies to cover all conceivable individual problems and to appear attend to them. To begin with, the pastor employs a theme or aspect of the faith developed throughout the year, with practical purposes in mind, to achieve predetermined objectives and to resolve the specific problems of the believers. These are practical and real issues, with special focus on the principal day-to-day problems of the great majority of the people.

Therefore, the church knows very well how to respond to the people's religious feeling, especially in offering through the worship services adequate opportunities to live and express their feelings, including every type of sentiment and emotion – joy, struggle, aggression, and anger. In the "free" prayer segments of the church service, which are guided by the pastor, an invitation is made to the believers to pray with a loud voice, sometimes very loud. With microphone in hand, the pastor interprets what he supposes or knows the people want to say.

With great flexibility, the PMCPL emphasizes physical and psychological illness and other real problems of daily life (unemployment, the lack of a green card). It promises the people material and spiritual help and radical change in their lives: the poor will have money; the illegal immigrants will have the needed green card; the sick will be healed by the Holy Spirit – and all by means of the divine cure, or their liberation from evil spirits through exorcism. The PMCPL believes that demonic forces cause people to lose control and, thus, that it is necessary to expel the devil from them. Because of this the church performs exorcisms, which are performed in special worship services (for example, in vigil and worship with special guests). These are purgative acts accompanied with violent expressions, often screams, such as: "In the name of Jesus, get out of here, Devil! Out, out, out, Devil! Burn, Devil, burn! Stamp out the Devil!"

Demonology is an important issue in the context of neo-Pentecostalism (Mariz 2000). Demons are the ones guilty of evil. Humans are not seen as sinners, but as the victims of the actions of demons. As Lehmann (1996) has noted, "The word *libertação* has a dual meaning: 'liberation' of individuals from the devils possessing them but also liberation of the evil spirit within the individual from the body, which in some sense imprisons it."

CONCLUSION

Although the flow of Brazilian emigration to the United States has slowed significantly in recent years, the process of evangelical conversion of Brazilian immigrants is ongoing, and consequently, their churches are still expanding in the New York area. No matter how serious the current economic crisis or how long the Brazilian evangelical community has lived in the United States, most do not want go back to Brazil. They have established small businesses and continue to be a highly entrepreneurial people – a trait that has served them well as they navigate the pluralizing urban religious landscape of New York.

The main theme and purpose of this chapter is to discuss, from an anthropological and religious ecology perspective, the significant presence of Brazilian immigrants and their evangelical churches in the context of the religious plurality of the New York Metropolitan Area. I have focused on the presence and spatial visibility of the Brazilian immigrants (where they live and work) and their evangelical churches, which are creating important changes in this religious urban landscape. By focusing on the establishment and growth of Brazilian churches in the New York area, as well as on the leadership, history, structure, and rituals of a specific church, the Igreja Pentecostal Missionária de Língua Portuguesa, I have attempted to show how new movements and organizations are transplanted into New York's religious ecology. In ecological terms, the Brazilian church plants represent an "incursion" of outside resources and leadership into the neighborhoods of the New York Metropolitan Area. But such transplants are not necessarily done in competition and conflict with other congregations of the host neighborhood. As suggested by the level of cooperation between Brazilian and Portuguese congregations, there was more of a "network of religious interchange" than of competition between these organizations (Eiesland 2000).

The Brazilian evangelical churches have created an enclave within a larger enclave through their expressive worship and strong community life. The processes of ethnic succession and cooperation with other churches, particularly Portuguese congregations, have strengthened their outreach, giving their church-planting strategy a global dimension. Such strategies may not be unique to the Brazilian churches, but this case study in Brazilianization suggests how religious innovation takes place both inside and outside a given religious ecology. In the religious ecology framework, these enclaves are good examples of the interactions that take place between immigrants and their surrounding environment, generating a process of ethnic succession that also reveals a cooperative dimension.

The growth of PMCPL also demonstrates two factors: the importance of the charismatic religious leader and of the transnational networks based in New York. Astoria is an ecological environment filled with Brazilian ethnic businesses and residents. The flourishing ethnic enclave drew Pastor Zeny to choose this location as the center of the PMCPL movement. The movement was funded by a charismatic immigrant pastor who was originally inspired by a transnational evangelical event hosted by the Billy Graham crusade in Rio de Janeiro. Pastor Zeny believed that he was called by the Holy Spirit to be a pastor and therefore came illegally to the city to minister to Brazilian and later Portuguese immigrants. Pastor Zeny realized his evangelical vision by starting at the "sinner city," the immigrant city and center of the world, to further pursue his mission transnationally to Portugal and even to the rest of Europe.

ACKNOWLEDGMENTS

I would like to thank Maxine Margolis, Tony Carnes, Paul Freston, and Peggy Levitt for their helpful comments on an earlier draft of this chapter. Of course, for errors and other faults that remain – and there are undoubtedly some – I am solely responsible.

NOTES

1. Albeit in a different ethnic context, however evangelical, see Kwon (1997).

REFERENCES

Badgley, Ruey. 1994. "Brazucas in Bean-town: The Dynamics of Brazilian Eth-nicity in Boston." Senior honors thesis in Anthropology. Connecticut College, New London.

Beserra, Bernadete. 2003. *Brazilian Im-migrants in the United States: Cultural Imperialism and Social Class.* Los Ange-les: Scholarly Publishing.

Bloch-Hoell, Nils. 1964. *The Pentecostal Movement.* London: Allen & Unwin.

Carnes, Tony, and Anna Karpathakis, eds. 2001. *New York Glory: Religions in the City.* New York: New York Univer-sity Press.

Chesnut, A. 1997. *Born Again in Brazil: The Pentecostal Boom and Pathogens of Poverty.* New Brunswick, NJ: Rutgers University Press.

Coleman, Simon. 2000. *The Globalization of Charismatic Christianity: Spreading the Gospel of Prosperity.* Cambridge: Cambridge University Press.

Droogers, André, et al., eds. 2006. *Play-ful Religion: Challenges for the Study of Religion.* Delft, The Netherlands: Eburon B.V.

Ebaugh, Helen R. 2003. "Religion and the New Immigrants." In *Handbook of the Sociology of Religion,* ed. Michele Dillon. Cambridge: Cambridge Uni-versity Press.

Eck, Diana L. 2001. *A New Religious America: How a "Christian Country" Has Become the World's Most Reli-giously Diverse Nation.* San Francisco: Harper Collins.

Eiesland, Nancy. 2000. *A Particular Place: Urban Restructuring and Reli-gious Ecology in a Southern Exurb.* New Brunswick, NJ: Rutgers University Press.

Freston, Paul. 1997. "Charismatic Evan-gelicals in Latin America: Mission and Politics on the Frontiers of Protestant Growth." In *Charismatic Christianity: Sociological Perspectives,* eds. S. Hunt, M. Hamilton, and T. Walter. New York: St. Martin's Press.

———. 2008. "The Religious Field among Brazilians in the United States." In *Be-coming Brazuca: Brazilian Immigration to the United States; Impacts on Econo-mies, Identities, and Cultural Practices,* eds. Clémence Jouët-Pastré and Letícia Braga, 255–68. Cambridge, MA: David Rockefeller Center for Latin American Studies, Harvard University; distr. by Harvard University Press.

Haddad, Yvonne Yazbeck, Jane I. Smith, and John L. Esposito. 2003. *Religion and Immigration: Christian, Jewish, and Muslim Experiences in the United States.* Walnut Creek, CA: Altamira Press.

Herman, Max. 2007. "Ethnic Succes-sion." In *The Encyclopedia of Race, Ethnicity, and Society,* ed. Richard T. Schaeffer. Thousand Oaks, CA: Sage.

Holy Bible: The Old and New Testaments. 1971. Oxford: Oxford University Press.

Jouët-Pastré, Clémence, and Letícia Bra-ga, eds. 2008. *Becoming Brazuca: Brazil-ian Immigration to the United States.* Cambridge, MA: David Rockefeller Center for Latin American Studies, Harvard University; distr. by Harvard University Press.

Kwon, Victoria H. 1997. *Entrepreneur-ship and Religion: Korean Immigrants in Houston, Texas.* New York: Garland.

Lehmann, David. 1996. *Struggle for the Spirit: Religious Transformation and Popular Culture in Brazil and Latin America.* Cambridge: Polity.

Levitt, Peggy. 2007. *God Needs No Pass-port: Immigrants and the Changing American Religious Landscape.* New York: The New Press.

Margolis, Maxine. 1994. *Little Brazil: An Ethnography of Brazilian Immigrants in New York City*. Princeton: Princeton University Press.

———. 2009. *An Invisible Minority: Brazilians in New York City*. Gainesville: University Press of Florida.

Mariz, Cecília Loreto. 2000. "The Devil and the Pentecostals in Brazil." In *The Religious Phenomenon: An Interdisciplinary Approach*, eds. Donizete Rodrigues and P. del Río, 43–50. Madrid: Aprendizaje.

Marrow, Helen. 2003. "To Be or Not to Be (Hispanic or Latino): Brazilian Racial and Ethnic Identity in the United States." *Ethnicity* 3, no. 4: 427–64.

Martes, Ana Cristina. 2007. "Neither Hispanic nor Black: We Are Brazilian. In *The Other Latinos: Central and South Americans in the United States*, eds. José Luis Falconi and José António Mazzoti, pages 231–56. Cambridge: Cambridge University Press.

———. 2011. *New Immigrants, New Land: A Study of Brazilians in Massachusetts*. Gainesville: University Press of Florida.

Martes, Ana Cristina, and Carlos Rodrigues. 2004. "Church Membership, Social Capital and Entrepreneurship in Brazilian Communities in the U.S." In *Ethnic Entrepreneurship: Structure and Process*, ed. Curt Stiles and Craig Galbraith, 171–201. New York: Elsevier.

Martin, David. 1990. *Tongues of Fire: The Explosion of Protestantism in Latin America*. Oxford: Blackwell.

McClymer, John. 2006. "Religion and Ethnicity." In *A Companion to American Immigration*, ed. Reed Veda, 513–27. Oxford: Blackwell.

Pew Forum on Religion and Public Life. 2008. "Changing Faiths: Latinos and the Transformation of American Religion." http://www.pewforum.org/Changing-Faiths-Latinos-and-the-Transformation-of-American-Religion.aspx. (accessed March 23, 2012).

Pluss, Caroline. 2009. "Migration and the Globalization of Religion." In *The Oxford Handbook of the Sociology of Religion*, ed. Peter Clarke, 491–506. Oxford: Oxford University Press.

Portes, Alexandre, ed. 1995. *The Economic Sociology of Immigration: Essays on Networks, Ethnicity, and Entrepreneurship*. New York: Russell Sage Foundation.

Ramos-Zayas, Ana Y. 2008. "Between 'Cultural Excess' and Racial 'Invisibility': Brazilians and the Commercialization of Culture in Newark." In *Becoming Brazuca: Brazilian Immigration to the United States*, ed. Clémence Jouët-Pastré and Letícia Braga, 271–86. Cambridge, MA: David Rockefeller Center for Latin American Studies, Harvard University; distr. by Harvard University Press.

Rodrigues, Donizete. 2002. *The God of the New Millennium: An Introduction to the Sociology of Religion*. Lisbon: Colibri.

———. 2003. "The Catholic Charismatic Renewal Movement in Brazil: The Case of Father Marcelo Rossi." In *Rite and Power*, ed. Anders Ruuth, 99–114. Uppsala, Sweden: Faculty of Theology, Swedish Institute of Mission Research.

———. 2006. "Universal Church of the Kingdom of God." In *Encyclopedia of New Religious Movements*, ed. Peter Clarke, 593–95. New York: Routledge.

———. 2010. Brazilian Immigrants and Pentecostalism in New York City. Unpublished manuscript, Columbia University, New York.

Sales, Teresa. 2003. *Brazilians Away from Home*. New York: Center for Migration Studies.

Suro, Roberto. 1999. *Strangers among Us: Latino Lives in a Changing America.* New York: Vintage Books.

Vásquez, Manuel A., and Marie F. Marquardt. 2003. *Globalizing the Sacred: Religions across the Americas.* New Brunswick, NJ: Rutgers University Press.

Warner, R. Stephen, and Judith G. Wittner. 1998. *Gatherings in Diaspora: Religious Communities and the New Immigration.* Philadelphia: Temple University Press.

Weber, Max. (1921) 1965. *The Sociology of Religion.* London: Methuen.

6

Building and Expanding Communities: African Immigrant Congregations and the Challenge of Diversity

Moses Biney

The importance of religious congregations in the life of immigrants has been well noted by many scholars (Herberg 1960; Williams 1988; Warner and Wittner 1998; Ebaugh and Chafetz 2000; Guest 2003). In addition to spiritual support, immigrant congregations are said to provide their members and even nonmembers with communities and social spaces where their home cultures can be maintained and reproduced, with opportunities for networking and for accumulating social capital and skills for civic engagement.

Immigrant congregations are typically particularistic. They tend to be racially and culturally homogenous. They are often communities created by and for migrants from particular racial and ethnic groups or geographical areas. Their main commitment is often to assist in the adaptation of the immigrant members to life in the United States (Biney 2007, 2011; Guest 2003). This is why some scholars refer to them as ethnic enclaves. Within these communities, they point out, identity is negotiated (Warner and Wittner 1998) and ethnicity is maintained and reproduced (Ebaugh and Chafetz 2000). These observations, though largely true, tell only part of the story; they overemphasize the homogeneity of immigrant congregations. What I aim to do in this chapter is to reveal the complex dynamics and tensions between homogeneity and diversity that exist within these congregations, and the attempts by such congregations to open up their communities to diverse populations.

I argue that post-1965 African immigrant congregations, despite the odds against them, are striving to create more inclusive spaces for worship and social life. To demonstrate this thesis, I describe and analyze the organizational, worship, and community life of four congregations in the New York Metropolitan Area, all with largely African immigrant memberships: Day Spring Church on Roosevelt Island, St. Mary of Zion Ethiopian Orthodox (Tewahedo) Church in Manhattan, Redeemed Christian Church of God Chapel of Restoration in the Bronx, and First Presbyterian Church in Irvington, New Jersey. These case studies show the challenges and struggles these congregations undergo to create more culturally and morally diverse communities.

AFRICAN IMMIGRANT CONGREGATIONS

Using Eiesland and Warner's framework of a multilayered religious ecology, it is important to start with the demographic makeup of African immigrant congregations. (Eiesland and Warner, 1998) Since the 1980s the United States has seen the emergence and growth of religious congregations made up predominantly of African immigrants (Biney 2007; Olupona and Gemignani 2007; Hanciles 2008). In many American cities and towns such as New York, Washington, and Miami, one is sure to see churches, mosques, and a few shrines (patronized by adherents of African indigenous religions) that serve as worship places and sometimes social spaces for first- and second-generation African immigrants. The New York Metropolitan Area, the most populous urban region in the United States with an estimated population of about 18,815,988 (2007 estimate), covering twenty-three counties in New York, New Jersey, Connecticut, and Pennsylvania, is home to numerous African immigrants and their congregations. Generally, the congregations are dispersed in various neighborhoods throughout the metropolitan area.

In New York City, these congregations are particularly concentrated in several adjoining community districts in the Bronx: Melrose, Morrisania, Claremont, Corotana Park, Highbridge, Concourse, Morris Heights, University Heights, Fordham, Mount Hope, East Tremont, Bathgate, Belmont, and West Farms. In Manhattan, they are found mostly in Central Harlem. These community districts, according to the New York Department of City Planning, are populated largely by blacks and Hispanics. Community District BX 3, for instance, has 30,201 of its total population listed as black. Also about 40 percent of CD BX4's population of 139, 563 is black. These blacks surely include persons from Africa and the Caribbean. The areas mentioned are also mostly distressed neighborhoods with high poverty and crime rates. During my research, I visited congregations such as the Pan African Church of God in Christ, the Presbyterian Church of Ghana in New York, the Redeemed Christian Church of God International Chapel, The Holy Order of the Cherubim and Seraphim Church, The Light Mosque of Faith, and others.

All these congregations and many others I know of have to constantly deal with the paradox of homogeneity and diversity that characterizes American society. They always have to seek a balance between their mission to African immigrants on one hand and, on the other, persons from other racial and ethnic groups in the neighborhoods within which they are located. Also, as is demonstrated in the description of the four congregations, they have to strive constantly to keep together different ethnicities and generations within their congregations. Before we look at the congregations described in this chapter, it is important to examine aspects of the social and religious context within which they have emerged and operate. I specifically look at the issue of diversity in America and its impact on congregational life.

THE AMERICAN RELIGIOUS LANDSCAPE AND
THE THEORY OF RELIGIOUS ECOLOGY

A critical change in the American sociocultural and religious landscape since the late nineteenth century is the emergence of great diversity. Scholars who have studied this change indicate that it is unprecedented and particularly obvious in areas of ethnicity and religion (Eck 2001; Wuthnow 2005). In direct contrast to the 1950s, when Protestants, Catholics, and Jews were the main religious groups in the United States (Herberg 1960), the American religious landscape now contains a plethora of world religions (Eck 2001; Levitt 2007). Religions such as Hinduism, Buddhism, and varieties of Islam and Christianity that were unknown to many ordinary Americans have now gained ground and followings in many American cities. Robert Wuthnow, in his *America and the Challenges of Religious Diversity* (2005), points out that the current degree of religious diversity in America is new. He further indicates that historically, Americans of European descent always viewed religions other than Christianity from a distance. This is no longer the case. Now, they live in the same neighborhoods with those who profess these other religions. "Hindus, Buddhists and Muslims," Wuthnow (2005) writes, "now live in significant numbers within the boundaries of the United States itself and despite the fact that many are immigrants and thus differ in cultural heritage from residents of longer duration, most are middle class, college-educated professionals who live in the same kinds of neighborhoods as other Americans, send their children to the same schools, vote in the same elections, shop at the same shops and watch the same programs on television" (38).

In addition and often associated with religious diversity is ethnic diversity. As indicated in Wuthnow's description, many of the adherents of these new religions have migrated from various cultures to the United States. America now has a host of varied cultures. Much of this diversity is seen in cities such as New York.

Cities are centers of complex networks. Described as a "geographical plexus" (Massey et al. 1999), the city facilitates the movement of people, goods, customs, and values. Another feature of cities, relevant to our country's purpose, is the heterogeneity of its people in terms of race, ethnicity, age, class, religion, belief, and sexual orientation. Eiesland and Warner (1998) introduce the concept of the open-ended character of the congregation environment: its extension from the local neighborhood to the global community and from the immediate present to the past and future. New York City and the adjoining urban areas where I conducted my research present a typical picture of the diversity that exists in many American cities and its implication for congregational life within African immigrant churches. Such numerous cultures obviously create a heterogeneous city life. While this heterogeneity is very evident, it has nonetheless not erased identities, particularly cultural ones. My contribution in this chapter is to demonstrate that heterogeneity has engendered and continues to engender what I call "involuntary homogeneity" in the congregational environment of New York. By this I mean that the heterogeneous nature of urban life often provides the conditions and opportunities for persons with the same or similar culture or beliefs to band together to form their own communities.[1] This is one of the many reasons that Africans in the New York Metropolitan Area have formed congregations.

Diversity, particularly the racial and ethnic diversity in America, has always generated different and often contradictory attitudes. America, as scholars have pointed out, has always been characterized by two somewhat contradictory visions – homogeneity and diversity (Myrdal 1944; Richardson 1988). Although the nation has always claimed to be a land of freedom and opportunity for all peoples, it also views itself as a "melting pot." For most of its existence, the United States has been a racialized country. By "racialized" I mean what Michael Emerson and Christian Smith (2000) describe as "a society wherein race matters profoundly for differences in life experiences, life

FIGURE 6.1. Day Spring Church, Roosevelt Island, New York.
Photograph courtesy of author.

opportunities, and social relationships" (7); or in the words of Bonilla-Silva and Lewis (1997), a "society that allocates differential economic, political, social, and even psychological rewards to groups along racial lines; lines that are socially constructed" (474); a society where "racial considerations shade everything" (Bonilla-Silva 2006, 1).

Specifically, as Emerson and Smith show in their research (2000), in America race determines income, housing, health care, and the like. The power of race has both direct and indirect implications for religious congregations. For instance, it affects where religious congregations are located and, of course, who their members are likely to be. It is not by accident, then, that most of the African immigrant congregations are located in areas populated by blacks and have largely black memberships.

Anthony Orum and Xiangming Chen, in their essay "The World of Cities: Places in Comparative and Historical Perspective" (2003), draw attention to the importance of place in human life. They define places as "specific locations in space that provide an anchor and a meaning to who we are." Places (such as cities and other such human settlements), they argue, provide (1) "a sense of individual identity," (2) "a sense of community," (3) "a sense of past and future," and (4) "a sense of being at home, of being comfortable, of being, as it were, in place." Although not specifically mentioned in Orum and Chen's work regarding the relationship between humanity and place, one important thing that can be deduced from it is the fact that places are dwellings for social structures such as individualism, community, race and racism, ethnicity, diversity, classism, poverty, wealth, and power and powerlessness, and arenas where these structures and institutions interact with one another. In other words, in every place, social structures both facilitate and inhibit action. The African immigrant congregations thus have their missions cut out for them by the places where they are physically located, as well as the composition of their membership. Like other congregations, they have to interact with these social structures and either adapt to or revolt against them.

In the following four case studies, I focus on the challenge of diversity, including languages and culture practices, and the roles of churches in structuring the interaction of people in the ecological setting I just described, in effect, covering the second and third layers of the religious ecology.

DAY SPRING CHURCH, ROOSEVELT ISLAND, NEW YORK

Day Spring Church, a Pentecostal congregation with a predominantly Nigerian membership, worships on the West Channel side of the East River on Roosevelt Island, New York. Its chapel, built with gray gneiss, a steep slate roof, and stained glass, was originally erected in 1924 as the Episcopal Church of the Holy Spirit and at one time served as a place of worship for Metropolitan Hospital patients. The church, founded in March 2003 by Pastor Olu Obed, an Ibo from Nigeria, his wife, and a few former members of the Redeemed Christian Church of God, has a total membership of about one hundred with an average attendance of eighty. The composition is 50 percent women, 30 percent men, and 20 percent children.

Attached to the chapel is a four-bedroom rectory house, currently used as temporary classrooms for the Lilies Christian School, founded and run by Associate Pastor Elsie Obed, wife of the head pastor. The sanctuary seats between 180 and 220 persons (the pastor told me it is able to accommodate 240 people). On each side of the center aisle are four rows of red chairs, nicely arranged. A lectern (used for preaching, reading of scripture, and announcements) stands on the platform (altar area) of the sanctuary. On the platform are two flags – one of the United States, the other of the church. Small paper flags representing twenty-three countries – Ghana, Nigeria, Barbados, Japan, Zimbabwe, Guinea, Jamaica, Russia, Kenya, Togo, Namibia, Sierra Leone, Trinidad and Tobago, Puerto Rico, Burundi, Guyana, Israel, Cameroon, the United Kingdom, Niger, Panama, Rwanda, and the Philippines – adorn the walls of the chapel. When I visited, gathered on the left side of the platform was the eight-member choir (praise team).

Between fifty-five and sixty people were attending the service the Sunday morning I worshipped at the church. About 70 percent of these worshippers were female. They were of diverse ages – from about four years old to sixty or thereabout. Although the majority of the worshippers were black, they were from many different countries. I personally spoke to three African Americans, three Ghanaians (incidentally I had taught one of them in a high school in Ghana years ago), two Nigerians, one person from the Democratic Republic of Congo, and one person from Trinidad and Tobago. I could not be certain of the professions and occupations in which the church members engaged, but from looking at how people were dressed and from later discussions with the pastor I was made aware that they belonged to diverse professions including diplomats, business executives, teachers, janitors, and others. Three women came in wheelchairs. As each of them arrived at the entrance of the chapel, members of the church promptly assisted them in entering the sanctuary. The main worship service began at 10:05 AM (Sunday school study was at 9:00 AM). Just before the worship service began, we were given copies of the *Day Spring News* (volume 4, issue 11), which contained the pastor's sermon for the day (or a version of it) and announcements. A note at the end directed those who wanted to obtain a copy of the full version of the sermon to see the Tape Department. These church magazines and tapes, I learned, are circulated not only among congregation members but also in Roosevelt Island Township and other places in New York and New Jersey.

The first half hour was devoted to singing praise songs. The leader of the praise team led the singing with support from the band (organ and drum accompaniment). No typical African instruments were played, and all the songs were sung in English. No hymn or song books were used. Words of the songs were projected onto a screen from a laptop computer. The singing and dancing were vibrant. From the pulpit Pastor Olu Obed introduced me to the congregation and also welcomed a member who had returned from a diplomatic assignment in Israel. He then led us to pray for the families of all those who had died during the attacks on September 11. Prayers were said aloud, with the pastor and others "speaking in tongues" at various points. This was followed by announcements and an offertory time lead by Pastor Elsie Obed.

Eventually, it was time for the sermon, and Pastor Olu returned to the podium. He reminded members of the church's mission to the poor and needy and asked that those who were able to make donations help the people of Niger who were facing severe famine and also people who had been displaced by Hurricane Katrina. Almost everybody present came forward to place a donation in a designated bowl.

In his sermon, entitled "Repentance from Dead Works," Pastor Olu spoke at length on repentance and reconciliation. It was essential, according to him, that each person be accepted before God. Since God blesses people based on his acceptance of their works, all must repent from "dead," "vile," or "deceitful works." "God chooses those he blesses and he maintains a standard, a yardstick for those he blesses. . . . God gives a testimonial and attests to the character of the person he blesses based on his [God's] righteousness," Pastor Olu intoned. Obviously this was an evangelical sermon aimed at conversion and also to reinforce with members the importance of holiness.

There was more singing for about five minutes, and then all of us said the benediction in the form of the "sharing of grace." The worship service finally ended at 12:20 PM, after which refreshments were served. There was cordial interaction between members as they enjoyed food and drinks. As I was leaving the church premises at 1:00 PM, a large portion of church members still remained, showing no sign of being in a hurry to leave.

A month prior to this participant observation at the church, I had visited Pastor Olu and interviewed him regarding the founding, mission, and challenges of the Day Spring Church. One of the crucial points of our discussion was the desire and effort by Day Spring to become a truly multicultural and multiracial congregation. He revealed that there was always a struggle within his congregation regarding how much attention must be devoted to African cultural needs. When I asked how his church deals with this dilemma, he replied,

> We cannot deny that the church has an African flavor, but we are cautious of how much of African culture we incorporate in our church life. This is because of my experience with the Redeemed Christian of Church of God (RCCG). When we started RCCG, we felt too comfortable with African immigrants. We therefore focused much on Africans, particularly Nigerians, and unconsciously shut people from other cultures out. What you do with such an approach is that you predetermine the size of your church and the scope

FIGURE 6.2. First Presbyterian Church, Irvington, New Jersey.
Photograph courtesy of author.

of your ministry. At Day Spring Church we want to avoid that. Day Spring
Church is a church of new beginnings. We believe that everyone, no matter
who they are, can have a new beginning in the Lord Jesus.

Let me say at this point that we do not specifically target African immigrants, even though many Africans are attracted to the church because
its leadership is largely African. Our goal is to have a multicultural church
in which all persons are welcome. We want the church to be open to all
peoples. Thus we don't emphasize a particular culture. For instance, we discourage the use of the vernacular in formal services. Yet we reinforce some
values such as respect for adults, communal life, and others which are very
important for Africans and also resonate with people from other cultures.

FIRST PRESBYTERIAN CHURCH, IRVINGTON, NEW JERSEY

A brick signpost announced the presence of the church, First Presbyterian
Church of Irvington (hereafter FPC), as I turned the corner at Berkley Terrace and Grove Street. It was Sunday morning, and people were arriving for

the morning worship service. The street in front of the church was lined with flashy, expensive-looking cars. I turned left and parked at the Berkley Terrace Elementary School parking lot. As I walked to the church, I saw others, many of them in familiar African garb, going there too. I shook hands with a number of them and entered the church building.

Adorning one of the walls on the first floor of the building was an artist's impression of a projected new building for FPC. The picture, possibly drawn in the 1950s, showed a huge chapel extending from Berkley Terrace to Grove Street. It was meant, according to the building plan, to consist of a sanctuary, a conference center, and a number of offices. Captured in the picture were also men and women – all Caucasian – wearing dark suits and expensive-looking skirts and blouses. They were all tall and slender and wore hats. The picture thus depicted what looked to be a white church in a white suburban and affluent neighborhood. In many ways this artist's impression of what First Presbyterian was to be hardly reflected what it is now. The first conspicuous difference is that the current church building is only about one-third the size of the massive building in the picture. As I later learned, the projected building could not be completed due to a fall in membership and the related lack of resources. The church ran out of funds after building the offices and therefore converted one of the offices into a sanctuary. A second difference is that the church's white membership and neighborhood have now been replaced by blacks. U.S. Census Bureau statistics for this district in 2000 showed a black population of 81.7 percent as compared to 9.0 percent white and 8.4 percent Latino. About 53 percent of the total population of 60,695 are female, according to these statistics. The average age of the residents is thirty-one years. Another feature of Irvington is that it has a high poverty level.

FPC is bordered on the east (toward Eastern Parkway) by private homes, on the west by Grove Street, on the south by Berkley Terrace Elementary School, and on the north by more private residences. Across Grove Street toward Ellis Street and up toward 19th Street are areas described by a resident as "infested with drug peddlers and addicts and prostitutes." A number of people I had the chance to speak with during my research in the area consistently identified the township with these vices. Shawn, a young man of about twenty who works at the barbershop close to the church, described the area around 19th Street as "very, very bad." Lomotey, a Ghanaian and now naturalized American and former resident of Irvington, would never recommend that any friend buy a house in Irvington, particularly around the Grove Street area, for the same reasons. Eastern Parkway, which runs close to the area, facilitates the transport of drugs into Irvington, according to some observers. The leaders and members of the First Presbyterian Church are not unaware of the drug and crime problem in the area. In fact, they have sometimes been robbed of their belongings and had their cars broken into. One of the elders of the church told me that on one occasion the car of a guest preacher they had invited for a Sunday morning service was stolen from the front of the chapel.

According to a short history on the church's website, FPC began in 1891 as a mission chapel in a predominantly German-speaking real estate development known as Manhattan Park in the Village of Irvington. This became the Manhattan Park Chapel, an offspring of Memorial Presbyterian Church of South Orange. On June 24, 1897, the chapel was purchased from Memorial and the new congregation of thirty-seven members was named Manhattan Park German Presbyterian Church. The church prospered and, due to changes in the immigrant community, began offering services in English. The World War I era brought many changes to the church, including dropping "German" from its name. The English-speaking project became a full congregation that eventually became known as the Faith Presbyterian Church of Irvington. These two congregations merged in December 1948 and became known as the First Presbyterian Church of Irvington. Groundbreaking for the current building took place on January 3, 1954, and was completed two years later. Dedication of the present sanctuary occurred on November 22, 1964.

The turbulent 1970s and '80s were difficult for many urban churches, including First Presbyterian. In 1988 the Presbytery of Newark reassessed the mission of the church, whose membership was down to eighteen. In early 1989 at the invitation of a member of First Presbyterian, several members from the dissolved Kilburn United Memorial Presbyterian Church came to worship, and together the congregations managed to keep First Presbyterian open. As part of a specific mission goal of the Presbytery to reach out to new populations, the Rev. Dr. E. Obiri Addo was called to lead a redevelopment effort. Under his pastoral leadership, FPC has in the past twenty years seen a great redevelopment. It currently has a membership of more than four hundred. The adult membership is made up of about 60 percent Ghanaians, 20 percent Nigerians, 10 percent Kenyans, 5 percent Caribbeans, 2 percent American-born citizens (mostly African American), and 3 percent from other African countries, among them Liberia and Sierra Leone. Women constitute 55 to 60 percent of the membership.

FPC considers itself a "multi-cultural and inter-generational congrega-tion." Its mission statement, approved by the 2003 church session on Decem-ber 19, 2003, reads: "First Presbyterian Church of Irvington is a fellowship of believers redeemed by God through the sacrifice of Jesus Christ. As a multi-cultural and inter-generational community held together by the Holy Spirit, we are part of the greater world church." Although this vision of the congregation is yet to be fully realized, it in many ways characterizes FPC's community and worship life. The church at this point can best be described as pan-African. Its composition imposes on the church leadership and mem-bers the need to negotiate the rather tenuous relationship between preserv-ing the identities of the cultural groups represented in the church and at the same time maintaining unity. In my interview with the senior pastor of the church, Dr. Addo admitted that this is a tightrope walk. According to him, some members of the church left to join other African churches because the congregation uses the English language for its service. Some in the church (particularly the Ghanaians, who were members of the Presbyterian Church of Ghana) have complained that the worship services are unlike those back home. Some have particularly complained of the lack of time given to danc-ing as it is practiced at home and in other African churches. The goal of FPC, however, according the head pastor, is not to replicate the worship style of members' former congregations in Africa and elsewhere. It is not only the African immigrants who wish that the church be more reflective of "home." Some African American members wish that its worship and liturgical prac-tices were more American, particularly something closer to those of South-ern Baptist churches. Reverend Kennedy, the associate pastor and minister of education, indicated that earlier, some of the African Americans did not particularly like the fact that African immigrants were growing in numbers and were gaining more and more control over the congregation. They there-fore left and joined other, "normal" African American churches. Although the situation has changed since then, some hot-button issues remain in the church. The crucial thing for the African immigrants is language. A ma-jority of the members are first-generation immigrants who are often quick to converse in African languages, especially in Twi, a Ghanaian language. This behavior often annoys some other members, particularly the African Americans.

The need to preserve unity in the members' diversity is often emphasized during services. During one service, Dr. Addo spent about ten minutes talk-ing to members about this need:

> Our church is open to all cultures. All cultures represented here must be
> who they are but must also be sensitive to others. For this reason every
> member is free to speak his or her language or dialect, but please be mindful
> of the fact that other members may not understand your language. Since
> English is one language everybody in this church understands, let us use it in
> communication more often, especially when some around us do not under-
> stand our particular dialect but may want to join in a discussion.

Dr. Addo suggested that flags for all the countries represented in the church would be displayed in the church's Founders Hall. Also to further promote unity in diversity at FPC, songs in African dialects are often translated into English before they are sung. I recall one particular incident during a worship service when the leader of the church's Centennial Band, when his attention was drawn to it, apologized to the congregation for not translating a song the band had sung in Twi.

One important strategy that FPC has devised to bridge the cultural gaps between members is the creation of "communities" within the congregation. These communities are based on the geographical location of members' homes. The communities, eight in all, are meant to be a variation of the "cell group" concept. Unlike the members of typical cell groups, members of these communities do not meet in people's homes but in the church once every month. It was hoped that these "geographical communities" would help bridge the different "cultural communities" since persons from different cultural backgrounds would belong to one community.

On the second Sunday of every month, between thirty and forty minutes of the worship service are devoted to community meetings. For instance, on April 9, 2006, which was Palm Sunday, there was a community meeting dealing with the topic of "What do I expect from my community in times of joy or sorrow/distress? Whom do I contact?" Each community, according to information in the bulletin, was to discuss expectations and identify two contact persons. These persons must have great discernment and be wise enough to handle confidential information with empathy. These would be the community links with the pastoral staff.

In my interview with Dr. Addo after the service, he made clear that his and the church's vision was to "reach out to all peoples irrespective of race, ethnicity, age, or sexual orientation." Aside from its theological importance, having diverse cultures represented in the church membership was also pragmatic. He pointed out that so-called "ethnic" churches have a very short lifespan, particularly in the United States. "We have to learn from this, and other immigrant groups such as the Koreans," he said. "Most of the Korean churches which were organized as 'ethnic' churches are now using English for services and opening up to people from other cultures. Those which started as multicultural churches have grown to become big churches."

Outside the church community, particularly in its immediate vicinity, however, FPC is considered and referred to as "the African church," a clear indication that it is yet to be recognized by the largely African American population as part of the larger community. Despite the fact that the congregation offers a meeting space for the East Ward Block Association, and once each year organizes a Safety Summit and Flea Market with the association, few in the immediate neighborhood actively participate in the church's activities. Nonetheless, the church continues to have its doors open to the neighborhood through its computer training classes, music school, and other services.

ST. MARY OF ZION ETHIOPIAN ORTHODOX (TEWAHEDO) CHURCH, NEW YORK, NEW YORK

The church building is quite large – it extends from 30th to 31st Street (with its main entrance on 31st Street). Situated between 7th and 8th Avenues, the church is close to Madison Square Garden, Penn Station, and other businesses, making the area around the church quite busy. Both human and vehicular traffic are heavy in the area. The streets behind the church are littered with paper and junk food wrappers. St. Mary of Zion uses the building of St. John the Baptist Roman Catholic Church.

I arrived at the church at 11:50 AM and entered the spacious basement of St. John's building. Of the basement's two large rooms, one is used for services by the St. Mary of Zion Orthodox Church. The preparatory service, mainly a time of prayer and chanting, had just started. As I entered a room adjacent to where worship services are held (it looks like a cafeteria with chairs around the tables), I was met by two women dressed in white linen bordered with green trim from their midsections to their heads. One took off her shoes and entered the place of worship, while the other remained in the outer room. I asked her for Father Tribenu, my contact person. "Father what?" She asked. Obviously she hadn't recognized the name, so I asked whether this was the Ethiopian service. She answered in the affirmative and asked me the first name of the priest I was looking for. I didn't know. She thought for a while and told me I needed to wait since the worship service had started. I asked whether I could join the service and whether I needed to take off my shoes. She smiled and said yes. "Are you bringing some charity?" she asked me. I said no and tried to explain the purpose of my visit. I took off my shoes and joined the preparatory service, deliberately choosing to sit at a chair very close to the entrance.

The room was not very spacious. It had about a hundred single chairs arranged to face the altar area. The altar was an elevated platform covered with a rich maroon and gold carpet. On the walls and also standing on the floor of the platform were large and medium-sized paintings of Jesus, Mary (separately and together), and other figures (I could not see clearly who they were from where I sat). Hanging on the two outer pillars of the platform were small wooden statues of Mary (on the left) and Jesus (on the right). The platform is divided into two sides by a velvet maroon curtain. Behind the curtain was an altar that looked like a small but elevated bed. On it was something that looked like an urn, a large Bible, and other liturgical books and golden incense holders. The priests and assistants officiated from this section of the platform.

About ten people had arrived when I entered. Most of them were women clad in white linen. A few of the men also had on the white linen (wrapped from their shoulders to their midsections). The seating was largely gender segregated, with men and women sitting on separate sides of the sanctuary. The children had their meeting in a room in the basement, but a few young ones kept coming up – sometimes running and making noise.

Except for some English translations of the prayer and parts of the liturgy, the entire service was conducted in Amharic and Ge'ez. I had no interpreter, so I could not understand most of what was said. For the most part, during this preparatory service and the main service that followed, a high level of solemnity and seriousness was maintained that is absent from many of the Protestant worship services I have observed.

The pre-service was essentially a time of preparatory prayer and chanting. Two priests and their two assistants lead the prayers, interspersed with readings from the Bible and songs. The worshippers often responded to or repeated some of what the priest said and sometimes bowed or knelt down. More people continued to arrive. After the preparatory service, which lasted about thirty minutes, the priests and assistants went inside the inner section of the altar area and drew the curtains behind them. They were, as I understood, preparing for the main service. After about three minutes the curtain was opened and the main service began. Almost all of the worshippers, including me, stood. My attention was drawn particularly to a middle-aged woman who came in with two teenagers (a boy and a girl). She stood while her children sat during the service. At one point she asked them to stand.

They grudgingly obeyed (their reluctance obvious in their faces), but sat down again only five minutes into the liturgy. Obviously, they would have preferred to be somewhere else.

The first part of the service was a long liturgy that took over an hour. This involved long recitations of what I presumed to be portions of the Bible, prayers, and songs. The text of the prayers, in both Amharic and English, were displayed on a screen in the center of the room. The priest went in and out of the inner altar area. From time to time he walked around the altar. The head priest at different times raised different crosses – a smaller wooden one covered in velvet and a larger, golden one. At specific times during the liturgy a second priest came around with incense. All these procedures were repeated a number of times. I could barely understand the recitations but tried to follow the genuflections as I saw the others do.

The recitation segment was followed by communion. At this point the elements were wrapped in velvet linen and brought from the altar. Two men in the front row opened umbrellas, one gold and the other velvet, and went up to the stage to cover the heads of the priests who held the elements. Some of the children and a section of the worshippers went to the front and were served with the elements. One of the priests carefully broke bread and placed it on the tongue of the communicant while another poured some sort of liquid – I am not sure whether it was wine – onto a spoon and gave it to him or her. I thought every worshipper was going to be served with the communion elements, but surprisingly only a few received it. I could therefore not verify what was served for the communion. Baskets were then passed round twice to collect offerings, and the sermon followed. I understood virtually nothing since it was delivered entirely in Amharic. After the sermon a group of worshippers (a choir of some sort) and the priests gathered on the platform and led the entire congregation in singing songs. I could not sing because neither the words nor the tunes were familiar to me. This went on for about ten minutes, after which a closing prayer and benediction were said. The head pastor stood in front of the platform holding the small velvet cross. One by one, worshippers passed by to be touched on their foreheads with the cross.

After the service, I was invited "for coffee." We went into one of the rooms farther into the basement, where many people had gathered to drink tea and coffee and eat bread. I was offered tea and homemade Ethiopian bread. Both tasted quite strange to me, but I managed to eat it. The atmosphere in the room was one of friendliness as members spoke happily in Amharic, some hugging each other. I had conversations about the church with Manaseh, a man who looked to be in his forties and who lives in Newark, New Jersey. He told me that the church was established about fourteen years ago and that its members mainly resided in New York, New Jersey, and Connecticut. This Sunday many people had not attended the church, he said. He was not sure why. The second pastor, with whom I spoke briefly, told me he had lived in Germany for many years and had been in the country for only a year and a half.

After about fifteen minutes, Father Tribenu joined us. He was served with tea. I asked for a summary of his sermon. In somewhat halting English, he explained that he had been preaching about the use of time. Based on Luke 2:25–38, he argued that Simeon and Anna spent all their time in the temple of the Lord and for this reason they saw Jesus. "We must all spend more time with God – in church generally serving God." he told me. "See, there are 168 hours in the week. Out of this we generally work 40 hours and are supposed to sleep 40 hours a week. What do we do with the rest – 88 hours? How much of it do we use in serving God? We waste a lot of time doing other things but serving the Lord."

I asked him if his church plans to reach out to non-Ethiopians or persons who can neither speak nor understand Amharic. He responded that the church was open to anybody who was willing to worship with them, but at this point, its mission focus was Ethiopians, particularly those who are or have been part of the Ethiopian Orthodox Church. According to him, many of these in the United States are "slacking" or leaving the faith due to the economic and social pressures in the United States. "American life is too loose; we must get our people to worship God truthfully," he said.

I then asked him whether the church intended to hold services in English in addition to Amharic and Ge'ez anytime soon. He told me this was a big challenge since most of the liturgical language and songs and *kidase* (traditional chanting) cannot be easily translated without losing their theological and liturgical value. On the other hand, he realizes the need for the members' children and children's children who don't particularly understand the language and religious culture to stay in the church.

As he spoke, some of the children chased one another around while others sat in a corner conversing, apparently not too concerned about their parents' religious fervor or the future of their church. One or two sat with earphones in their ears listening to what looked like iPods or cell phones. Clearly, this was a new culture that Father Tribenu and the others had to embrace. And indeed he said the church was trying. The children, he said, had

FIGURE 6.3. Redeemed Christian Church of God
Chapel of Restoration, Bronx, New York.
Photograph courtesy of author.

their own separate services, where they were taught scripture and liturgical practices in ways they can understand. Only time will tell how things will play out. We talked for a while longer, and I asked permission to leave. He then invited me to their Good Friday service, which, he said, was the highpoint of their liturgical life.

REDEEMED CHRISTIAN CHURCH OF GOD CHAPEL OF RESTORATION, BRONX, NEW YORK

It was about 12:00 PM on August 2, 2005, and I had come to visit with Pastor Daniel Ajayi-Adeniran to ask him about the church he leads, the Redeemed Christian Church of God Chapel of Restoration, located on Morris Avenue in the Bronx. It had been difficult to contact him, so I was happy to meet on a weekday instead of a Sunday, always a busy day for him.

Redeemed Christian Church of God, founded in Nigeria, West Africa, in 1952, came to New York in 1995. The Chapel of Restoration at the time of

my interview was one of the twenty-one RCCG congregations in New York
City. Pastor Ajayi-Adeniran (also known as Pastor Sunday) told me the story
of how it began:

> [I] arrived in the United States in 1995 and settled in Brooklyn. The only Re-
> deemed Church in New York (also the first one to be founded in the state),
> was on Roosevelt Island [at the time], so I joined it. I was there for a couple
> of months. Then, some members were coming all the way from Bronx to
> Roosevelt Island for worship, so I was sent by my pastor to start a branch in
> Bronx. We started meeting at 205th Street. on Grand Concourse in North
> Bronx and then later moved to Fordham Avenue. As our numbers increased,
> we rented this present building. Whenever we moved, however, we left a
> small congregation at the original place. So we now have three congregations
> in Bronx. This particular congregation was therefore formed in 1997, but we
> moved here in March of 2002. This building was an abandoned auto shop
> which was almost in ruins. We acquired it and renovated it as you can see.
> [He showed me pictures of what the building used to look like – dilapidated,
> waterlogged, and dirty.] We signed the lease for rent with the option to
> buy in September 2001, completed with its renovation in March 2002, and
> moved in the same month.

The mission of the church, according to the pastor, was to make it possible for
all to hear the Word of God and also to plant as many churches as they can so
that people will have places of worship so close to them that they would have
no excuse for not attending church. This was not going to be easy, he admitted. When the Europeans came to Africa and other places with the Gospel,
he pointed out, "they had the money and resources to propagate the Gospel
and also convert people through the provision of health care, education, and
other social services. On the contrary we come with very limited economic
resources to people who are wealthy and who have all the material things they
need. Some even consider Africans as inferior people. It is therefore very difficult to attract people other than Africans into the church."

I asked him if he believed that America was a "mission field" for his
church. His face lit up, and he was obviously excited. He paused for a few
seconds and then answered, "Yes, I always tell my members that God does not
make mistakes. He therefore made no mistake in bringing us here at this time.
Whatever circumstances that brought us here, God requires us to be his missionaries in this land. I therefore encourage members to share the word with
their neighbors and invite them to worship services." He was quick to point
out, however, that this does not mean America lacks churches or preachers.

In fact, America has many churches: many of the world's largest Christian ministries, large seminaries, and eloquent and knowledgeable preachers are in the United States, yet many of them have turned away from the foundations of the Christian faith. What is lacking in America is the belief in prayer, holiness, the power of the Holy Spirit and zealousness for the word of God. These, according to him, were "old landmarks" that need to be revisited.

During our conversation, I could not help but admire Pastor Ajayi-Adeniran's passion for evangelism and his strong conviction that he could reach out to all cultures. I therefore asked him if he had been able to draw persons other than Africans into his church. He responded:

> A major challenge is how to become attractive to non-Africans or even non-Nigerians and also how to worship in such a way that we can satisfy the needs of the African immigrants who are in the majority and still make the non-Africans feel at home.
>
> You know, in America the membership of congregations often depends on people in the location. This area is made up of mainly blacks and Spanish people. There are hardly any whites who live here. There was one white sister in the church, but she stopped coming because she said she didn't feel very comfortable when she comes to this neighborhood. Though we have a few Hispanic and Caribbean brothers and sisters in the church, we cannot deny that the church has an African flavor. Many of the members are immigrants from Africa, and so even our accent and worship style show that we are Africans.
>
> Though the congregation is made up of predominantly Nigerians, we still have the vision of attracting people from other cultural and racial backgrounds. For this reason, I ask my members, particularly the Nigerians, not to use vernacular at church. The choir is also not supposed to sing any vernacular songs. We conduct service mainly in English. Also we had a Spanish young man who used to stay with us in our home. He had a little problem and was sent to jail, but before then he was interpreting my sermons into Spanish during Sunday services. Fortunately, he is coming back from jail soon, and we will surely continue the interpretation of my sermons into Spanish.

DIVERSITY, CHALLENGE, AND OPPORTUNITY

It is evident from the accounts of the four churches presented that they and others with significant African immigrant membership are faced with the challenges of diversity both within and outside their respective moral communities. Specifically, the challenge is twofold: first, how to extend their mission and ministries to their neighborhoods, particularly to people from different

ethnicities and races, without sacrificing the needs of the first-generation immigrants, who constitute the bulk of their membership, and second, how to
manage diversity within their faith communities. The locality of each congregation is very different from the others, providing a unique comparison of African churches in the Greater New York area. The ways in which each pastor
deals with these challenges are likely to be as diverse as their neighborhoods.

The common characteristics evident among the people in these church
communities might suggest a tendency toward pan-African congregations.
Yet my data demonstrate that certain diversities challenge such an emerging
pan-African Christian solidarity. Common to all the congregations is the
challenge of racial and ethnic diversity. Although Day Spring Church has
some African (non-Nigerian), Asian, Caribbean, and Caucasian members,
well over 50 percent of the congregation's members are Nigerian. In fact, when
I asked a resident of Roosevelt Island for directions to the church, he referred
to it as "the Nigerian church." Many non-Nigerian members were staff of the
United Nations on-duty tour who live in the UN apartments on the island.

Having majority Nigerian membership, however, does not make the
church any less diverse, for the Nigerians are not of the same ethnic group.
At least two prominent Nigerian ethnic groups with different languages and
cultural norms – Ibos and Yorubas – were present in the congregation. I found
similar ethnic dynamics in the Redeemed Christian Church of God Chapel
of Restoration, where about 90 percent of the congregation was Nigerian. At
FPC, where about 60 percent of the membership was Ghanaian, the Ghanaians consisted of several language groups such as Twi, Ga, and Ewe.

In these congregations, diversity revolves around language and cultural
norms such as showing respect, eating, and gender roles. While observing
these norms, particularly the use of African dialects, may make the respective speakers feel at home, ironically this is also often a source of contention.
To address this problem, all the congregations except St. Mary use English
as the language for formal worship. The Day Spring Church and Redeemed
Church expressly discourage the use of ethnic dialects during worship services and even in conversations in the church. First Presbyterian, on the other
hand, allows its members to speak their dialects in informal situations but
encourages members to be mindful and even sensitive to others who may not
understand those dialects.

Another challenge common to all the congregations examined is in-
tergenerational diversity. First-generation immigrants are generally wary of
American youth culture, aspects of which they consider depraved. In my

conversations with the pastors of these congregations, they all spoke about the need to assist the younger members of the church in making wise choices. At the top of their agenda was the need to provide them the necessary education. At Day Spring, Associate Pastor Elsie Obed runs an elementary school for that purpose; Pastor Ajayi-Adeniran (Redeemed) has similar plans; at First Presbyterian there are computer training classes and music classes in addition to Sunday School. At St. Mary of Zion, Father Tribenu is very much aware of the differences between generational cultures in the church. He and some of the parents I spoke to admit that they had to give young people a lot of "freedoms" they never had or could even dream of having when the parents were young.

The young people, for their part, saw things differently. Some saw the church generally as a place where they could meet with some of their family's friends; others were interested in the worship services but felt uncomfortable in a space they considered to be more for their parents than for themselves.

CONCLUSION

African immigrant congregations have both benefited from and been limited by their neighborhoods. In areas with higher concentrations of African immigrants, congregations may have a strong base on which to draw, yet this can prevent them from meeting their stated goal of reaching out to other ethnic groups. Those congregations in more pluralistic neighborhoods depend on commuter members, at least initially, but this tendency can work against the formation of neighborhood ties that could facilitate outreach and ministry in their communities. African immigrant congregations vary in terms of religious beliefs, denominational affiliation, membership, racial and ethnic composition, organizational structure, location, and worship and other social programs. These congregations are shaped not only by their mission but also by the social structures they confront. In many cases, they deal with similar structures, prominent among which is the challenge of diversity. In this essay, I have demonstrated how four congregations with majority–African immigrant members are dealing with the challenge. My purpose here is not to suggest that the challenge of diversity is peculiar to African immigrant congregations. Diversity in the United States presents an American dilemma that all institutions, including religious congregations, have to deal with.

What I argue in this chapter is that African immigrants are struggling to build communities that can accommodate other cultures different from their own. Though largely concerned with helping their members survive in America, these African religious congregations are not oblivious to the challenges of the larger society, particularly the immediate neighborhoods within which they are located. Even though their actions may have very minimal results, they are surely challenging the American ethos regarding diversity.

NOTES

1. A similar view has been expressed by Omar McRoberts. I thus agree with McRoberts's argument that city life engenders participation in subcultural life and reliance on homogenous institutions. See McRoberts (2003, 43).

REFERENCES

Biney, Moses O. 2011. *From Africa to America: Religion and Adaptation among Ghanaian Immigrants in New York*. New York: New York University Press.

———. 2007. "Singing the Lord's Song in a Foreign Land: Spirituality, Communality, and Identity in a Ghanaian Immigrant Church. In *African Immigrant Religions in America*, ed. Jacob K. Olupona and Regina Gemignani. New York: New York University Press.

Bonilla-Silva, Eduardo. 2006. *Racism without Racists: Color-Blind Racism and the Persistence of Racial Inequality in the United States*. Lanham, MD: Rowman & Littlefield.

Bonilla-Silva, Eduardo, and Amanda Lewis. 1997. "The New Racism: Toward an Analysis of the U.S. Racial Structure, 1960s–1990s." Unpublished manuscript.

Ebaugh, Helen, and Janet Chafetz. 2000. *Religion and the New Immigrants: Continuities and Adaptations in Immigrant Congregations*. New York: Altamira Press.

Eck, Diana. 2001. *A New Religious America: How a "Christian Country" Has Become the World's Most Religiously Diverse Nation*. New York: HarperCollins.

Eiesland, Nancy L., and Stephen R. Warner. 1998. "Ecology: Seeing the Congregation in Context." In *Studying Congregations: A New Handbook*, ed. Nancy T. Ammerman et al. Nashville: Abingdon Press.

Emerson, Michael O., and Christian Smith. 2000. *Divided by Faith: Evangelical Religion and the Problem of Race in America*. New York: Oxford University Press.

Guest, Kenneth. 2003. *God in Chinatown: Religion and Survival in New York's Evolving Immigrant Community*. New York: New York University Press.

Hanciles, Jehu. 2008. *Beyond Christendom: Globalization, African Migration, and the Transformation of the West*. New York: Orbis Books.

Herberg, Will. 1960. *Protestant, Catholic, Jew: An Essay in American Religious Sociology*. New York: Doubleday.

Levitt, Peggy. 2007. *God Has No Passport: Immigrants and the Changing American Religious Landscape*. New York: The New Press.

Massey, Doreen, John Allen, and Steve Pile. 1999. *City Worlds*. New York:

Routledge in association with the Open University.

McRoberts, Omar. 2003. *Streets of Glory: The Church and Community in Black Urban Neighborhoods*. Chicago: University of Chicago Press.

Myrdal, Gunnar. 1944. *An American Dilemma*: New York: Harper & Bros.

Olupona, Jacob K., and Regina Gemignani, eds. 2007. *African Immigrant Religions in America*. New York: New York University Press.

Orum, Anthony, and Xiangming Chen. 2003 *The World of Cities: Places in Comparative and Historical Perspective*. Malden, MA: Blackwell.

Richardson, Allen E. 1988. *Strangers in This Land: Pluralism and the Response to Diversity in the United States*. New York: Pilgrim Press.

Warner, Stephen R. 1994. "The Place of the Congregation in the American Religious Configuration." In *American Congregations*, vol. 2, ed. J. P. Wind and J. W. Lewis. Chicago: University of Chicago Press.

Warner, Stephen R., and Judith G. Wittner, eds. 1998. *Gatherings in the Diaspora: Religious Communities and the New Immigration*. Philadelphia: Temple University Press.

Williams, Raymond B. 1988. *Religions of Immigrants from India and Pakistan: New Threads in the American Tapestry*. Cambridge: Cambridge University Press.

Wuthnow, Robert. 2005. *America and the Challenges of Religious Diversity*. Princeton, NJ: Princeton University Press.

PART THREE

Entrepreneurial Innovation
and Religious Institutions

7

Changing Lives One Scoop at a Time:
The Creation of Alphabet Scoop
on the Lower East Side

Sheila P. Johnson

It is a warm and sunny Sunday morning on East 11th Street, in what is known
as "Alphabet City" (Pekarchik 2001) on New York's Lower East Side.[1] Sun-
light gleams from the windows of the restored four-story walk-up tenement
that houses The Father's Heart Church and Ministry Center (Father's Heart),
built in 1857 as the People's Home Church and Settlement. The first congregants arrived from Russia in 1919, determined to provide a religious and moral
education for their children and evangelize their fellow Slavic immigrants.
In the following years, the progenitors and their ecclesial offspring would be
confronted with critical structural decisions that would affect their organizational identity. The Father's Heart would have to re-invent itself to insure its
survival. Some eighty-six years later, it would morph into a marketplace ministry with entrepreneurial strategies founded on principles of religious social
capital, prophetic social activism, and community engagement. The creation
of an ice cream business, Alphabet Scoop Ice Creamery, would become an
important aspect of the ministry's long-term survival strategy.

Reflecting the new urban landscape, with its slick corporate branding
and attractive exteriors, the Alphabet Scoop Ice Creamery, a for-profit social-
purpose business owned and managed by The Father's Heart, occupies an
attached street-level commercial space located on the first floor of the "Faith
Annex." On the same block, trendy clubs, independent clothing designers,
Zagat-rated restaurants, and multimillion-dollar condominiums jockey for

position alongside bodegas, storefront churches, and a handful of properties as yet untouched by the surge of the well-heeled, demographically homogeneous, upwardly mobile professionals who seem poised to consume a neighborhood ripe for occupation.[2]

The primary objective of this chapter is to examine how a faith-based, market-oriented nonprofit organization functions in a large urban center. This chapter extends the theoretical model of religious ecology beyond its current application to the concept of the "free market." I treat the "free market" as a metaphorical social space (White 1992) as a site where goods are created, produced, exchanged, and consumed.[3] It may be further conceptualized as "the outgrowth of how to provide the means for human sustenance and then with gradual, material improvement through time, the satisfaction of an ever widening range of desires" (Santelli et al. 2002, 67). Economic theory and religious ecological theory are seldom addressed together. Nonetheless, I endeavor to demonstrate how changes in religious ecology, a propos of its network of interdependent institutions (e.g., the political arena, the market, and moral and cultural social spaces) (Santelli et al. 2002) can cause new market phenomena to emerge, satisfying a previously overlooked need while simultaneously transforming both the free market and the community.

I will note the ways in which this organization harnesses social capital – through the creation of Alphabet Scoop, the for-profit wholesale and retail ice creamery and youth job training program – and how The Father's Heart successfully introduces a prophetic dimension to the public realm of commerce and community development and promotes social and civic engagement within a diverse religious and secular ecology.[4] The intention is to elucidate through observation and interviews the role The Father's Heart plays in addressing social and distributive inequalities and in mitigating the alienation and separation that commonly arises between church and community.

EXILED TO ALPHABET CITY

I am seated in a cavernous four-story-high room that serves as combination sanctuary–soup kitchen–social service outreach center or family and youth center (where KidZone™ meets, as discussed later in this chapter), depending on the time and day of the week.[5] A raised platform, flanked by American and Israeli flags, sits at the far end of the freshly painted aqua- and white-walled room. A traditional baptismal pool for full immersion rests in front of a hand-painted pastoral-themed mural depicting a little white lamb grazing peacefully in a broad green field. Although the years have muted its colors, the mural remains both a symbolic and a transcendent reminder of the Lamb of God – Jesus Christ. Otherwise, there are no crosses or human representations of Jesus. Eight enormous pendant lights are suspended from the ceiling. As he descends the four steps leading down to the base of the platform, Pastor Perry Hutchins is drenched in sweat from having led the highly expressive style of praise and worship music that he is known for. There is no air conditioning.

The small multicultural congregation, no longer mourning the loss of its beautiful oak pews, sits obediently on gray metal folding chairs. The pews, donated to another church, were among the first fixtures to go when the ministry shifted its focus in 1998 from a traditional, cloistered approach to prophetic social activism. Senior Pastor Charles "Chuck" Vedral steps forward and makes an announcement that electrifies the congregation. Now nearly everyone is standing. Crying with joy, shouting and "getting the Holy Ghost," they collectively and individually respond to the good news.[6] An article about Alphabet Scoop is in the *New York Times* Sunday edition (Schwarz 2005). Pastor Chuck passes the article around. It features a color photo of an awning tastefully emblazoned with the store's name, Alphabet Scoop, juxtaposed against a forty-foot, 1930s-style neon cross suspended three stories up, which proclaims "Jesus Saves." Just two days earlier, the store hosted its grand reopening. Apparently, the promises of God to bless them had been endorsed by the *New York Times*.

"In the world, yet not of it" is a "particularism of exilic consciousness"[7] – a community engagement praxis that The Father's Heart has extended to marketplace activity. It requires that the church remain faithful to its sacred and ethical commitments while facilitating dialogical relationships with the secular world. It also requires a remarkable adaptability that ensures survival through perplexing and difficult times. Jesus Martinez, associate pastor and general manager of Alphabet Scoop, stands before the predominantly minority congregation and, quoting Jeremiah 29:4–7 – "A Letter to the Exiles" – urges the congregation to follow the example of Israel when it was exiled to Babylon and "set up camp right where you feel out of place. Camp yourself right where you are and declare God's plans to prosper you." He reminds the congregation that, "even in the midst of exile, God instructs the children of Israel to build homes, and plan to stay; plant gardens and eat the food they provide; marry and have children." Countless *Amen*s echo throughout the sanctuary. Pastor Martinez then exhorts the congregants to "work for the peace and prosperity of the city where I sent you in exile and pray for it. For its welfare will determine your welfare."

This jeremiadic homily (Bercovitch 1978) contextualized the hardships experienced by the congregation by helping its members to make sense of their present troubles and create an optimistic outlook for the future.[8] The message was implicit: the church could not afford to live in passive isolation; instead, it must relate to its neighbors in a redemptive manner. But it could not imitate or integrate the dominant cultural ecology characterized by upper-middle-class gentrification and pleasure seeking and epitomized by the explosion of expensive rental properties, luxury condominiums, fashionable clothing boutiques, liquor licenses,[9] and binge drinking.[10] Rather, the church must take responsibility for the peace and prosperity of the city, penetrating and co-existing with society while simultaneously remaining true to its Christian culture.[11] The church hoped to close the cultural divide between these two worlds by establishing a business that would benefit both itself and the community.

The service ends with an announcement that "the ice cream store is now open for business, *but not business as usual*" (author's emphasis).

As I step through the large glass entryway that separates the ice cream store from the main church building, I enter an inviting 160-square-foot space that itself looks like a lime green and raspberry sherbet confection. Two large blackboards mounted behind the counter list fifteen gourmet flavors. A countertop is available for seating; four customers already occupy its stools. It is standing room only. A display on one wall holds samples of branded hats and T-shirts for sale. Christian kitsch is nowhere in sight, and you won't find "Heavenly Vanilla" or "Praise the Pineapple" on the menu, either. Flavors like "Street Haiku" and "Banana Stampede" are staples here. Their registered service mark – the clever brainchild of the pastors and a pro bono consultant – simply states that they are "Saving Lives One Scoop at a Time."

One could not help but wonder how the ministry could straddle both worlds – of religion and capitalism, of spirituality and materialism – participating in an economic system that it had relentlessly criticized for its celebration of profit and oppression of the poor, yet still retaining its values and integrity. Specifically, how can the ministry accommodate quid-pro-quo capitalist principles by generating profits on the one hand (as we presume it must to remain viable) and, on the other, accommodating the needs of its "at-risk" youth employees and remaining ethically and ideologically discrete?[12] And, in light of the ministry's economic interdependence with the larger community, how can it safeguard against corrupting its creative social gospel of free-market enterprise? These musings underscore the ambiguous nature of religious-market interactions. Put simply, the question is: What is the church doing in the ice cream business? Pastor Carol Vedral, posted serenely at the cash register, responds:

> Right. I wonder too. But it helps that it is being opened by a nonprofit and not the church. But it could still be opened by a church. It could easily be opened by a church. It would be a great benefit. Ephesians 3:10 says that God's intention is that now through the church His manifest wisdom will be revealed to the powers and authorities. I believe that God wants to reveal his wisdom in everything that's going on through His people. And the Church has taken a very religious approach to that, where it has to be through the traditional means we've always used, such as concentration on Sunday services, Bible study, and Sunday school. But I think some in the body are very creative in doing these social enterprises as well as just pure business. What's wrong with godly businesses? I feel like the whole culture of industry has gone to greed. We cut jobs so that the top people can make millions and millions and millions. How many millions does a person need? So I believe that the influence of godly people upon culture has to be in everything . . . not just the traditional church outlet that we are familiar with. We have to be salt and we have to be light, but you know, we have to get out there.[13]

Although the theological framework of her argument is unconditional in its denunciation of greed and excess consumerism, Pastor Carol articulates a Christian social ethic that seeks to engage the market by creatively revisioning consumption as social action. McDannell (1999) asserts, "If we immediately assume that whenever money is exchanged religion is debased, then we will miss the subtle ways that people create and maintain spiritual ideas through the exchange of goods and the construction of spaces" (6).

THE RELIGIOUS ECOLOGY

The Father's Heart is embedded in an "ecological frame" (Eiesland and Warner 1998, 41) that determines how it acts and is acted upon by its environment. Eiesland and Warner conceive of this environment as a having an "open-ended character that extends from the immediate local neighborhood to the global community and from the present to the past" (1998, 41). Its theoretical scope includes not only religious relationships but also the "economic, political, and educational contexts within which congregations exist and relate globally" (42).

Alphabet Scoop may be conceptualized as an interface or "layer" in the social fabric of Alphabet City, consisting of "a complex web of people, meanings, and relationships; alterations in any one of which can result in social ramifications elsewhere." This tripartite socio-economic model consists of substrata or "layers" defined by the culture, demography, and organizations that flavor the local ecology. The configuration of these layers embodies and expresses the "characteristics of the people in the community; its shared systems of meaning, values and practices, and the systems of roles and relationships that structure the interactions of the people in the community" (Eiesland and Warner 1998, 41–42). Although tension between these "layers" seems inevitable, particularly when bipolar value and meaning systems chafe and spark against one other, new, cocreated outcomes may be surprisingly creative. Alphabet Scoop is an expression of this cocreativity; and whatever the existence of Alphabet Scoop comes to mean to the community is being mutually constructed by the culture, people, and organizations in Alphabet City. This does not imply that these "tensions" are easily overcome.

Implicit in Pastor Carol Vedral's critique of consumerism and greed is a hierarchical notion of "otherworldly" versus "worldly" values. McRoberts (2003a) challenges the prevailing notions of mutual incompatibility between sacred and secular worldviews, and argues that the "otherworldly/worldly dichotomy" has multidimensional complexity that expresses the essence of prophetic social activism and engagement:

> Beneath most typologies of religious organizations is the notion that some churches are oriented toward earthly matters, while others completely turn their backs to secular human affairs, seeking solace in the promise of a better world to come. . . . This assumption obstructs social scientific understanding of . . . organized religion in general, in at least two important ways. First, it suggests that religious people cannot use ostensibly otherworldly ideas for secular activist purposes. If some theologies are taken to be political opiates (recall that Karl Marx dubbed religion the "opiate of the masses"), others are considered amphetamines for activists. Moreover, both are thought to act unambiguously. That is, no religious tradition can be both worldly and otherworldly. No church can change orientations, chameleon-like, to fit the context or issue at hand. The second limiting assumption is that seemingly otherworldly religious practices (such as "shouting" or "getting the holy ghost") do not have practical, even political, implications for the faithful. (413)

McRoberts's observations have important theoretical implications, particularly for socially active fundamentalist congregations like The Father's

Heart that struggle with a dialectic of religious dualism – the idea that spiritual practice and public engagement can be thought of as independent entities much as spirit and body are conceived as discrete. The Father's Heart is unequivocal in its theology: the Bible stands as the inerrant word of God,[14] and the purpose of the church is to proclaim the Gospel to the community.[15] This struggle reflects what Baggett (2002) refers to as the "double-edged nature" of congregations: "Congregations are not, first and foremost, social service organizations. Most congregations say they exist primarily to promote the spiritual well-being of their members through worship and opportunities for spiritual growth, followed by fellowship, or cultivating a caring community of fellow believers"[16] (430).

McRoberts conceives of a kind of hybrid intersubjective religiosity that challenges the fundamental theological convention that "man cannot serve two masters" and retain his ethical purity.[17] He suggests that a disjuncture occurs when congregations ignore the possibility of merging spiritual and public life and undermine opportunities for the expression of fluid and dynamic models of radical religious relationality – a new spiritual enterprise – that has the power to unleash moral agency. As McRoberts (2003a) states:

> The tension between the two [spiritual and public life] is never resolved, but is experienced in every era by religious actors who struggle to remain true to the transcendent amidst the pressing social, political, and economic exigencies of their time. Lincoln and Mamiya (1990:12) concede that "[t]he otherworldly aspect, the transcendence of social and political conditions, can have a this-worldly political correlate which returns to this world by producing an ethical and prophetic critique of the present social order. In some instances, eschatological transcendence can help to critique the present." (412–13)

A type of ecological transcendence emerges as boundaries between The Father's Heart Ministries and the world outside its doors acquire permeability. Ammerman and her colleagues (1998) refer to this "boundaryless" aspect of the church culture and identity as conducive to groups that "emphasize being part of the culture . . . and shun the strictness and intolerance seen in other groups. Their openness to the community illuminates an ethic of inclusion" (98). The Father's Heart vis-à-vis Alphabet Scoop stands as a critique of the capitalist culture, particularly the egocentric lifestyles of the mainstream gentry who are attempting to control existing social and spatial arrangements in Alphabet City.

THE WAKE-UP CALL: FROM OTHERWORLDLY EXCLUSIVITY
TO WORLDLY PROPHETIC SOCIAL ACTIVISM

From its early origins in the Slavic Pentecostal tradition (and identification as the Russian Ukrainian Polish and Pentecostal Church) to its Americanization as the Evangelical Christian Church, the ministry cleaved to an otherworldly relational stance, focusing its mission on evangelicalism and individual moral reform to the exclusion of all other concerns. Unbeknownst to the members, they were about to face a perfect storm of demographic and structural forces that would bring about a sea change, dislodging both leadership and membership from decades of parochial insularity. HIV/AIDS, poverty, homelessness, and food insufficiency would catapult the ministry into the "worldly" realms of grant-seeking, fund-raising, nonprofit incorporation, community capacity enhancement, and sustainable community development.

In 1984 New York City had the highest rates of acquired immunodeficiency syndrome (AIDS) in the world,[18] and the Lower East Side was an HIV/AIDS epicenter. Tragically and seemingly overnight, The Father's Heart lost nearly 25 percent of its membership to the epidemic. Inclusive and welcoming in its response, the church opened its doors to members and nonmembers suffering from HIV/AIDS, ministering to the sick, dying, and bereaved. The disengagement strategies engendered by us-them dichotomies were unworkable. The reality of HIV/AIDS could not be ignored. The road to faith-based activism was thus uncompromisingly paved. "Colloquially," McRoberts (2003a) writes,

> the term "faith-based activism" refers to extroverted forms of social action originating in religious institutions. Churches with food pantries and shelters for battered women, or that build homes and run welfare-to-work programs, or whose leaders organize marches and protests, are considered "activist." It is assumed that religious beliefs and practices are no obstacle for these churches – there is no contradiction between faith and activism. (412)

A salutary effect of the AIDS epidemic was the creation of social capital vis-à-vis "bonding and bridging ties" that generated nationwide collective social action. According to Agnitsch, Flora, and Ryan (2006),

> Both bonding and bridging social capital have been deemed important in terms of community action. Woolcock argued that the presence of both local, embedded (bonding) and external, autonomous (bridging) ties was crucial in successful community development. He contended that, "[T]o

overcome the numerous collective action problems entailed in coordinating 'developmental' outcomes, actors – and the groups of which they were members – had to be able to draw on both 'embedded' [bonding] and 'autonomous' [bridging] ties." The commitment is a function of bonding, and the ability to act is largely a function of bridging.

How do theories of bonding and bridging apply to The Father's Heart? In 1984 the Evangelical Christian Church established CARES (Christian AIDS Relief Services), sending Christian church workers into the adult and pediatric AIDS wards of municipal hospitals to comfort and advocate for the sick and dying. They partnered with God's Love We Deliver to deliver food to homebound persons.[19] For the first time in the church's history, it engaged in secular development activities, launching a successful public awareness and fund-raising campaign aimed at churches and diverse philanthropies and businesses throughout New York City that generated hundreds of thousands of dollars in direct funding for pediatric AIDS research for Harlem Hospital, New York City Health and Hospitals Corporation, along with innumerable in-kind donations.[20]

The social capital generated by the church's AIDS ministry is a function of its facility at mediating the tension between sacred and secular realms, its insertion in the local ecology (bonding ties), its agility in dealing with "external, autonomous actors," and its ability to create networks of concern (bridging ties). According to Putnam (2000), the goal orientation of social capital differs significantly from physical or human capital. Putnam writes, "By analogy with notions of physical and human capital – tools and training that enhance individual productivity – social capital refers to features of social organization such as networks, norms, and social trust that facilitate coordination and cooperation for mutual benefit" (2000, 107).

If one assumes that bonding ties remain stable and that the group contains its otherworldliness within a more expansive sociopolitical framework, this theory fits nicely with Coleman's assertion (2003, 33) that religious organizations are primary incubators for social capital in America. How then, might bonding ties be affected when religious communities are in the birth pangs of transition from the otherworld to this-world? In the case of The Father's Heart, intrabonding ties were weakened. By 2002 the church census of two hundred members had dwindled to twenty as a result of the shift to prophetic social activism and incorporation as a faith-based 501(3)(c) public charity.

The church's new mission statement spoke directly to structural inequities and aimed "to break the cycle of dependency and poverty by providing hunger relief, job training and referrals to those in need."[21] Despite suffering its own internal losses of human capital, The Father's Heart was nevertheless propelled onto the streets of Alphabet City. But the streets were changing and the demographics were shifting in new and (for some) exciting ways. Even now, The Father's Heart was loosely constrained by traditional missionary modes and objectives. Its objective was "to educate, train and prepare volunteers to provide programs designed to meet the immediate and long-term needs of individuals and families in crisis; to demonstrate the good news of God's love by going out into the streets of our community."[22] Christian workers still needed training, but the training ground was shifting to the streets.

The ministry has made itself known in the community, primarily through its ambitious feeding program.[23] The Father's Heart Church is interested in spiritual salvation, but offers, "in the meantime, preemptive and palliative social services, to treat the causes and consequences of youth violence."[24]

GENTRIFICATION 101

To understand the impact of the community on The Father's Heart, one must examine local demographic patterns. Population shifts and modifications provide an important context for understanding how ecological changes affect The Father's Heart. Eiesland and Warner (1998) state, "As the population characteristics in the community change, so do the systems of meaning, values and symbols. Demographic change seldom comes without some discomfort and. . . . Viewed from an ecological frame, conflict and discomfort are the natural and expected consequences of continued existence, and, indeed, vitality" (80). Delgado (2004) affirms, "The notion(s) of sustainable development . . . incorporate(s) the idea of change and uncertainty" (46).

Seismic shifts in the urban ecology of The Father's Heart – the result of changes in urban housing policy, social disaggregation, and the gentrification that began in the late 1970s[25] and intensified in the 1990s[26] – created a culture based on class segmentation. According to Waste (1998), U.S. urban policy paved the way for the gentrification observed in Alphabet City, and aggravated conditions of hunger, poverty, and homelessness. Waste observed that "the slum clearance and urban renewal efforts of the [Housing] Act [of 1949] actually intensified urban poverty by removing numbers of substandard but low-priced rental housing units and greatly concentrating the urban poor into high-rise, low-income public housing projects, and into existing but uncleared poverty neighborhoods" (1998, 45).

Alphabet City housing characteristics substantiate this premise. Characterized by low-rise, pre-war tenement housing built in the late 1890s, most buildings are typically five-story walk-ups. (In accordance with local zoning laws, six-story buildings are required to have elevators; hence the proliferation of five-story walk-ups.) One hundred years later, many residents still share communal hallway toilets. Due to low building heights, this neighborhood is very sunny, and year-round the temperature seems warmer than that of nearby Midtown Manhattan. Alphabet City is home to thirteen public housing sites, including the massive Jacob Riis Housing Project superblocks, which run from 5th Street to 12th Street between Avenue D and the East River Drive;[27] and the Lillian Wald Houses, which encompass 1st to 4th Streets between Avenue D and the East River Drive. Campos Plaza, a New York City Housing Authority development built some twenty years ago, includes senior citizen and low-income housing as well as a massive parking lot for Housing Authority equipment and residents' vehicles. Located as they are on the perimeters of the neighborhood, these housing configurations have essentially isolated a predominantly nonwhite minority population from its affluent surroundings and constructed a new kind of ghetto. Waste suggests that the implications for the inner-city inhabitants are dire:

> Sometime around 1990, the basic fabric of American cities changed dramatically. The new post-1990 ecology of American cities is characterized by a seemingly permanent crisis involving persistently high levels of poverty, hunger, homelessness, violent crime, infrastructure deterioration, fiscal stress . . . inner-city neighborhoods have become isolated urban reservations where an ever-expanding number of American children grow up poor, hungry, and increasingly, victims of violence. (1998, 1)

As Von Hassel (1996) confirms, gentrification significantly altered the landscape of New York City:

> Rents skyrocketed during the 1970's and 1980's; between 1978 and 1985 median rents of all tenant households increased by 93 percent; for the poorest households – those with annual incomes under $3,000 – there was a 147 percent increase. The high rate of conversions of rental buildings to luxury condominiums and cooperatives during the 1980's has further exacerbated the growing gap between the total supply of low-rent units and households needing such housing. (12)

The neoclassical Christadora House, at 147 Avenue B, was the first major condominium conversion in Alphabet City.[28] This towering building features eighty-five condominium apartments, a concierge and doorman, a health club and pool, and a bird's-eye view of adjacent Tompkins Square Park, where the 1980s riots took place. Pop singer Madonna was one its first residents.

There are 410,000 housing units in Alphabet City – approximately 26 percent of which are occupied by low-income residents, including 24,000 children under the age of five who are living below the poverty level.[29] At least twenty newly constructed luxury condominiums are located in Alphabet City, some adjacent to major public housing developments. On East 4th Street and Avenue D, two bedroom–two bath condominiums with prices starting at $555,000 are on sale directly across the street from the Jacob Riis Housing Project. The largest condominium project, located on East Houston Street and Avenue A, is a twelve-story high-rise with thirteen commercial storefronts including Baskin-Robbins, FedEx/Kinko's, H&R Block, Subway, and AutoZone. Three major nearby institutions – New York University, The New School, and Cooper Union – provide the pool of potential tenants that the developers are tapping.

Income Profiles and Poverty Status data for Alphabet City are revealing.[30] The median incomes for both families and households within Alphabet City are significantly lower than those in all of Manhattan and the five boroughs of New York City (NYC) as a whole. The median household income in Alphabet City is 32 percent below that for all of Manhattan and 17 percent below the median for NYC as a whole.

Similarly, the median family income in Alphabet City is 40 percent below that for all of Manhattan and 29 percent below the median for NYC as a whole. This income disparity suggests that a significantly greater percentage of households and families in Alphabet City have incomes below $10,000 than do households and families in all of Manhattan and in NYC as a whole. Similarly, at the other end of the income scale (i.e., annual income greater than $100,000), we find the reverse. A consequence of this income disparity is that a significantly higher percentage of families in Alphabet City live below the poverty level (26%) compared to the percentage of families in all of Manhattan and in NYC as a whole that live below the poverty level (18% for both).

The unemployment rate for residents of Alphabet City (7.5%) is lower than the rates for all of Manhattan (8.5%) and for NYC as a whole (9.6%). In addition, the employment rate for Alphabet City females is higher than it is for males, which is the opposite of the situation in all of Manhattan and in NYC as a whole, where the employment rate for males is higher than it is for females. This is especially significant in light of the fact that median incomes are lower in Alphabet City and poverty is more prevalent. These indicia suggest that Alphabet City residents work more but are paid less than residents of all of Manhattan and of NYC as a whole, and may indicate that many Alphabet City residents comprise what is referred to as the "working poor."

As increasing levels of concentrated poverty and social problems converged with changing housing configurations and the loss of affordable housing, aggrieved communities endured increasing levels of human suffering, and social capital was squandered. Sites (2003) maintains, "The dominant thrust of this period of neighborhood change can be understood, of course, as a story of gentrification – even of hypergentrification – in which a largely working-class and lower-income minority community was increasingly being made into an urban playground for the young, white and affluent" (96). Overall, these demographic outcomes contributed to the weakening of bonds and ties in the once neighborly, inclusive culture of Alphabet City. The Father's Heart was confronted with a Herculean task. As Orsi (1999) says, "It has been one of the challenges of contemporary inner-city Protestant and Catholic churches to find ways of reconnecting these environments, in which many of their congregants make their homes, with the life and movement of the cities surrounding them" (35).

Putnam (2000) decries the decline of neighborhood-based social connections. By linking good-neighborliness and social trust to informal social capital, he suggests that a kind of social decapitalization arises as bonds and ties are eroded, ultimately neutralizing social relations and reinforcing a downward trend in neighborliness. Citing a correlation between educational levels and social trust, Putnam asserts that "the overall decrease in social trust is even more apparent if we control for education" (2000, 110–11).

As a former longtime resident and urban pioneer in Alphabet City, the author remembers community gardens, jazz clubs, and families that looked out for one another's children. Unfortunately, this may be a somewhat romanticized recollection, because the characterization of Alphabet City as a grim, crime-ridden neighborhood is accurate insofar as it signifies physical and civil deterioration.

Thirty years ago, the social fabric of Alphabet City was under siege. As Pekarchik (2001) describes it,

> Alphabet City . . . was synonymous with the sleazy underbelly of the city. To the Empire City's middle class, it was a no-go zone: bizarre, scary, sometimes

FIGURE 7.1. The Father's Heart Ministry and Alphabet Scoop Ice Creamery.
Photograph courtesy of author.

[*sic*] dangerous. Drug deals were transacted openly or in crack emporiums in
condemned buildings. The dealers' whispered litany of "smoke, dope, coke"
followed pedestrians down the streets. Neighbors kept chickens penned
in tiny plots of land. Pit bulls strained against leashes. On summer nights
people sat outside watching TVs run on power hijacked from streetlights.
Taxis were nonexistent. On Sundays, junk was sold on the sidewalks as if at
an open-air bazaar. Squatters brushed their teeth in the spray from water
hydrants. And recurrent tension between police and activists in Tompkins
Square Park erupted into full-blown riots.

In Alphabet City, urban population trends may be contextualized in the
light of earlier population movements and spatial transformations. Many
groups have attempted to claim this land, beginning with the white ethnics
from Ukraine and Poland who emigrated to the United States in the late
nineteenth and early twentieth centuries,[31] followed by the Puerto Ricans
who designated this area "Loisaida" in the early 1960s (Ševčenko 2001, 295),
and the urban homesteaders who fought to remain stably housed through

the 1990s. Alphabet City's affluent professional class is now staking the same claim to Alphabet City as its indigenous predecessors (with mixed results) as this "destination" neighborhood gains instant notoriety for quality-of-life complaints and the inability of the police to preserve civil society. The Lower East Side has one of the highest rates of noise and 311 complaints about the nightlife than any community in the city.[32] The local police precinct, despite having quadrupled its cabaret unit in recent years, is still overwhelmed with the regulation and oversight of these existing locations and does not have the resources to monitor increases in traffic congestion and numbers of people on the streets, or to address crime.[33]

How did Alphabet City's populace respond to these dystopian signs? In 2007, the community rallied around quality-of-life issues instigated by the proliferation of liquor licenses in the neighborhood, appealing to The Father's Heart to lead the charge against environmental offenses perceived as threatening the area's hard-won family-like culture. Networks of concerned groups consolidated as The Father's Heart fought side by side with long-standing community residents and businesses, nearby neighbors, the 11th Street Block Association, and the 9th Police Precinct, all agitating for a new kind of "Prohibition,"[34] and successfully advocating for a permanent moratorium on the issuance of liquor licenses by the State Liquor Authority (SLA) in the neighborhood. Shortly thereafter, the following report appeared in a weekly community newspaper.

> The State Liquor Authority rejected a wine-and-beer license application
> for a bar planned at the site of a former vintage clothing shop at 174 Avenue
> B at E. 11th St. According to Susan Stetzer, Community Board 3 District
> Manager, neighbors pointed out a slew of "discrepancies" on the applica-
> tion. Previously, the S.L.A. rejected a full liquor license for the bar because
> the spot's within 200 feet of a church. Stetzer said the applicant denied that
> they knew the church – Father's Heart Ministries, which sports a large, il-
> luminated white cross (with "Jesus Saves" inscribed in neon) projecting over
> 11th St. – was there.[35]

The above civic action demonstrates how The Father's Heart success-fully mediates social activism in Alphabet City and acts as an "institutional agent that can impact the trajectory and outcome of neighborhood collective action" vis-à-vis the horizontal networks embedded in Alphabet City.[36] It extends the empirical evidence that Putnam (2001) developed on the role of social networks, demonstrating that civic engagement increases government accountability. As Putnam wrote, "the quality of governance was determined by longstanding traditions of civic engagement (or its absence) . . . and suggests that the norms and networks of civic engagement [also] powerfully affect the performance of representative government" (2001, 106–107).

Taking into account the cultural and socioeconomic demography of the area, The Father's Heart would have to find a way to appeal to the larger community and leverage its social programming, prophetic authority, and concerns beyond the church's walls. Alphabet Scoop eventually became the vehicle for this broad appeal. The ministry's influence would be driven by successful horizontal and vertical integration strategies.[37]

THE FUTURE NEVER LOOKED SO SWEET: THE GENESIS OF ALPHABET SCOOP

In the late 1990s, the ministry operated a combination Christian bookstore and candy store in the space now occupied by Alphabet Scoop, but with little success. This venture was unsustainable because its income was derived from the primarily low-income congregation. In 2001 The Father's Heart received the pro bono business services of a volunteer from McKinsey and Company who served in their soup kitchen and pantry. In his role as a professional strategist, he determined that the ice cream and frozen dessert industry yielded highly favorable performance and profitability outcomes. "After all," as Pastor Carol says, "who doesn't like ice cream?"[38]

Several factors led to the selection of this business model, including the ministry's keen insights into and awareness of community needs, the ministry's historical ties to the community, and the market research The Father's Heart conducted. Ministry leaders examined ice cream industry trends, attended ice cream technology events and conventions, and conducted research on every aspect of ice cream production, sales, and marketing. They assumed the Alphabet City subneighborhood, with its contingent of young, upwardly mobile professionals, would provide the customer base.

In January 2002, after gaining consensus among the church's Board of Trustees and the support of the congregation, the leadership of The Father's Heart met with a consultant to develop a business model for a combined for-profit ice cream store and nonprofit job training program that would be owned and operated by the ministry in Alphabet City. The ministry had contemplated operating, among other potential ventures, a secret-recipe fried chicken wing outlet, but a decision was made to establish an ice cream business with backroom capacity for manufacturing ice cream for wholesale, retail, and catering and restaurant sales. The ice cream business would serve as an opportunity structure for unemployed adults, by providing life and job training skills that would prepare them for economic self-sufficiency. The business name: The Father's Heart International Ice Cream and Coffee Store.[39]

Subject to the same indiscriminate structural forces that have shaped The Father's Heart, The Father's Heart International Coffee and Ice Cream closed after one year of operation. The leadership attributes the closure to "unexpected environmental factors" such as the presence of a major utility construction site near the entrance of the newly opened store, but other factors prefigured business failure and jeopardized its success (Austin, Stevenson, and Wei-Skillern 2006). These factors include (1) undercapitalization, (2) limited resource mobilization, (3) lack of business expertise, and (4) an undifferentiated organizational identity.

In the interim, The Father's Heart continued to operate its soup kitchen and pantry on Saturday mornings, and on Tuesday nights KidZone™, its gang prevention and youth development program for children and youth ages four to eighteen. The latter program provides a place for youth to connect with one another and with positive adult role models. It is designed to reduce the risk factors that lead to gang involvement.

The failed ice cream venture came to the attention of a Manhattan-based marketing firm whose employees originally came to the ministry to bag groceries for the Saturday morning feeding program. That experience led them to provide consultant services to the ministry and, over eight weeks, to develop a new branding strategy. They, along with architects, electrical and plumbing contractors, and ice cream consultants all worked pro bono to make Alphabet Scoop a reality. McRoberts (2003b) would refer to these "connections between neighborhood and extra-neighborhood institutions . . . as 'vertical networks that draw resources to the community while presenting neighborhood affairs to a broader public'" (123). These connections create positive outcomes in bottom-line performance. Between 2003 and 2008, net income for Alphabet Scoop increased by 717 percent (McRoberts 2009, 90).[40]

THE SOCIAL GOSPEL OF FREE-MARKET ENTERPRISE

It has been demonstrated that Alphabet Scoop is a product of the socioeconomic and demographic shifts in the community that The Father's Heart discerned. Its presence mediates both the capitalist structure in which it is embedded and the associated "invasion and succession" phenomenon common to gentrified neighborhoods.[41] The concept of Alphabet Scoop operationalizes the ecological schema of relatedness and interdependence that exist between Alphabet City and the ice cream store. The very existence of Alphabet Scoop is evidence of the ministry's broad appeal. Its presence is a stabilizing factor that signifies that the community is a nice place in which to live.

As suggested earlier, population shifts inevitably alter meaning systems, values, and symbols, but in the case of Alphabet Scoop, the ministry was able to incorporate the ethos of Alphabet City without compromising its ethical principles. Notwithstanding the renaissance of Alphabet City, it is ironic that gentrification has provided the economics that makes Alphabet Scoop a viable enterprise. The incongruity of selling $3.00 ice cream cones and $4.50 pints in a site literally flanking a ministry-operated soup kitchen is not lost on ministry leaders.

Alphabet Scoop creates a congruent linkage between religion and capitalism. For our purposes, "capitalism is based on the righteous pursuit of self-interest, of achieving a better life in this world through productive effort, on the dignity of both manual and intellectual labor and on the rights of creators to profit from their efforts" (Bragg 2002) If there is any inherent contradiction between religion and freedom, it is not reflected in the beliefs of our founding fathers. In fact, the system of capitalism allows for "freedom of" and "freedom from" religion. As James Madison said, "While we assert for ourselves a freedom to embrace, to profess and to observe the religion, which we believe to be of a divine origin, we cannot deny an equal freedom to those whose minds have not yet yielded to the evidence which has convinced us" (quoted in Jelen, Cochran, and Segers 1998, 133). By selecting a social-entrepreneurial business model, Alphabet Scoop disassociates itself from the unconstructive aspects of the capitalist culture, such as unemployment, while addressing the marginalization of "oppressed" youth denied access to opportunities and resources, and also articulating the essentialism of American culture.

ENGAGING YOUTH OUTCOMES

In creating KidZone™, The Father's Heart returned to its original social agenda – children and families. The decision to employ youth recruited from KidZone™ was inspired by youth development needs that the ministry discerned. On balance, most of the children and youth who receive services at The Father's Heart reside in nearby public housing projects. Since its inception, Alphabet Scoop has employed more than ninety local youth; all nine current Alphabet Scoop employees reside in the Jacob Riis and Campos Plaza public housing projects and attend public educational institutions in Alphabet City.

A study conducted by the New York City Department of Education suggests that educational outcomes for Alphabet City youth are troubling. In 2005, only 67 percent of Alphabet City youth graduated from the local high school.[42] Only 30 percent of 11th- and 12th-graders took the Scholastic Achievement Test. Average verbal and mathematics scores were low (392 and 397 respectively). Police incident data suggest that crimes committed against persons and property are relatively high compared to schools of similar size; incidents of criminal and noncriminal police involvement were 39 percent higher than similarly sized schools.[43] Forty-three percent of students entering 9th and 10th grades were over age for the grade, and 43 percent of this group was eligible for free lunch.[44] Overall, 71 percent of students enrolled in grades 9–12 in the 2005–2006 school year were eligible for free lunch;[45] 71–80 percent of the students lived in families receiving public assistance.

As stated earlier, a substantial number of these youth receive services or participate in youth programming at The Father's Heart. Many faith-based community programs often neglect three key factors in reaching at-risk youth: scheduling, parental involvement, and co-religiosity. The Father's Heart initiated regular social activities for families to promote parental involvement, and it linked parents and children to volunteer activities. To eliminate barriers to parental involvement, it scheduled youth and volunteer activities on weekday evenings and Saturdays. Children, youth, and adults who come to The Father's Heart, do not have to be co-religionists; all may "come as they are." This inclusive approach is critical to high levels of volunteerism and program and business success. Countering forces associated with the social disaffection of poverty, this model facilitates social and civic engagement by providing opportunities for altruism as parents "give back" to the ministry and the community and as the community responds in kind.

Engagement is multidirectional at Alphabet Scoop. By working through the marketplace to address social development goals, the enterprise provides alternative access to opportunity structures for youth and synergies between the church and the "world." Its professionally produced brochure states:

> Alphabet Scoop is a socially conscious ice creamery located in the heart of Alphabet City. We are offering high quality ice cream while serving as a job training program in which at-risk youth are equipped with life skills that will serve them as they mature and advance in school and the job market. Every time you buy our ice cream you will be helping a teen stay off the streets and away from gangs.

Alphabet Scoop's website also highlights its vertical engagement capacities. As the website stated: "ABCscoop.com was constructed pro bono by Pace University students as part of the Web Design for Non Profit Organization course. The semester long course teaches students the basics of web construction as well as the importance of civic engagement."[46]

THE VALUE AND VIRTUE OF DOING GOOD

In adopting a hybrid model of social enterprise that aims to create both social and economic value, and in implementing a community enhancement strategy that connects individual growth and development to community betterment, Alphabet Scoop generates "an ecological perspective [that] reinforces the interrelationship between individual progress and community progress" (Delgado 2004, 43). As an engagement tool, Alphabet Scoop helps strengthen connections between consumers who want to "do good" by providing an outlet for altruistically self-interested consumerism. By appealing to self-interest and goodwill, Alphabet Scoop balances mission and market. And, as they re-invest profits in missions, operational expenses, and business development, the operators transfer "assets" between purely commercial and purely philanthropic enterprise configurations (Alter 2007).

By employing "at-risk" youth, Alphabet Scoop attenuates the risks associated with a declining youth labor market. As Kolberg asserts, "If our economy is to grow as it is capable of growing, we must be able to use the talents of virtually all our young people, because the number coming into the labor force is declining" (quoted in Kronick 1997, 48). The dual focus of the ministry's sustainability strategy strengthens the embedded, "mission-centric" social purpose of Alphabet Scoop and provides unrestricted income to fund the operations and social programs of The Father's Heart and provide employment for youth at risk.[47] The social impact is measurable in terms of "learned, transferable skills, and gained soft skills such as communication, punctuality, and ability to work with a team, that individuals may lack due to disadvantaged circumstances" (Alter 2007, 68).

FIGURE 7.2. Working at Alphabet Scoop.
Photograph courtesy of Alphabetscoop.com.

Overall, outcomes for Alphabet Scoop graduates improve as a result of mentoring and employment opportunities at the ice creamery. Nineteen-year-old employee Samantha Crespo is Alphabet Scoop's main ice cream maker. Sam has worked at Alphabet Scoop since she was fifteen years old. She attends Landmark High School, aspires to become an entrepreneur, and credits Alphabet Scoop with instilling in her a sense of responsibility and the ability to present herself well in all situations.[48] Not only is Samantha apprenticing as a master ice cream maker, but she also plans to pursue a career in criminal justice following high school graduation.[49]

Dropout statistics among high school students employed at Alphabet Scoop are enviable. With a 0 percent dropout rate, all Alphabet Scoop employees remain in high school until graduation. Ariel Morales, eighteen, won a full scholarship to study filmmaking at Hampshire College. This past summer Pastor Carol Vedral reported that Ariel was in demand for multiple internships.[50] His brief web bio stated:

Ariel has been a part of Alphabet Scoop since he was 14 years old. In his spare
time, Ariel studies karate, kung fu and combat. He enjoys fixing computers
and making films. He plans to be a director or a cinematographer when he is
finished with school. Ariel credits Alphabet Scoop with helping him manage
his time and improving his communication and listening skills. He has also
successfully been employed at Aldo Shoes and D&Q Computers.[51]

One of the first graduates of Alphabet Scoop's job training and mentoring program was recently promoted to first mate by a local cruise line. This
young man continues to volunteer at Alphabet Scoop. His current success
is due to the synergies that this ministry generates, as he was able to secure
employment through an individual who stumbled into the church for prayer
and who happened to be employed by the cruise line. This former supplicant
continues to lend his time and energy to Alphabet Scoop through volunteering and acting as an employment source for The Father's Heart.

A PLACE TO CALL HOME

By simultaneously strengthening engagement dynamics between the ministry
and youth, parents and community, The Father's Heart has demonstrated
its efficacy and efficiencies at shattering, in purely practical ways, the other-
worldly/worldly hierarchies that prompt alienation and separation. In March
2009, Alphabet Scoop received a $60,000 interior design makeover, courtesy
of New York University and Macy's and launched a new flavor – Macy's Cher-
ries Jubilee.[52] The makeover was facilitated through a network of vertical
relationships that extend from graduate interior design competitions to corporate sponsorships. Alphabet Scoop and its employees frequently provide
on-site catering services at the corporate offices of Victoria's Secret. And, as
a result of their relationship with Extreme Realty, a full-service commercial
real estate firm whose owner and staff regularly volunteer at KidZone™, they
recently signed a ten-year lease for 3,500 square feet of office space in a newly
constructed luxury condominium one block north of the current facility. For
$100 per month, the ministry occupies a ground-floor, multimillion-dollar du-
plex space with a private entrance. Without benefit of a public relations agent,
Alphabet Scoop appears regularly in print and televised media including the
New York Times, Time Out New York, The Villager, ABC Eyewitness News,
WNBS, and NY1. Most of these opportunities were orchestrated by members
of the ministry's volunteer corps.[53]

The case study that is the focus of this chapter illustrates how a small, underfunded, understaffed, faith-based organization can create social and capital impacts that affect the trajectory of political and environmental outcomes by creating material infrastructure vis-à-vis a for-profit business that responds to the practical, spiritual, and humanistic needs of the community.

The creation of Alphabet Scoop has allowed The Father's Heart to harness commercial power and connect socially engineered business solutions to urban political and spatial outcomes. Although gentrification and structural issues continue to proliferate, Alphabet Scoop brings a social justice perspective to Alphabet City's emerging landscape, crying out for those who cry and transforming The Father's Heart ministry and the religious ecology to further the social gospel.

NOTES

1. "Alphabet City" is defined as a neighborhood in between the largely Puerto Rican housing projects by the East River and Greenwich Village to the West. The lettered avenues (A, B, C, and D) of the East Village were built primarily on reclaimed harbor. East River Park and the FDR Drive form its eastern boundaries; East Houston Street it's southern; Avenue A it's western, and East 14th Street its northern boundary. See Pekarchik (2001).

2. UrbanDigs.com, "Cool Pads for 2007," http://www.urbandigs.com/2007/01/cool_pads_for_2.html (accessed May 5, 2009).

3. Harrison C. White, a theorist of social process, defines the free market as a social space "continually being rebuilt and torn down, over and over again, with everyday and demographic contingencies at the root of both tearing down and reproducing" (White 1992, 307).

4. This diverse religious ecology includes 32 houses of worship: 41% Pentecostal (85% of which provide services exclusively in Spanish); 19% Catholic; 16% Baptist; 6% Eastern Orthodox and Evangelical; 3% Lutheran, Presbyterian, Jehovah's Witness, and denomination unknown. Just outside the borders of Alphabet City, within a few short blocks of each other, are a synagogue and a mosque. There is evidence of other spiritual activity in Alphabet City consisting of Santeria, New Age, Wicca, and the ubiquitous psychic readers. Barna Group, "One in Three Adults Is Unchurched," March 28, 2005, http://www.barna.org/barna-update/article/5-barna-update/182-one-in-three-adults-is-unchurched (accessed April 18, 2005). These data were "based upon telephone interviews conducted in January 2005 by The Barna Group using a random sample of 1003 adults. According to The Barna Group, the maximum margin of sampling error associated with the sample of parents is ±3.2 percentage points at the 95% confidence level."

5. The author attended the church service as a researcher-observer on April 17, 2005.

6. Good news (*euangelion* in Greek) is proclaimed to people trapped in oppressive situations.

7. Particularism of exilic conscious-ness is a diasporic reflection on the need for those of "the faith" to maintain a discrete religious and social identity and value system and apply a humane social ethic to all mankind. See McRoberts (2003b, 61).

8. According to Bercovitch, "the American jeremiad (a rhetorical form) was designed to join social criticism with spiritual renewal, public to private iden-tity and the shifting signs of the times to traditional metaphors, themes and sym-bols" (1978, xi).

9. According to Community Board No. 3, which regulates land use issues in Alphabet City, there are five licensed establishments on Avenue B between 10th and 11th Streets, four of which have full on-premises liquor licenses; there are five other licensed establishments on Avenue B between 11th and 12th Streets, four of which have full on-premises liquor licenses, and sixteen licensed establish-ments between 10th and 14th Streets overall, excluding retail licenses.

10. According to the New York City Department of Health and Mental Health, "binge drinking is more common in the Lower East Side than NYC overall, and both men and adults with higher incomes are more likely to binge drink than any other residents in the commu-nity. Estimates of binge drinking repre-sent the risk of immediate alcohol-relat-ed problems such as alcohol poisoning, injury and violence." Moreover, "alcohol related hospitalizations have increased by 35% in the past decade. . . . In 2003–2004 the average annual alcohol-related hospitalization rate was higher than in New York City overall (520/100,000 vs. 439/100,000)." See Karpati et al. (2006).

11. Rev. A. R. Bernard, sermon, No-vember 9, 2003, Christian Cultural Cen-ter, Brooklyn, NY.

12. According to Morris (2000), an ex-tensive range of factors qualify youth for an "at-risk" designation, including "low achievement, retention in grade, behavior problems, poor attendance, low socioeco-nomic status, and attendance at schools with large numbers of poor students" (4) The author suggests that the use of the "at-risk" signifier and the stigmatiza-tion inherent in this designation create assumptions that these youth personify society's near-failures.

13. Pastor Carol Vedral, personal in-terview with the author, April 10, 2005.

14. The Father's Heart Church, "What We Believe" (statement of faith), http://www.fathersheartnyc.org/church/we_believe.htm (accessed May 3, 2009).

15. The Father's Heart Church, "His-tory," http://www.fathersheartnyc.org/church/history.htm (accessed May 3 2009).

16. Baggett's (2002) and Ammerman's research (n.d.) indicates that although congregations are involved in social ser-vice activities, their primary goal is "the spiritual well-being of the membership; group worship and building up a caring, functioning internal community."

17. "No man can serve two masters. For either he will hate the one, and love the other: or he will sustain the one, and despise the other. You cannot serve God and mammon [wealth, riches]." See _The Holy Bible_, Douay-Rheims Study Bible, 1989.

18. New York City Department of Health AIDS Surveillance (1986).

19. God's Love We Deliver is a New York City nonprofit organization that provides nutrition and educational ser-vices to persons living with HIV/AIDS.

20. The author participated in develop-ment activities and authored a renewable grant for CARES.

21. The Father's Heart Church, "His-tory," 5. Printout in author's possession.

22. Ibid.

23. On average the ministry serves breakfast to five hundred people every Saturday morning.

24. The Father's Heart Church, "History."

25. Research by Liz Ševčenko (2001) confirms the deteriorated condition of Alphabet City in the 1970s. By her count, there were "100 vacant lots and 150 vacant buildings in the thirty-six block area between Avenue A and the East River and between Houston and 14th Streets" (295).

26. Andrew Reicher, of the Urban Homesteading Assistance Board, a community housing group, dates the original influx of "gentry" to the mid-1990s, and explains that it was catalyzed by the creation of new housing in what had formerly been warehouses or empty buildings. Strongly contributing to the neighborhood's ability to grow in the 1990s was activism from locals, including squatters, to control drug sales and crime. Says Gregory Heller, a member of Community Board 3, which represents the neighborhood: "On some blocks, gardeners and squatters drove the drug dealers off the block. Little did they know that they would open the door to gentrification and their own eviction" (Pekarchik 2001).

27. "Jacob Riis Houses on Manhattan's Lower East Side has 13 buildings, 6-, 13-, and 14-stories high. The 11.73-acre complex has 1,187 apartments housing some 2,903 residents. Completed January 17, 1949, it is between East 8th and East 13th Streets, Avenue D and F.D.R. Drive. Jacob Riis II on Manhattan's Lower East Side has six buildings, 6-, 13-, and 14-stories tall. There are 577 apartments housing some 1,402 people. The 5.94-acre complex was completed January 31, 1949 and is between East 6th and East 8th Streets, Avenue D and the F.D.R. Drive" (New York City Housing Authority n.d.).

28. "Christadora House," Wikipedia, http://en.wikipedia.org/wiki/Christodora_House (accessed May 6, 2009).

29. Pollution Report Card for the Community Index for Zip Code 10009, Scorecard: The Pollution Information Site, http://www.scorecard.org/community/index.tcl?zip_code=10009&set_community_zipcode_cookie_p=t (accessed April 19, 2005).

30. United States Census Bureau, 2000 Census, Census Tracts 22.02, 26.01, 26.02, 28, 30.02, 32, and 34, http://www.census.gov/census2000/states/ny.html (accessed February 15, 2005).

31. This area was known as the "New York Ghetto," and Jacob Riis, namesake of the aforementioned massive public housing project, referred to the neighborhood as "Jewtown."

32. Calling 311 connects one to New York City's centralized citizen service center. A resident may call the center for general information about government services or report a leaking fire hydrant, file a complaint against the NYPD, or the like.

33. New York City Manhattan Community Board, "September 2007 Full Board Minutes, Meeting of Community Board #3." In a hearing held on September 23, 2007, the State Liquor Authority and Economic Development Committee of Community Board No. 3 (CB3) denied a restaurant wine and beer license to an applicant who opened a restaurant within 200 feet of the Father's Heart. In denying the application, CB3 affirmed the community's right to limit the number of establishments serving alcoholic beverages, citing the "cumulative impact of noise and nighttime vehicular and pedestrian or patron traffic from existing establishments; demonstrated community opposition and strenuous objections by the overburdened local precinct, along

with the applicant's inability to garner community support."

34. In 1919, the Eighteenth Amendment of the U.S. Constitution was ratified, prohibiting "the manufacture, sale or transportation of intoxicating liquors within the United States and territory subject to the jurisdiction thereof." See "U.S. Constitution: Eighteenth Amendment," FindLaw, http://caselaw.lp.findlaw .com/data/constitution/amendment18/ (accessed May 3, 2009).

35. Scoopy's Notebook 2007.

36. Quotation in ibid. Horizontal networks represent connections among neighborhood institutions that help to focus existing resources to address neighborhood problems. See Omar (1999, 125).

37. Partnering with social service agencies, nonprofit organizations, and secular organizations, The Father's Heart has networked with faith-based community organizations, churches, and government, corporate, and private organizations, including the Food Bank for New York City, NYC Coalition Against Hunger, City Harvest, America's Second Harvest, Chinese American Planning Council, Department of Youth and Child Development, New York Cares, Beth Israel Continuum Health Partners, the Food Stamp Outreach Project, World Vision, Habitat for Humanity, JPMorgan Chase, the U.S. Department of Agriculture, Stuyvesant Square Chemical Dependency Treatment Program, WorkForce NYC, and the Stromberg Consulting Group, to name but a few. After 9/11, the church's strategic location in Alphabet City, excellent reputation, and mobilization capabilities positioned it to become a FEMA (Federal Emergency Management Administration) site.

38. Vedral, personal interview.

39. "History of The Father's Heart International Ice Cream and Coffee Store" n.d. (printout in author's possession).

40. Data derived from analysis of "Alphabet Scoop Balance and Expense Sheet," provided to author.

41. The Chicago School of Urban Sociology developed a theory to explain how ethnic and racial turnover occurs in neighborhoods over time. I have appropriated this term to denote race- and class-based turnover and explain how large-scale racialized, class-based turnover works in neighborhoods over time.

42. New York City Department of Education, "East Side Community High School," in 2005–2006 Annual School Report Supplement, http://schools.nyc .gov/Accountability/data/AnnualSchool Reports/default.htm (accessed March 26, 2009).

43. "East Side Community High School Comprehensive Information Report," in New York State Report Cards, NYStart.com, http://schools.nyc.gov /SchoolPortals/01/M450/AboutUs /Statistics/default.htm (accessed March 26, 2009).

44. Ibid.

45. New York City Department of Education, "Progress Report Overview, 2009–2010," for Eastside Community High School, http://schools.nyc.gov /SchoolPortals/01/M450/AboutUs /Statistics/default.htm (accessed March 26, 2009).

46. "About the Website," Alpha betscoop.com, http://www.alpha betscoopicecream.com/web.html (accessed May 5, 2009).

47. According to Alter (2007), the business activities of mission-centric social enterprises are closely related to their mission.

48. "Meet the Team" Alphabetscoop .com, http://www.alphabetscoopicecream .com/bio.html (accessed May 5, 2009).

49. As reported to the author by Pastor Carol Vedral, summer 2008.

50. Ibid.

51. "Meet the Team."
52. Ibid.

53. In 2005, 7,500 volunteers served at The Father's Heart.

REFERENCES

Agnitsch, Kerry, Jan Flora, and Vern Ryan. 2006. "Bonding and Bridging Social Capital: The Interactive Effects on Community Action." *Journal of the Community Development Society* 37, no. 1: 1–16.

Alter, Kim. 2007. "Social Enterprise Classification." In *The Four Lenses Strategic Framework*. http://www.4lenses.org/book/export/html/92 (accessed April 16, 2012).

Ammerman, Nancy T. n.d. "Doing Good in American Communities: Congregations and Service Organizations Working Together." Research Report from the Organizing Religious Work Project. Hartford Institute for Religion Research, Hartford Seminary, Hartford, CT. http://hirr.hartsem.edu/orw/orw_cong-report.html#preview (accessed August 26, 2011).

Ammerman, Nancy, Jackson W. Carroll, Carl S. Dudley, and William McKinney. 1998. *Studying Congregations: A New Handbook*. Nashville: Abingdon Press.

Austin, James, Howard Stevenson, and Jane Wei-Skillern. 2006. "Social and Commercial Entrepreneurship: Same, Different, or Both?" *Entrepreneurship: Theory and Practice* 30, no. 1: 1–22.

Baggett, Jerome P. 2002. "Congregations and Civil Society: A Double-Edged Connection." *Journal of Church and State* 44, no. 3: 425–54.

Barna Group, The. 2005. "One in Three Adults Is Unchurched." March 28. http://www.barna.org/barna-update/article/5-barna-update/182-one-in-three-adults-is-unchurched (accessed April 18, 2005).

Bercovitch, Sacvan. 1978. *The American Jeremiad*. Madison: University of Wisconsin Press.

Bragg, John. 2002. "Q&A on the Ethics of Christianity vs. Capitalism." The Center for the Advancement of Capitalism. http://www.capitalismcenter.org/Philosophy/Commentary/02/11-03-02.htm. (accessed April 13, 2012).

Coleman, John. 2003. *Religion as Social Capital: Producing the Common Good*. Waco, TX: Baylor University Press.

Delgado, Melvin. 2004. *Social Youth Enterprise: The Potential for Youth and Community Transformation*. Westport, CT: Praeger.

Eiesland, Nancy L., and Stephen R. Warner. 1998. "Ecology: Seeing the Congregation in Context." In *Studying Congregations: A New Handbook*, ed. Nancy Ammerman, Jackson W. Carroll, Carl S. Dudley, and William McKinney. Nashville: Abingdon Press.

Father's Heart Church, The. "History." http://www.fathersheartnyc.org/church/history.html (accessed May 3, 2009).

———. "What We Believe" (statement of faith). http://www.fathersheartnyc.org/church/we_believe.htm (accessed May 3, 2009).

Holy Bible, The. Douay-Rheims Study Bible. 1989. James Gibbons, ed. Charlotte, NC: Tan Books and Publishers.

Jelen, Mary, Ted G. Cochran, and Clarke E. Segers. 1998. *A Wall of Separation? Debating the Public Role of Religion*. Lanham, MD: Rowman & Littlefield.

Karpati A., X. Lu, F. Mostashari, L. Thorpe, T. R. Frieden. 2003. "The Health of the Lower East Side." *NYC*

Community Health Profiles 1, no. 32: 1–12. http://www.nyc.gov/html/doh/ downloads/pdf/data/2003nhp-man hattang.pdf (accessed April 19, 2012).

Kronick, R. F. 1997. *At-Risk Youth: Theory, Practice, Reform.* New York: Garland.

McDannell, Colleen. 1999. *Material Christianity: Religion and Popular Culture in America.* New Haven: Yale University Press.

McRoberts, Omar. 2003a. "Activism in an Urban Religious District." In *A Handbook of the Sociology of Religion*, ed. Michele Dillon. Cambridge: Cambridge University Press.

———. 2003b. *Streets of Glory: Church and Community in a Black Urban Neighborhood.* Chicago: University of Chicago Press.

McRoberts, Omar. 2009. "Beyond Savior, Victim, and Sinner: Neighborhood Civic Life and Absent Presence in the Religious District." *The Civic Life of American Religion*, ed. Paul Lichterman and Charles Brady Potts. Stanford, CA: Stanford University Press.

Morris, Robert C. 2000. *Curriculum for At-Risk Students.* Carrollton: State University of West Georgia.

New York, State of. 2006. "East Side Community High School Comprehensive Information Report." New York State Report Cards. NYStart.com. https://reportcards.nysed.gov/ (accessed March 26, 2009).

New York City Department of Education. "East Side Community High School." In 2005–2006 Annual School Report Supplement. http://schools.nyc .gov/Accountability/data/Annual SchoolReports/default.htm (accessed March 26, 2009).

New York City Department of Education. "Progress Report Overview, 2009–2010" for Eastside Community High School. http://schools.nyc.gov /SchoolPortals/01/M450/AboutUs /Statistics/default.htm (accessed March 26, 2009).

New York City Department of Health AIDS Surveillance. 1986. "The AIDS Epidemic in New York City: 1981–1984." *American Journal of Epidemiology* 123, no. 6:1013–25.

New York City Housing Authority. N.d. "NYCHA Housing Developments." NYC.gov. http://www.nyc.gov/html/ nycha/html/developments/manriis .shtml (accessed April 16, 2012).

Olsen, E. C., G. Van Wye, B. Kerker, L. Thorpe, T. R. Frieden. 2006. *Take Care Lower East Side: NYC Community Health Profiles.* New York City Department of Health and Mental Hygiene.

Orsi, Robert A. 1999. *Gods of the City.* Indianapolis: Indiana University Press.

Pekarchik, Karin. 2001. "Alphabet City: The ABC's of Gentrification." *Bloomberg BusinessWeek.* 11 June. http:// www.businessweek.com/magazine /content/01_24/b3736044.htm.

Pollution Report Card for the Community Index for Zip Code 10009. 2005. Scorecard: The Pollution Information Site. http://www.scorecard.org /community/index.tcl?zip_code=10009 &set_community_zipcode_cookie _p=t (accessed April 19, 2005).

Putnam, Robert. 2000. "Bowling Alone: America's Declining Social Capital." In *The City Reader*, ed. Richard T. LeGates and Frederic Stout. New York: Routledge.

Santelli, Anthony J., Jr., Jeffrey Sikkenga, Rev. Robert A. Sirico, Steven Yates, and Gloria Zuniga. 2002. *The Free Person and the Free Economy: A Personalist View of Market Economics*, ed. Stephen J. Grabill. Lanham: Lexington Books.

Schwarz, Karen. 2005. "Nourishment for the Soul: Hot Fudge Optional." *New York Times.* April 17.

Scoopy's Notebook. 2007. *The Villager* 76, no. 34 (January): 17–23. http://www.thevillager.com/villager_194/scoopysnotebook.html (accessed February 1, 2009).

Ševcěnko, Liz. 2001. *Mambo Montage: The Latinization of New York*. New York: Columbia University Press.

Sites, William. 2003. *Remaking New York: Primitive Globalization and the Politics of Urban Community*. Minneapolis: University of Minnesota Press.

United States Census Bureau. 2000 Census. http://www.census.gov/census2000/states/ny.html (accessed February 15, 2005).

UrbanDigs.com. Cool Pads for 2007. http://www.urbandigs.com/2007/01/cool_pads_for_2.html (accessed May 5, 2009).

Von Hassel, Malve. 1996. *Homesteading in New York City, 1978–1993: The Divided Heart of Loisaida*. Westport, CT: Bergin & Garvey.

Waste, Robert J. 1998. *Independent Cities: Rethinking U.S. Urban Policy*. New York: Oxford University Press.

White, Harrison C. 1992. *Identity and Control: A Structural Theory of Social Action*. Princeton: Princeton University Press.

8

Navigating Property Development through a Framework of Religious Ecology: The Case of Trinity Lutheran Church

Nadia A. Mian

Walk through the streets of any city, and the spires, domes, and minarets of churches, mosques, synagogues, and temples are common indicators that distinguish houses of worship from any other building on the street. Architecture identifies religious institutions through their unique physical markers, symbolizing the presence of religion and faith. But what happens when these institutions are no longer recognizable? As buildings age and begin to require extensive repair, congregations are increasingly unable to afford the massive cost of renovation. Coupled with a decrease in religious membership, and constant shifts in neighborhood demographics, they struggle to survive.

In New York City, many congregations are faced with the task of learning how to care for their aging structures and, as a result, are turning to property development. One common model of faith-based property development involves tearing down the existing structure and rebuilding a mixed-use facility with the church occupying the lower level of the building and housing located on the levels above. These mixed-use buildings generally meld in with the surrounding environment, and their religious components are indistinguishable. But before development even takes place, what steps are taken to ensure that such property development is best for the church? How do churches organize themselves internally? How is the community taken into account? While the reasons for engaging in development are clear, the process of deciding whether or not development is the right course of action is a more ambiguous.

In need of serious structural repairs, Trinity Lutheran Church (herein referred to as Trinity), located on the Upper West Side of Manhattan, was faced with similar questions as it pursued the quandary of development. This chapter explores the decision-making process the church went through as it decided whether or not to develop its property. The development team, as well as the congregation, understood that as a religious organization the church affects and is affected by its surrounding environment, which includes not only religiously affiliated relationships but also social, economic, and political associations. Trinity had a clear understanding of the local religious ecology, and the demographic, cultural, and organizational environment played a critical role in its decision-making process and heavily influenced the congregation's final choice not to redevelop its property.

In detailing Trinity's journey, first, I provide an overview of faith-based property development in New York City. Second, through observations and interviews, I narrate the pre-development process the congregation went through as it navigated the world of real estate and negotiated its options in discussions with the congregation, community, experts in the development field, and other churches. Finally, I argue that Trinity's decision-making process regarding property development comes from an analysis of the demography of the church and community, examination of the church's own identity and history as a congregation, cooperation with other organizations, and the impact of urban land use policies in New York City. In this particular case, the framework of religious ecology guides my analysis of Trinity's exploration of its development options. I conclude with some thoughts for expanding on the theory of religious ecology to include the role of agency within the framework.

EXPLORING FAITH-BASED PROPERTY DEVELOPMENT

As land in New York is a valuable and scarce commodity, religious institutions recognize that property is a powerful asset they own that can be utilized in various ways to help not only their own struggling institutions but also the community and city. However, religious response to property development has changed over the years, from a social justice orientation to a market-driven response.

During the postwar, post-industrial period, the involvement of religious institutions in property development was a social response to the rising welfare needs of urban residents. Religious institutions instigated community development as they responded to the decline of urban neighborhoods, a rise in poverty, and the need for affordable housing. In this tradition, faith-based development has generally been done in three ways: through congregations, faith-based community development corporations (CDCs), or through national denominations (Vidal et al. 2001). Each option focuses on nurturing the needs of a neighborhood through social and economic development. Well-known examples in New York City include Abyssinian Baptist Church and Abyssinian Development Corporation in Harlem, Greater Allen African Methodist Episcopal Cathedral in Queens, and the work of the Industrial Areas Foundation in the South Bronx and Brooklyn with the creation of the Nehemiah Affordable Housing Project. National organizations, such as Habitat for Humanity, have been building affordable housing for decades through sweat equity programs designed to instill civic pride, as well as providing a place to live (Shook 2006). These faith-based organizations partnered with various public and private entities to create housing, establish local businesses, and provide residents with employment and training.

However, property development and investment through real estate now function differently. In the past forty years, the trend of selling and leasing property and air rights has become more common. Present engagement in real estate is a response to the declining physical and social state of urban religious institutions. The increasing number of faith-based real estate developments can be attributed to a combination of low congregational membership (which means less in donations), high maintenance costs for historic structures, and the scarce and therefore high value of land in New York City (Vitullo-Martin 2006; Eckstrom 2006).

In this type of faith-based development, the first priority is to sustain the institution, followed by that of the community. By selling or leasing property or air rights (the undeveloped space above a building), or both, to private and public developers, religious institutions are able to stay in their neighborhoods, procure revenue to save their institutions, and possibly expand their social ministries to help the community. Property development involving religious institutions generally follows two models: one involving market-rate commercial and residential construction, and the other involving civic-minded development, such as affordable housing. With both types of development, space is reserved for the religious institution including room for conferences, a library, and offices. The development is beneficial for the institution and its developing partner, as each gains new space and revenue. Religious institutions use the new space and revenue to increase mission work, offer increased services to the community, and possibly even attract new members.

Since its inception in 1705, Trinity Episcopal Church in Lower Manhattan has been one of the largest landowners in New York City. In the nineteenth century, the church began leasing its properties for commercial and residential purposes. As the economy shifted from manufacturing to service-oriented industries, Trinity Episcopal converted the industrial space into premium office space, and now "holds six million square feet in 18 buildings" (Trinity Episcopal Church 2008). The church's response to changing economic trends in the city through its real estate holdings was important as it helped to configure and maintain the status of the area as a financial district.

In the 1970s, St. Peter's Lutheran Church in Midtown Manhattan instigated a new type of relationship between real estate development and urban churches when it negotiated a $9 million dollar deal with Citigroup that resulted in a brand new office tower for the corporation and a new building for the church (Eckstrom 2006). The case of St. Peter's differs from Trinity Episcopal in that Trinity leased its external property holdings while maintaining its original structures, whereas St. Peter's used the land on which the church was built to create a whole new development that includes an office tower and retail space. The precedent-setting deal between St. Peter's and Citigroup has been cited as a successful property development.

Like Trinity Episcopal and St. Peter's Church, other religious institutions that own property are becoming more active by selling or leasing their land to developers in multimillion-dollar deals. In Bay Ridge, Brooklyn, the Bay Ridge United Methodist Church sold its property to a developer for approximately $9 million due to the church's deteriorating condition. In its place will stand a new church structure, as well as a school (Jon Donlon, interview with author, July 23, 2009). General Theological Seminary on 9th Avenue in Manhattan sold its air rights to the Brodsky Organization for over $30 million because of the crumbling state of the historic structure. The deal resulted in the construction of retail and market-rate housing, as well as new space for the church (Stowe 2007). In the Bronx, Senda De Benedicion Church sold its air rights to the South Bronx Overall Economic Development Corporation to build a condominium, which will include space for the church (Satow 2006). In another example, religious institutions in Washington, D.C., are being lobbied by affordable housing activists to sell or lease their vacant property. As Michelle Boorstein (2007) writes, "The renewed interest accompanies what some call a spiritual crisis in affordable housing. It is particularly pronounced in Washington, where available land is rare and prices have been booming."

FIGURE 8.1. Trinity Lutheran Church.
Photograph courtesy of author.

However, it has been difficult to attract the interest of religious institutions in
helping to provide affordable housing. As housing advocate Dominic Moulden
argues, "To compare it to 20-plus years ago, no one today is saying, 'We don't
need to make a profit because this is God's land and we are stewards, we don't
need to make a penny.' I don't think there is a lot of that going on" (quoted in

Boorstein 2007). Religious institutions are now more concerned with making a profit in order to remain viable, in addition to serving their mission and helping the community.

As the preceding examples reveal, real estate transactions involving religious institutions are becoming more common in New York City. In *The Real Deal*, a local real estate magazine, Jen Benepe (2007) states that "churches and synagogues sold more property than any other nonprofit group in 2005, though it was only worth $45 million." According to my own research, at least seventy-five houses of worship are currently involved in development deals. As Reverend Robert Brashear of West Park Presbyterian Church argues, "Real estate is the most important, cutting-edge issue for urban ministry" (Satow 2006).

A VILLAGE ON THE UPPER WEST SIDE

Located on the northwest corner of 100th Street and Amsterdam Avenue, Trinity Lutheran Church (referred to as Trinity) on Manhattan's Upper West Side is a century-old church sandwiched between a brand-new luxury rental apartment building and the New York City Department of Health, which plans to tear down its current building to construct a new facility. The low-income, high-rise Frederick Douglass housing complex faces Trinity to the north, as does the 24th Precinct of the New York Police Department. While crime rates in the area have drastically gone down in the past twenty years, the area still has problems with drug activity (NYPD, CompStat, 24th Precinct). Farther down the street, to the east, between Central Park West and Columbus Avenue, is a group of buildings situated on a superblock known as Park West Village. Many of the congregants of Trinity live in these buildings, as well as Frederick Douglass housing. The seven buildings comprising Park West Village were constructed as part of Robert Moses's slum clearance plans in the 1950s. The area was comprised of tenements and single-room-occupancy apartments until Moses razed the buildings to construct what was first called Manhattantown and later West Park Apartments (Horsley, n.d.). During that period, while entire neighborhoods were being demolished and rebuilt, Trinity survived, but only because the pastor at the time had connections to City Hall and saved the church (Trinity meeting, October 28, 2008). More than half a century later, several more new buildings are going up across from Park West Village. The area is being renamed Columbus Square by developers and is set to include a thirty-story apartment building and four smaller residential buildings. In addition, there will be 320,000 square feet of retail space that will include a Whole Foods grocery store, Duane Reade Drugstore, Crumbs Bakery, and other shops (Rasenberger 2007).

These new developments do not represent those who currently live in the community or those who attend Trinity. According to a document issued by the New York City Department of City Planning that compiles census data on Community District 7, the area surrounding the church is incredibly economically, socially, and racially diverse, with a majority of the population either Hispanic, African American, or white. The neighborhood is also home to a large number of families with children (New York Department of City Planning, Manhattan Community District 7). Approximately 29 percent of residents in the census tract encompassing the church live below the poverty level, which is high compared to the rest of the Upper West Side. There is a high rate of unemployment, and most do not own their homes. The foreign-born population ranks immigrants from the Dominican Republic, China, and Germany as the largest groups residing in the area, with Spanish being the language spoken at home for the largest proportion of those nonproficient in English (New York Department of City Planning, Manhattan Community District 7).

KNOW THYSELF

In the story of Chicken Little, a falling apple bops the title character on the head, leading him to believe the sky is falling. In 2004 a slate tile fell from the roof of the church, almost hitting a passerby on the head. Although Chicken Little followed no process or method in informing the rest of his community of the event, for the next four years, Trinity Church would conduct research, compile data, and communicate its findings in a series of presentations to the church and community before deciding what should be done about its building. Trinity's current identity and its expectations for the future were key to knowing how development would affect its potential as a congregation. What was the church's mission and vision? What did it need to effectively carry out its mission? What was the role of the church building in this respect?

Trinity's current pastor, Heidi Neumark, knows something about real estate development. In the 1980s, she was one of the founding members of the South Bronx Churches (SBC), an ecumenical group that helped revitalize the South Bronx through community organizing. The SBC, with the aid of the Saul Alinsky's Industrial Areas Foundation, a community-organizing network group, "successfully fought for improvements in school safety, subway maintenance, supermarkets, and community policing. They forced the demolition of unsafe buildings, the fencing of vacant lots, and the creation of neighborhood parks" (Stuart, with Heinemeier 2006, 203). In 1990 the SBC worked with a multitude of private, public, and social agencies to implement the Nehemiah Strategy of affordable home ownership. The group's organizational efforts paid off, and "from 1992 to 1996, SBC built 512 homes (224 single-family homes and 288 condominiums) primarily on contiguous lots. In the second phase, which was largely in-fill housing and ran from late 1998 through 2003, SBC built 205 two-family homes and 44 single-family homes for a total of 454 dwelling units" (Stuart, with Heinemeier 2006, 200). In an interview with Pastor Heidi (as she is called by her congregation), I asked about the Nehemiah Strategy, and whether or not she had initiated a similar organizational strategy at Trinity when thinking about development. She said: "In the South Bronx it wasn't just speaking with the congregation; it was speaking with many people, but the similar thing is, I think that people impacted by a decision should have a voice in the decision, and that was one of the reasons why early on we not only had a conversation within the congregation but also with the community around us" (interview with author, March 3, 2009).

The process of figuring out whether or not to develop Trinity's property was organized by the loosely defined "development team" made up of church council president Lydie Raschka, treasurer Joy Gramolini, Finance Committee member Jennifer Graves, and Pastor Heidi. She provided direction and advice in a consensus-based approach. In an organizational process similar to that of the SBC, people were continually brought together at each stage of decision making to comment on or question what was happening. Pastor Heidi explained her efforts in the Bronx: "We followed very traditional community organizing: we worked with the Industrial Areas Foundation, a professional community organizer, and one of the first steps was doing thousands of one-on-one individual conversations, and having house meetings. . . . That was a strong priority; that was something we were interested in exploring and doing in the South Bronx." But Pastor Heidi was not interested in continuing her work in the South Bronx on the Upper West Side. This time, this place, this project – this was a whole other experience.

I arrived on Tuesday, October 21, 2009, at 11 AM for my first meeting with church council president Lydie Raschka and treasurer Joy Gramolini. Joy greeted me in front of the building. The front of the Late Gothic Revival church was gated and locked, so we went around to the west entrance, down the stairs, and in through the basement. The hundred-year-old church was surrounded by scaffolding. Scaffolding kept people walking by safe from falling debris and helped absorb vibrations from construction next door. The stained-glass windows inside the sanctuary had been taken down and put into storage as a result of the vibrations. The spires on the steeple had also been taken down as a safety precaution, so they too did not fall and endanger anyone.

As we entered through the basement (or undercroft, as it is also known), there were a men's/women's bathroom and church offices, as well as a large meeting space that serves as a shelter for lesbian, gay, bisexual, or transgendered (LGBT) teens every night. The shelter has approximately ten beds, of which nine are currently filled. There is also a kitchen, and one of the bathrooms has two shower stalls for the teens to use. The small church offices are filled with books, papers, and filing cabinets. There are two rooms, one for the general office and the other for Pastor Heidi.

We walked upstairs to the enormous sanctuary. Light filled the space, but only because the stain glass windows had been removed and replaced with regular windows. Faux marble pillars line the room and rows of pews face south toward the altar.

Lydie met us soon after and we began our conversation. She brought with her a large yellow construction board on which she had written a brief timeline of the church's condition over the past few years. Simply put, the building suffers from structural issues. While it was not being condemned, it was in a state of physical disrepair. After the episode with the falling slate in 2004, the Department of Buildings fined the church $800, and the scaffolding was put up around the building. It was costing almost $1,500 a month to maintain the scaffolding.

In 2005, the church began exploring options for repairing the steeple. For the next two years, the development team met with structural engineers, developers, church leaders involved in development, affordable housing advocates, and the congregation to better understand the state of the building and the options available to them. The development next door had not helped matters.

In 2006, construction of a new luxury condominium development by the Chetrit Group, a real estate developer, began next door to the church. When vibrations from construction threatened the stability of the stained-glass windows, Chetrit offered $150,000 to remove the windows and place them in storage. The church's endowment is approximately $300,000, with an annual ongoing deficit of $30,000, which meant finances were limited. Trinity asked building conservator Bill Stivale to prepare a restoration report documenting the extent of the disrepair and damage. Stivale's report indicated that a full repair of the sanctuary and exterior would cost almost $8 million. Lydie mentioned that during this time, Trinity learned that the Department of Health next door would also be conducting a $24 million renovation, and the Ryan Health Center (which rented space from the Department of Health) would move into the second floor of the Chetrit building. An Associated Supermarket would be located on the first floor.

Surrounded by construction, Trinity took steps to learn more about its own property development options. As it turned out, selling the air rights (the undeveloped space above a building) in order to raise money for the building was not an option. Trinity was separated from the Chetrit building by a narrow alleyway designated as "parkland," and the Department of Health was not interested in purchasing the church's unused development rights. According to zoning regulations, air rights can be transferred only through a zoning lot merger, which joins two adjacent lots into a single lot. Only under certain circumstances, such as the case of preserving historic buildings or open space, can a zoning lot merger take place if the lots are *not* adjacent to one another (New York City Department of City Planning, Zoning Glossary).

Lydie and Joy argued that even if Trinity were to redevelop the church building, it would not consider building market-rate housing, because that option did not reflect the church's social justice mission. Still pursuing the option of some form of development, the leaders met with Ron Drews of Lutheran Social Services, a private, nonprofit social service agency, about low-income housing. They also entertained a proposal from Laura Jervis, of the West Side Federation for Senior and Supportive Housing, which builds affordable housing. Neither option went beyond the discussion stage.

In 2008 Trinity held a meeting with the community and local politicians to inform them of the issues surrounding the building and the options the church had explored. With approximately one hundred people in attendance, the community was split; some accepted the idea of redevelopment, while others wanted to see the church preserved. Ironically, it was clergy who argued that the building was an albatross because of the high maintenance costs and should be demolished. Hesitant to develop, architect and engineer Robert Litchfield was hired to review Bill Stivale's conditions study. Litchfield argued that the building could be stabilized for the next ten to fifteen years for approximately $1.5 million. While this was still a large amount of money, it was more feasible than the $8 million suggested by Stivale. Litchfield's estimate was an amount that the congregation believed it could raise, and opened the door to explore another option: a capital campaign.

Understanding that the choice now lay between rebuilding and redevelopment (between raising money to fix the church and tearing it down to build something new), in 2008, the development team began holding "visioning sessions" with congregation members to explore the congregation's identity and future. Lydie explained that the church had a few months remaining before the congregation would make a final decision at its annual meeting in February 2009. With regard to rebuilding, Trinity began looking into applying to be a part of the National Park Service Historic Register. By doing so, the church would be restricted in terms of what could be physically done with the building, but would still be less restricted than if it were to apply for landmark status or join the area's historic district. Also, it would be able to apply for matching grants to pay for restoration. If Trinity chose to redevelop, it would look to partner with a group to construct affordable housing.

Over the next few months, beginning in January 2009, after meeting with a developer and other churches that had built successful housing projects, the development team explained its findings to the congregation in a series of meetings, Q&A sessions, and documents. In February, the congregation voted 56–5 not to develop its property but to pursue a capital campaign to restore the building.

NAVIGATING PROPERTY DEVELOPMENT THROUGH
A FRAMEWORK OF RELIGIOUS ECOLOGY

Church and Community Analysis

In the theory of religious ecology, context is key. In a handbook on how to study congregations, Eiesland and Warner (1998) utilize the ecological perspective. This framework, they argue, "is a theoretical and practical response to increased religious pluralism and the restructuring of religious life" (40). Knowing that a congregation occupies a specific space within a locale that may include many other institutions, people, and groups, they urge viewing the congregation as an interactive institution that "exists in relation to an environment" (41). Knowing and understanding the context one is situated within can influence a congregation's actions – especially if those actions may alter a neighborhood. The theory argues that religious institutions are wide in scope, have several layers, and have visible and invisible elements (Eiesland and Warner 1998). "Scope" refers to the open-endedness of a congregation; it is not an enclosed entity but has networks across time and space. Through these networks, there are similar conversations about issues and common practices, as well as cooperation and the exchange of information with other congregations and organizations that strengthen congregational identity and ministry (Eiesland and Warner 1998). Interaction with other organizations occurs at various levels through a complex web of people, meaning, and relationships. Finally, religious institutions must deal with invisible and visible elements, which can include more tangible elements like the church building more obscure, intangible issues such as property values.

In its decision-making process, Trinity considered the demographic profile of its church and community; its history and identity as a congregation; networks that included the community and other organizations and religious institutions; and urban land use policies. The importance of Trinity's place within the Park West Village community was definitely taken into account by the congregation during its process of inquiry. While the census had been taken almost ten years before, the data still reflected Trinity's members, a majority of whom lived in the community. When I asked members of Trinity to describe the demographic profile of their congregation, most replied using words like "diversity." As one woman explained:

> We have projects in this neighborhood; we have gentrification in the last twenty years on the Upper West Side. Kinda difficult to answer, but I think that the diversity of the congregation, of the fact that we do have people in the church who are in the projects, we do have working-class people, people who are struggling, but then we do have middle-class and upper-middle-class, so it does reflect the diversity of this particular urban neighborhood. (Suzanne Kaebnick, interview with author, January 25, 2009).

The demographic profile of the congregation mirrored that of the community. The congregation's awareness of its members' identity and the fact that they existed in relation to their external environment was further established through the "visioning sessions" held by the development team in the spring of 2008. Guided by Pastor Heidi and administered by Lydie, Joy, Jennifer, and church council members, these sessions were essentially focus groups that helped the congregation ascertain the church's future, with or without the building. Two questions were asked: What do you like about Trinity that you would like to see continue in the future? And, What do you envision for the future? In answering the first question, one member responded, "The most important thing to me is the friendly, welcoming community, the worship services, the social justice focus, Pastor Heidi's sermons, the children's programming, that we serve this community, have relationships with those in the projects and the diverse community that surrounds us" (Trinity visioning session, June 22, 2008). But when asked what they envisioned for the future, many congregants spoke to the state of the building as a pressing issue. One congregant wrote that they needed, "a clear vision for the building," and another felt like he or she was "getting tired of the lack of storage, the kitchen floor, all the little things that after a while do sort of get to you. They wouldn't keep me from coming, but it would be nice to have a better church building" (Trinity visioning session, January 16, 2009).

During the sessions, recurrent themes emerged. From a record of the responses, Lydie created a condensed one-page document that summarized in large print which themes came up most often, while not-so-prominent themes were shown in smaller print. Words like "Growth/Outreach," "Building," and "Mission" were written large, as congregants spoke to the issues numerous times. Congregants realized that the growth of their church (in terms of members and mission) was intrinsically tied to the state of their building, as well as to the rest of the community. The full record of responses was typed up and given to the congregation at the Q&A sessions and the annual meeting, along with the one-page document, and a table that listed the pros and cons of development. The complete packet of materials gathered by the development team was also mailed out to members who could not attend sessions to keep them informed.

Congregation members worried that the new, Columbus Square development would bring a wealthier demographic into the area. Trinity's congregants were aware of their unique position within an evolving community, as a stable institution viewed as a haven for accepting difference and encouraging diversity.

This awareness was reflected in the ministries and social services that the church provided to its congregants and the community. Like many churches, Trinity ran an after-school learning program providing tutoring to young children, as well as English as a Second Language (ESL) classes for adults. At the same time, Trinity remained committed to inclusiveness. As leader of a bilingual church with a large Latino presence in the community, Pastor Heidi advocated for immigrant issues; the church also offered Mujeres en Progreso, a women's support group geared toward Latino women, and rented out the undercroft for Quinceañera parties. There was also Trinity Place – the shelter described earlier for LGBT youth that the church had started a few years before, after Sylvia's Place, a local shelter, was unable to accommodate the increasing number of youth in need of a bed for the night.

Trinity's social justice position is not a new stance for the church. The theory of religious ecology argues that part of seeing a congregation in context is understanding not only place but history as well (Ammerman et al. 1998, 43), and Trinity's history is rooted in serving the underserved within the community. On the one-hundredth anniversary of Trinity's building, Pastor Heidi reminded the congregation of Trinity's place historically within the community in one of her sermons (January 25, 2009). She preached:

> In the late sixties, the neighborhood was beset with growing problems – an increase in poverty, drugs, gangs, and before long, AIDS. Pastor John Backe was sent to close the church. But Trinity didn't see the struggles of this community as a reason to close its doors; on the contrary, Trinity's doors opened to welcome other people and groups in the city who wanted to make a positive difference, to feed the hungry and heal the sick. Together Trinity members and friends and neighbors stood up to injustice and said, YES WE CAN!

Echoing the campaign slogan of now-president Barack Obama, Pastor Heidi encouraged her congregation to keep faith that the members could resolve their building woes by believing "Yes, we can!" "Like our founders 120 years ago and all the disciples at Trinity over the past one hundred years," she declared, "we face challenges. At times we may wonder how we are going to keep on keeping on. Well, you won't and I won't but WE is another story . . . YES WE CAN!" (sermon, January 25, 2009).

The building's history was documented in the application to the State and National Registrar for Historic Places. In the application, Pastor Heidi wrote:

> The history of Trinity is closely bound to the history of development in our community. . . . From its earliest days of struggle, Trinity showed a desire to respond to the needs of its wider community, recognizing the plight of children who "roamed the streets" and welcoming them to a school program. . . . As a new neighborhood rose up in the 60's and 70's, with the large Frederick Douglass Housing Project across the street, and Park West Village on the other side, Trinity remained more committed than ever to its diverse neighbors and their needs. The church opened its doors to scouting, neighborhood job training, high school equivalency classes, day care, a soup kitchen, a photography studio for ex-convicts and an off-off Broadway theatre. . . .

> Despite these challenges to our building, like our founders, we seek to offer sanctuary to those who are becoming increasingly marginalized in this community and city by present urban development trends.

It was obvious that Trinity's strong sense of its identity as a congregation came from understanding its history within the community, as well as its current position in the area. This distinct sense of identity guided the congregation on how important context is in its decision regarding the building, because whatever it choose would affect not only the church's mission but also the neighborhood. Trinity's was a mission-focused development process based on its identity and its purpose of social justice. These were recalled again and again by the congregation and development team. Even the church's preference for the type of development it would like to do was rooted in its identity and community. If the congregation were to choose to tear down the building, a mixed-use church and affordable-housing building would be constructed instead of a market-rate housing or commercial project.

Network City

If Trinity worked hard to understand the local demographics by analyzing its membership and exploring its history, it further expanded the scope of its religious ecology by speaking with local organizations, cooperating with the community board, and networking with other religious institutions. Omar McRoberts (2003) argues that churches "must extract resources from the local environment to survive. Resources include membership, money, legitimacy, and information" (10). During the development process, Trinity spoke with a number of groups it could potentially partner with. Speaking with these groups and individuals provided Trinity not only with the sense of legitimacy that pursuing property development as a church was an acceptable venture but also with the information the church needed to learn more about its options.

Through Lutheran Social Services, West Side Federation for Senior and Supportive Housing, and Con Edison's Renaissance Program, the development team at Trinity considered proposals for affordable housing. The proposals included creating a mixed-used facility, giving the church a few floors on the bottom of a building that would have affordable housing units on top. To increase the church's revenue stream, El Taller Latino Americano (The Latin American Workshop) was considered as a potential partner that would rent out current space in the church. To keep all options open, though the church was not inclined to do a commercial development, Dr. William Gordon of Gordon Atlantic Development was also consulted for his thoughts on what the church could do with its property. Surprisingly, Dr. Gordon advised that the church would be better off accruing various income streams from renting out its space than pursuing a redevelopment project.

Understanding their role within the community and advocating communication and open dialogue, Pastor Heidi and church council members attended community board meetings to learn what was going on in the area and to inform the board of their own building issues. Within the framework of religious ecology, interaction between a congregation and the community occurs at various levels, one of which is culture. Culture encompasses "the systems of meaning, values, and practices shared by members of the community and groups within the community" (Ammerman et al. 1998, 42). In attending community board meetings regularly, Pastor Heidi and the church council realized that church development issues had become prevalent in the community. Not all development projects had been done with community approval, and Trinity wanted there to be transparency and communication in its development process. Furthermore, Trinity also held a community forum, inviting neighborhood residents to come and hear the church's issues and voice their own thoughts on what the church should do.

Trinity discussed its options with at least three other churches that had been involved in development – Sion Lutheran Church and Church of the Resurrection in Harlem, and Fordham Lutheran in the Bronx. It was through discussions with Sion Lutheran that Trinity learned how to establish its development process. As Lydie recalls, "They basically said that we should follow at the same time about three different tracks – going with a high-end developer, low-income housing, capital campaign. Explore all these options at once, and then you'll see it narrow, something will emerge, which is what happened, and we came down to these two" (interview with author, January 21, 2009). With the options narrowed to a choice between a low-income housing development and a capital campaign, many congregants at Trinity were reluctant to pursue development after hearing about Sion's troubles. Sion's building had been condemned by the city, and the church had been working with a developer to build a new, mixed-use development. However, after the economic crisis, the developer backed out of the deal, and the congregation was left without a place to worship. Fordham Lutheran's development plans also went awry after the economic crisis, when the city could no longer finance the church's low-income affordable-housing project.

To gain more information and a more comprehensive idea of what development entailed, Pastor Heidi, Jennifer, and Lydie wanted to see a church development project that was complete and so visited Church of the Resurrection in East Harlem. Church of the Resurrection was an example of a market-rate building with church facilities on the lower levels. Reverend Kimberly Wright gave the development team a tour of the new building, shared her vision for the future, and talked about her experience with property development. Through shared networks and connections, Trinity was able to learn more about the development process, inform its community, and create potential partners.

Urban Development

Finally, urban development trends and processes in New York City played a strong role in Trinity's development process and final decision. Local development, zoning and air rights regulations, and policies and funding for historic buildings further affected and limited Trinity's options when it came to property development. Nancy Eiesland's *A Particular Place: Urban Restructuring and Religious Ecology in a Southern Exurb* (2000) examines how urban sprawl and intra-organizational changes in religion affect a local community and its religious institutions. Eiesland tells the story of a small exurb in Georgia, a formerly rural area that had to adjust to the effects of urban sprawl. She argues that urban restructuring and the creation of "edge cities and exurbs are also the result of numerous cultural, economic, and global factors that have facilitated deconcentrated metropolitan growth" (2000, 5). However, Eiesland's work does not address how specific urban and regional land use policies affect communities.

As development in Park West Village continues with the onslaught of new condominium towers and high-end retail stores, some religious institutions were using land use regulations to their advantage by selling their air rights and property. The area was slowly changing, and some argued that a decision of a neighboring church – one that Pastor Heidi said "made a lot of people angry" – accelerated gentrification of the area. In 2005, St. Michael's Episcopal Church, located directly across the street from Trinity on the west side of Amsterdam between 99th and 100th Streets, sold its air rights to Extel Development Corporation. The developer used the air rights to extend the height of Ariel East and Ariel West, two thirty-seven- and thirty-one-story, glass luxury condominium towers located on either side of Broadway at 99th Street.

What angered community residents and disappointed Pastor Neumark was the lack of transparency and communication between St. Michael's and Extel, and the rest of the neighborhood. As longtime resident Paul Bunten explained, "What has been an eye-opener for me is that the developer is allowed to exercise his property rights with no input from the community – that there really isn't a mechanism for it in these large-scale development programs that have such an enormous impact on the lives of people who already live there" (Rasenberger 2007). It was this type of harsh backlash that Pastor Neumark wanted to avoid with Trinity by having as much communication as possible among congregants, the church, and the community. As she explained:

> That was something that was missing at another church that made a decision which impacted the community and made a lot of people angry. My critique of that was not so much their right, certainly not their right to make a decision, nor even their decision, but the lack of conversation with other people about it. Yes, a church legally has a right to make a decision all by itself, but I don't think that's ethically the right thing to do. (interview with author, March 3, 2009)

Within the fifty-one blocks that define the Upper West Side, St. Michael's was not the only religious institution that had sold its air rights or tried to redevelop its property. West Park Presbyterian, located at 86th Street and Amsterdam Avenue, was trying to broker a deal with a developer to build condominiums on site, but by mid-2009 that deal fell through. Congregation Shearith Israel, at 70th Street and Central Park West, was also attempting to build a luxury condominium building. Both institutions were battling the community and the Landmarks Commission for the right to develop. In 2010 West Park Presbyterian was designated a New York City landmark, which means that development was no longer an option. A couple of blocks north of the Upper West Side boundary, at 112th Street and Amsterdam Avenue, the Cathedral of St. John the Divine sold two parcels of land to Columbia University and Avalon Bay Corporation to create mixed-income apartments in 2006.

Given all the church-related development projects in the area, Trinity was hesitant to pursue anything that would contribute further to the gentrification of the Upper West Side. However, even if it had wanted to do so, the church was constricted in its development options by local land use regulations regarding air rights and zoning. One easy but controversial method of gaining revenue for religious institutions is to sell air rights. In New York City, as explained previously, property owners are restricted to selling their air rights to adjacent buildings. Only a historic property or landmark can transfer its air rights to a property across the street. Since Trinity is not currently on the National Register for Historic Properties and is not a New York City landmark, it is limited by what it can do with its air rights. As previously mentioned, the church is separated from the Chetrit development by an alley designated as "parkland" in the city's zoning code, and the Ryan Health Center was not interested in purchasing its air rights. Also, according to local zoning provisions, transferred air rights can be used on major streets above 96th Street to extend the height of buildings and increase density, so it would have made sense only to sell the air rights to Chetrit, which faces Amsterdam Avenue. Furthermore, Pastor Heidi says that even if they were to develop, zoning restricts the building from being any higher than eight stories.

If Trinity had been a designated landmark, selling its air rights may have been easier, as the church could have "jumped" the alleyway and sold the development rights to Chetrit. However, Trinity was hesitant to become part of the area's historic district or be a New York City landmark. As Pastor Heidi argued, it becomes much more difficult to decide what you want to do with your property once it is a landmark. Instead, the church decided to go the less restrictive route and apply to be on the National Historic Register, which would still place limitations on what could be done with the church building, but would be far less restrictive than becoming a landmark or part of a district. Also, there was more funding available being part of the National Historic Register, and Pastor Heidi hoped that Trinity would be eligible for the matching grant program the National Park Service offered.

CONCLUSION

The ecological model proves useful in examining Trinity's pre-development process, as it analyzed and considered the relationship between the church and community, its social and political networks, and the effect of urban land use policies on religious institutions. However, there are still some factors not easily explained by the ecological framework.

While the theory of religious ecology allows for an understanding of the relationship between a congregation and its environment, it does not explain the role of agency on behalf of the congregation. In this particular case, while Trinity was very cognizant of the impact its actions would have on the community, the church did not "adapt" by opting against redeveloping its property; in light of its context, redevelopment would have been an acceptable choice to the church's building dilemma. If anything, Trinity challenged the current standard in deciding to launch a capital campaign. As McRoberts (2003) argues, "religious ecology does not consider fully the voluntary nature of religious life" (11). The members of Trinity volunteered their time to serve on development committees, run focus groups, have meetings, and finally vote on what to do with their building. All the choices made were done through careful analysis, but the congregation chose to pursue, not an entrepreneurial course, but one that would require additional resources from its members. In the ecological model, adaptation is altering in the face of forces beyond one's control. Lowell Livezey argued that adaptation was almost a form of acquiescence. Wedam (2008) writes, "For Livezey, adaptation sometimes connoted that organizations and individuals were unwilling to challenge various kinds of problematic social and economic structural conditions . . . it was this form of adaptation that Livezey found problematic. In contrast, groups that sought to confront systems that socially or otherwise disadvantaged them were defined as having 'agency'" (365).

By choosing to raise money to rebuild the church through a capital campaign, rather than through property development, the members of Trinity effectively voted against further gentrification of their neighborhood. This may not have been the intent of each of the congregation members as they voted to save the building, but the consequences of what development could do to the community was clear. The theory of religious ecology needs to provide more clarification and direction as to the role of individual actors and agency in how and why decisions are made and relationships are established.

For Trinity Episcopal Church, the tenuous state of the building brought to the forefront the church's place within Park West Village, its identity as a congregation focused on social justice, and its role within the community. Communication with other churches, community members, and developers helped the congregation to navigate the world of property and real estate. Furthermore, some of those networks helped to clarify the restrictions placed on any action the church might take in terms of land use and development. The decision not to tear down its building is not where Trinity's story ends, but where the church now enters a new phase in its history. Through the capital campaign, the congregation will continue to work within its religious ecology to strengthen its identity and rebuild.

REFERENCES

Ammerman, Nancy T., Jackson Carroll, Carl Dudley, and William McKinney. 1998. *Studying Congregations: A New Handbook*. Nashville: Abingdon Press.

Benepe, Jen. 2007. "Nonprofits in Black with Record Building Sales." *The Real Deal*. November 20. http://ny.therealdeal.com/articles/nonprofits-in-black-with-record-building-sales. Accessed November 20, 2007.

Boorstein, Michelle. 2007. "Putting Faith in Affordable Housing: Activists, Entrepreneurial Pastors Push Renewal of D.C. Churches' Efforts." *Washington Post*. June 23. http://www.washingtonpost.com/wp-dyn/content/article/2007/06/22/AR2007062202237.html (accessed March 25, 2012).

Donlon, Jon. Interview with the author. Brooklyn, NY, July 23, 2009.

Eckstrom, Kevin. 2006. City Churches Reap Real-Estate Cash. *Christian Century*. http://www.christiancentury.org/article/2006-05/city-churches-reap-real-estate-cash.

Eiesland, Nancy. 2000. *A Particular Place: Urban Restructuring and Religious Ecology in a Southern Exurb*. New Brunswick, NJ: Rutgers University Press.

Eiesland, Nancy, and R. Stephen Warner. 1998. "Ecology: Seeing the Congregation in Context." In *Studying Congregations: A New Handbook*, ed. Nancy T. Ammerman, Jackson W. Carroll, Carl S. Dudley, and William McKinney, 40–77. Nashville: Abingdon Press.

Horsley, Carter B. n.d. "The Upper West Side Book: Central Park West." *The City Review*. http://www.thecityreview.com/uws/cpw/cpw382.html. Accessed January 30, 2009.

Kaebnick, Suzanne. Interview with the author. New York, NY, January 25, 2009. Tape recording.

McRoberts, Omar M. 2003. *Streets of Glory: Church and Community in a Black Urban Neighborhood*. Chicago: University of Chicago Press.

Neumark, Heidi. Interview with the author. New York, NY, March 3, 2009. Tape recording.

New York Department of City Planning. Manhattan Community District 7. http://www.nyc.gov/html/dcp/pdf/lucds/mn7profile.pdf. Accessed January 20, 2009.

New York City Department of City Planning. Zoning Glossary. http://www.nyc.gov/html/dcp/html/zone/glossary.shtml. Accessed February 3, 2009.

NYPD (New York Police Department). CompStat, 24th Precinct. NYC.gov. http://www.nyc.gov/html/nypd/downloads/pdf/crime_statistics/cs024pct.pdf. Accessed February 15, 2009.

Raschka, Lydie. Interview with the author. New York, NY, January 21, 2009. Tape recording.

Rasenberger, Jim. 2007. "High Anxiety." *New York Times*. June 17.

Satow, Julie. 2006. "Religious Groups Pray for Guidance." *Crain's New York Business*. July 31, pp. 17–18.

Shook, Jill S., ed. 2006. *Making Housing Happen: Faith-Based Affordable Housing Models*. Atlanta: Chalice Press.

Stowe, Stacey. 2007. "Seminary's Renovation Juggles the Old, the New and the Financial." *New York Times*. December 19, p. C6.

Stuart, Lee, with John Heinemeier. 2006. "The Nehemiah Strategy: South Bronx Churches." In *Making Housing Happen: Faith-Based Affordable Housing Models*, ed. Jill S. Shook. Atlanta: Chalice Press.

Trinity Episcopal Church. 2008. The Trinity Real Estate Story.

http://www.trinitywallstreet.org
/welcome/?realestate (accessed November 12, 2008).

Vidal, Avis, Stefan Freiberg, Evelyn
Otchere-Agyei, and Milda Saunders.
2001. *Faith-Based Organizations in
Community Development.* The Urban
Institute, for the U.S. Department of
Housing and Community Development, Office of Policy Development
and Research. August. http://www
.urban.org/url.cfm?ID=409200. Accessed October 1, 2008.

Vitullo-Martin, Julia. 2006. "Can New
York Save Its Houses of Worship?"

New York: Center for Rethinking
Development, Manhattan Institute.
http://www.manhattan-institute.org
/email/crd_newsletter06-06.html (accessed May 6, 2012).

———. 2008. "Due to Ex-Spire: Historic
Churches Doomed." *New York Post.*
January 6. http://www.nypost.com
/seven/01062008/news/regionalnews
/due_to_ex_spire_678140.htm. Accessed July 1, 2008.

Wedam, Elfriede. 2008. "Religion in
Urban American Program: Chicago
Conversations." *CrossCurrents* 58,
no. 3: 363–68.

9

Hinduism at Work in Queens

Matthew Weiner

How does a Trinidadian Hindu woman named Chan Jamoona – a nurse, mother of four, and caretaker for her mother – become one of the most important civic and religious leaders in Queens? What does her story say about the changing nature of religious leadership? And what does being a good citizen and a Hindu and living in diverse Ozone Park, Queens, have to do with all of this? This chapter argues that community-based religious leaders are often very innovative – both in terms of how their leadership evolves and in terms of the entrepreneurial work in which they engage. This improvisational work is the result of a complex interplay between the changing and multifaceted leadership roles they fill, both in and between their small communities, and the ever-shifting urban contexts in which they reside.

By tracing the story of Jamoona, who created New York's first Hindu senior center, I offer an example of how religious leaders innovate. Through an analysis of this case study and by attending to several factors – including the religious and civic ecology of Jamoona's neighborhood, the social capital she helps to cocreate, and the way she lives her religious faith – I explain why she engages in her particular form of social entrepreneurship, and further argue that a better understanding of the social context in which religious communities reside helps to elucidate the way in which both religious innovation and the development of religious leadership emerge.

BACKGROUND

My argument about the role of local ecology and the creative nature of religious leadership is built upon an analysis of Jamoona's story through scholarship concerned with the development of religious and community life in civic contexts.[1] It was Tocqueville ([1840] 2000) who famously observed the way churches developed in America in response to particular situations, and connected this to the way active citizens groups created a form of social cohesion and local democratic practice. The field of congregational studies applies Tocqueville's observation about citizenship and local democracy to argue for the unique way religious communities practice this form of creative citizenry in contemporary contexts (Ammerman 1997; Warner 1993). Nancy Ammerman (1997) reaffirms that congregations, as voluntary organizations, are central to the current democratic spirit of the American experiment. Characterized by their voluntary nature, congregations are inherently diverse, and each is uniquely formed. James Luther Adams has developed a description of how voluntary religious organizations "function as a creative principle by making way for free interaction and innovation in the spirit of community" (quoted in Ammerman 1997, 2). Ammerman's explanation (1997) of the freedom, and thus the opportunity and necessity, of innovation in congregations helps explain the creative work of religious actors that operate in relationship with, but outside of, the congregations she describes.

The theory of religious ecology builds directly on congregational studies by noting how congregations are necessarily grounded in, are shaped by, and are shaping the local religious and secular social ecologies that they reside in (Eiesland 2000; Livezey 2000; McRoberts 2003). Religious ecology is an important analytical framework for looking at a Hindu leader in Queens, because the religious ecology here is diverse, very much in a state of recent flux, and a central factor in leading to Chan's creativity as a religious leader. Indeed, if religious ecologists hope that ecological language allows "religious groups at the local level to see themselves more clearly as potentially complementing one another, sometimes sharing resources" (Eiesland 2000, 17), then Chan's work is an example of this thesis at work. At the same time, my analysis of Chan at work stretches the analytical framework of how religious communities are defined – that is, not always as congregationally based – how they interact with each other, and the role of innovative leadership within them.

In a parallel trajectory that follows Tocqueville, scholars of social capital theory argue that civic participation through voluntary organizations creates networks of trust across difference, which allows for a creative and democratic response to problems. First articulated by the sociologist James Coleman (1988), the theory of social capital asserts the practical value of relationships and networks.[2] Its antecedents are found in the writing of theorists such

as Bourdieu (1985), Granovetter (1973), and others, who point to a form of
capital that resides in the relationships between people and within groups.
Coleman (1996, 1987) demonstrates that it is through relationships that social, economic, and political resources become available, norms and trust are
built, and public goods, beyond the actual actors' control or consumption,
are developed.[3] Within his basic thesis, Coleman (1988) identifies a twofold
typology for social capital: *bonding,* which emerges from close community and
family relationships; and *bridging,* which results from relationships with those
outside one's immediate and natural group. While bonding accounts for the
majority of any given person's network, it is the "bridges," or "weak ties" as
Granovetter (1973) calls them, that have particular "strength," because they
link agents to those outside their immediate community, thus providing mobility for the agent, and a form of social cohesion for the larger community. In
the case of religious communities, bonding social capital is a result of internal
religious community participation,[4] and interfaith and civic participation is a
form of bridging social capital. The example of Chan leads me to argue that
both forms of social capital and their interplay lead to a religious leader's ability to successfully improvise.[5]

Robert Putnam (1993) builds on Coleman's social capital theory by in-
terpreting it to be both a means by which to measure the civic health and
democratic vitality of a society, and a way to foster healthy communities
and nations. As a political scientist, Putnam analyzed different regions of
Italy that have identical government structures but experienced democracy
differently, and concluded that the vibrancy of local civic structures and the
networks they produce determines democratic health. In a following study,
Putnam (2000) applies these findings to American democracy, building on
Tocqueville's location of associations at the heart of American democracy.
Putnam defines social capital as the networks, norms, and trust built primarily through voluntary associations. While Coleman focuses on networks and
relationships in any social context (such as in schools, around neighborhoods,
and among diamond dealers), Putnam adds a dimension to social capital
theory through Tocqueville's focus on networks, civic groups, and associations
as they relate to civic structures, civil society, and democracy.[6] Putnam's work
has been tremendously influential both inside and outside the academy, and
his critics are many and wide ranging,[7] but the scholarship that relates most
closely to contextualized religious leadership as analyzed here is carried out
by sociologists of religion, who apply Putnam's social capital theory to ethnographic studies of the ways religious groups build civically oriented social

capital and foster democracy. While these sociologists focus on different aspects of Putnam's thesis, their critique is that Putnam does not provide an embedded sociological analysis, and therefore fails to adequately address the key factors of context and culture that generate particularity and that greatly influence the development of social capital. In other words, he does not apply a critique that is ecologically sensitive to the notion of social capital.[8] Building on this critique as it relates to this chapter, scholars of social capital attend little to the role of religious leadership within the fabric of networks of trust, and do not consider the role social capital plays in developing or shaping leadership. And yet the case of Chan demonstrates how very vital social capital has been in developing her role as a leader.

Religious improvisation as theorized by Robert Orsi (1999) is a useful means for identifying how creativity is sprung through social capital and religious ecologies. Orsi argues that religious communities in urban settings must innovate and improvise to respond to the new complexities that the cityscape presents. He notes the scholarly bias of seeing religion as corrupted by the urban setting, and quite correctly redraws the moral framework through which religion, and its ethical adaptability, is seen. The examples he draws on are individuals who change their theological and doctrinal postures to maintain their religious integrity, while inherently shifting the city's texture. I use the terms "entrepreneurial" and "innovation" interchangeably, but I want to focus on the role that context (a particular ethnic religious community that immigrates to a religiously plural and civically active cityscape) plays in Chan's religious agency, as she develops new social and religious structures; this in turn changes the city's social structures and the city's orientation toward religious difference, as well as redefining what it means to be a Hindu leader.[9] In the case study and following analysis, Orsi's attention to religious agency as the interplay between social structures and actors helps draw our attention to Chan's creative leadership in context.[10]

A HINDU CASE STUDY

Chan Jamoona is the founder of the first Hindu senior center in New York City. She comes to community work as a mother, a daughter, and a resident of Queens. This is how she explains it. In the mid-1980s her family – four children, her husband, and her mother – moved to the border of Richmond Hill and Ozone Park. They had come from Trinidad several years before and had lived in Washington Heights. Their new home was far-flung, off the far end of the A Train, but less expensive. More importantly, two friends from back home and a few other community members had already moved into the neighborhood, which was primarily Italian Catholic and Jewish.[11]

It was in this way that Chan's family became part of the small but growing population of Hindu, Muslim, and Christian Caribbean immigrants. She worked long hours in the early morning as a nurse at the Queens Hospital, and her mother, who lived with them, walked the kids to school. One day off from work, Chan walked with them. Her kids ran ahead and "rapped on the windows" of various homes where their friends lived and came out. By the time they arrived at school, there were a dozen kids – all new immigrants. Her mother had apples for them, "a whole bag," and handed them out "one by one" as they went to class. This was their routine, Chan's mother explained. Chan found it sweet, and said so. But her mother explained that the strategy avoided bullying.

Chan had no idea about bullying of newcomers, so that night she talked to her kids. "They were seven and ten, the two little ones," she explains, "and they told us how the brown kids would get beaten and battered by the others. So I told my kids, 'Listen, at school tomorrow, you get the phone numbers of all your friends. You tell them to tell their parents that I'm going to call, and you explain why.' So they did. They were great organizers themselves from the start.' And the next night, I called every kid's parents. They all understood, and they all wanted to do something. And so we set up a meeting."

"Where did you meet?" I asked.

"Right here," Chan says with a smile.

Chan and I are talking in her living room, where we meet from time to time. It is the place from which so much of her story of local leadership emerges. As usual, we sit across from each another, against the armrests, on the well-worn couch. The room shows the patina of a family that has for years been at the center of informal community. It also has the sign of regular and recent activity. A dining room table in the adjoining room, with a wall opening to this one, serves as a work space. Piles of folders sit precariously in a chair. A pile of papers on the table has spilled over. Veda, her youngest daughter, who is now a college graduate, works at the table on an audit of the senior center while we talk. It is clear from Chan's stories, the state of the room, and her interaction with Veda, that Chan's work is a family effort. The walls display family, a picture of Chan with Mayor Bloomberg, and various plaques and certificates. There is an American flag and a handwritten quote from the Declaration of Independence on a mini-chalkboard. To the left of the TV is a Hindu altar with gold statues of Ganesh and Krishna – Hindu deities.

"We use this place like a meeting hall." Her pointed finger drifts around, and she returns to the story of bullying. "We cleared all this away and had the kids and their parents here. Thirty or forty of us. Of all religions. There were Jewish and Irish families, too, who were concerned. We were just a little group then."

Such a meeting is hard to imagine in these times. Walking to her home from the train, I notice that Liberty Avenue is now thick with Caribbean- and Sikh-owned shops: Mr. Singh's Roti Shop, Hot and Spicy Caribbean Food, various Sari shops, but also delis, florists, and cell phone shops. The area is far more economically vibrant than it was when Chan first came. At that time, many of the now-busy storefronts were shuttered. The neighborhood did not have a high crime rate, but Chan explains that when they first came, there was trouble for them. Luckily, by the time she found out about her kids being bullied, she had already been involved in local affairs. "I've always been civically minded, Matt. So when I came, I just started."

I ask her how her being Hindu directs her civic work.

"It doesn't. It's about being civically minded . . . It's my upbringing. Serving and living in a community. Being aware of what's going on and trying to fill the spots. Being responsible. When I came, I joined the community board meetings and block associations. I substitute-taught at the schools to see which one was best."

And yet Chan was acutely aware of the important role of religious communities in her civic work, both engaging many of the Hindu mandirs (houses of worship) and their leadership, as well as the Muslim and Christian leadership. In fact, her first real community project was the result of what might be called a religious dispute, and started soon after she came. The annual Hindu Pagua parade, which went down Liberty Avenue, was in its earlier years and was resisted by local store owners. "The priest had found a lot of resistance," she explains. "Some were for it, but some would say, 'What is this pagan stuff?' Things like that. So I just went to each store and group [on behalf of the parade] and listened to their concerns and problems. I took two [young] men with me to all the meetings in the neighborhood. One young, arrogant guy and one more gentle guy. It was easier, more comfortable this way. We would just hang out, sip tea. It was lots of fun, doing things with each other like this. I liked the young man's arrogance, his frankness. Sometimes I'd have to tell him to stop, but he was straightforward, and the other was gentle." Now there is laughter in her voice. "That was the way to do it, so it was always a group effort.[12] Then I'd bring the ideas back to the temple, and we adjusted as we could. Also, we had more formal meetings. We presented our findings and ideas at the community boards. I also spoke often with the police department and made sure they knew we would go by the books, and include everyone." Chan is a multitasker, and yet "hanging out" is part of her style. It is also important to her to have a range of personality textures of people in her group. I am surprised to hear her say, with a smile, that she likes disagreement.

"You know, it's good to disagree. If we agree all the time, then you're not yourself. You have to agree to disagree. Then you can work it through. There were some, and they disagreed with us, and that's the way it was. But we came to know each other, at least, and I think we all know that. So you have to identify the disagreements. It's *not* good just to disagree for its own sake. Some people are like that, you know?"

The police were so impressed with Chan's work for the parade that they hired her to do community outreach for them.[13] As Arty Storch, the precinct captain of the police department put it, "She was my Hindu contact. My Hindu liaison, if you will." Chan concurs. "I was a liaison. I went to the Police Academy. I'd go to all the different houses of worship [with Captain Storch]. So that was seventeen years ago. So now I know all these places. At the time, I had a broken arm," she mimics how it was positioned. "And they'd drive me around."

Because of this experience, by the time she learned about her kids getting bullied, Chan was ready for action. "We had [the kids] give testimonials. Some parents knew, some didn't. One kid, a girl, told the story of a boy grabbing her braid and smashing her face into the ground." Chan makes a fist and rotates it in a circle, with a jerk at the bottom. She sucks in air. "Oh, it was *terrible*," her voice elevates, "and *really* got people angry. Because we were working for a common cause, everyone pitched in. Then we had more meetings, sometimes here, sometimes in the church, or the mandir, or the mosque. After we were organized, we had the police come, and we talked to them. Finally we had a meeting at the precinct itself." Indeed, as precinct captain Arty Storch explained it, Chan's involvement was key. "There were 'wolf pack' muggings. We knew they were happening, but couldn't stop them, and couldn't get the newer residents to trust us. Chan changed this." With everyone's help, the bullying stopped. "So now [as a result] I'm on all these boards and do all this work." Chan looks around. "It's because they know me from then. We fought together."

But it was another "fight" that more distinctly led to relationships between Chan and other religious leaders and to more formal relationships with local civic and government structures. During the same time as the bullying, new immigrants were buying houses. Often they didn't understand housing regulations and were caught off-guard by housing authorities who showed up unannounced, scaring the new homeowners, and fining them. "This was a real issue for the community," Chan explains. For her and others, it seemed that only new immigrants were getting targeted. No one had alerted them to the problem. Although the visits hadn't affected her personally, she felt she had to do something. "I put signs up everywhere for a meeting at my home. And people turned up in swarms." The meetings rotated through the houses of worship – Hindu, Christian, and Muslim – and the local library, and soon they met at the borough president's office, where they created a housing task force that included Chan, other religious leaders, home owners, and an architect.

The series of meetings also led unexpectedly to Chan's involvement in local city government. There was a recognized need for representation more reflective of Queens' increasing diversity. Until this point, she had primarily responded to problems by creating ad hoc groups and working to interface them with more formal civic structures. Now she was invited to join these very structures, to provide representation and input. When I meet Chan years later, she rattles off her numerous appointments and connections to local government. She is currently a member of the borough president's Immigration Task Force and the Queens General Assembly, but she also helps with the borough's domestic violence program. "You know, Matt, I've done so many of them, I forget what I've done and what I'm doing. Just the other day someone reminded me that I had done rape crisis intervention, and sure enough I have."

Chan's positions and appointments have spiraled and led to her engagement in numerous other programs. In any given week Chan attends a dozen meetings, both within the Hindu community and outside it, representing the Caribbean Hindu community. To be sure, her date book looks overstuffed. In a recent conversation, I asked her if she knew a certain organizer and a particular priest. "We will know them one way or another. Or they will know me. So many know me these days, and I know them all as well, somehow."

Jamoona's experience of responding to problems and working with various city agencies provides, besides important discrete community victories, examples of the impact of this work on the larger overlapping communities and the city's civic structure itself. The result of her community response to bullying was a safer neighborhood, but also a better relationship between the NYPD and the community it serves. The result of the basement controversy was a more carefully watched civic and legal structure, but also a more responsive borough president's office, which included members of the community in its official work. In both cases, the education was reciprocal: civic structures learned about community concerns and how to navigate them, but community members also learned about regulations (such as laws regarding basements).

Chan always explains her development as a community organizer by telling these stories – responding to her kids being bullied, helping to organize the Hindu Pagua parade, and working with city government in response to the basement issue – but while each case is its own inspiring example of community organizing, the larger significance is not understood until she explains what happened next. In part, it all began with her mother's friendship with other seniors in the neighborhood. At first her mother had a regular group of friends over for tea in the afternoons. But soon there were more friends, and Chan's home became a kind of meeting place for these elders. Chan was happy to have them and to keep her mother happy. "We'd buy bags of carrots and rice and spices, and my mother would cook for everyone. I couldn't believe how high my grocery bills were," she says, mimicking a look of amazement at a receipt in her hand. "But we all enjoyed it."

Chan explains her generosity as stemming from Hinduism, and what she learned from her father. "Hinduism teaches us openness. Not 'This is mine and mine alone.' My father was very generous. We had a big piece of land, with lots of crops. And he would let anyone come and take what they needed. It is important for Hindus not to be selfish."

But here in Ozone Park, while it brought joy to her home to host her mother's friends, she realized that something else was happening. "They would use my being a nurse as an excuse. They'd come to me and say, 'Chan, I have a hurt shoulder,' or something. But it was usually nothing. They just wanted to talk. They had complaints. 'Oh, my granddaughter has a nose ring, and the other one has a bellybutton ring. This one has short shorts, this one won't listen.'" But there was more to it than the generation gap. Chan realized that they came to her home because they felt they weren't wanted. "And when I inquired about them going to the local senior centers, they all complained." There were no senior centers that served vegetarian food – a requirement for many Hindus. And bingo, though seemingly lighthearted, was gambling that made many uncomfortable. There was a basic sense that none of these places were for "their community."

Meanwhile, Chan was feeling overstretched. "My house was full. It's a little old house with no space. My kids had to do their homework in the basement." Chan began thinking about what to do for her mother's friends, and praying for answers. "I prayed so hard," she explains. "These old people, their illnesses and loneliness, it worried me. So I asked, 'God what can I do?'"

Chan's daily prayers are intimate and responsive: they depend on what problems she is having and how her prayers are going. She begins each morning with traditional Sanskrit prayers, and when she's done, she asks for help. "I just say straight, 'God help me,' and then things come. They appear."

So with this problem of her mother's friends in her home, with no place to go, Chan prayed every day. She also talked with friends she had made in working for her kids' safety, the basement problem, and the Hindu parade, as well as people she knew through various projects with city government, most notably the Queens borough president's office.

Then she had an idea to create a senior center. "Once I had the idea, I knew I had to do it," she says. But while she had been community organizing for years, responding to needs, even creating an informal school, she had never created her own legally structured community organization. So she talked with friends from Catholic Charities and the borough president's office, and they provided guidance. Then, through her contacts she visited Jewish and Catholic senior centers to get a sense of how to create a space tailored to her community. "I was very impressed by what they had done," she explains. And as she studied, visited, and talked to friends, she "prayed hard about what kind of center to create." She had many meetings, both at the community boards in which she had been participating for some time and with many of the religious leaders whom she had met through responding to bullying and basements and while serving as liaison for the NYPD.

As she considered what the center would be like, she found a former rug store and rented it. Her mother and friends started using it. Soon, more seniors began to come. They got incorporated. Now, five years later, the senior center is at capacity. Chan is engaged in dozens of monthly meetings with the Department of the Aging, advocating for seniors' rights, improving the structure of services, and explaining her work to other religious and secular groups.[14]

An hour into our conversation during this visit, Chan and I have finished our soup. We get ready to go with Veda to the center. This is their usual routine. Sometimes Chan sleeps when she gets off work. "I try to get some sleep before going, but I'd rather talk with you today, Matt, than sleep." They discuss details about an audit, and think through how to handle a problem employee. Veda drives the white Land Cruiser with Chan alongside her.

The center is a one-story building, and inside is basically one large room, with tables around the perimeter and a rug in the middle. Seniors sit at the tables, and Chan's small staff crowd into two small, open-door offices on the far side from the entrance. A kitchen has been added on, and someone is cooking Caribbean food that reminds me of where we've just come from. Here Chan points to the kitchen and explains, "You see, this is the first vegetarian kitchen in a senior center in New York. Hard to believe?" she asks. "I find it hard to believe as well, but that's what they tell me."

Now in their office, Veda is talking on the phone, planning for an event next week, and greeting seniors. Someone brings us tea, and Chan continues to tell me her story. Soon after the center opened, they hired a van that would pick seniors up and drop them off at the end of the day. There were many Muslims and Christians who came as well, but most everyone was Caribbean. Chan got seed money and guidance from the borough president's office, as well as assistance from the many people she had worked with over the years.

The program next week is about hate crimes. It will be not only for her seniors but also for the larger community. The NYPD, Queens DA's office, and the Queens borough president's office will all be in attendance. What do hate crimes have to do with a senior center? Clearly, for Jamoona, social responsibility is an integrated response. Her center, she explains to me, now serves as a platform for other important work, such as this. In fact, her first social action work was in response to her community being attacked for its identity.

Jamoona is a community organizer and social entrepreneur, but the senior center developed in response to a need from the Hindu community, and also through Hindu prayer. While she often says her work is secular, and is seen in that way by most civic leaders, she also understand herself and her work as Hindu. "There are many kinds of yoga, and I chose Karma yoga. You know, they say with karma, that what comes around goes around. My parents were great Karma yogis. They were great doers. My father wanted his kids to go to school. At that time most thought girls shouldn't, or they'd play around too much with boys. [He and my mother taught me] that we needed to do something good for humanity. Our senior center is a success because of her. She would call if someone wasn't around. She would notice if something wasn't right. Karma yoga is working not for the fruits of your action, not for a pat on the shoulder.

"Krishna says, 'Whoever comes to me, and *what*ever you are' – so we accept and work with you. You are that. Souls are in everyone.[15] So you have to work with people where they are, and not to reject them."

"And what if you disagree with them?"

She smiles, I think because she knows that I know she works in spite of problems she may have with some – both within her faith and across faith lines. What Chan says next is both translatable and commonplace, yet uniquely understood by Hindus. "Krishna says you gotta do what you gotta do. Sometimes, Matt, it's not pretty."[16]

ANALYSIS

The religious entrepreneurship of Jamoona's leadership depends on many interconnected social factors. My analysis briefly notes four interconnected factors. First, Jamoona's work depends on the religious, social, and civic ecology she resides in, in terms of what triggers her activity, the way she conceives of her ideas, and how she mobilizes resources. In other words, while Jamoona is a particularly creative religious actor, we cannot understand her work outside the urban location or religious plurality in which she does it. Her earlier efforts to respond to kids being bullied and the basement crises were the result of new immigrant populations coming into the primarily white Richmond Hill and Ozone Park neighborhoods. In these examples, Jamoona gathered the religiously diverse Indo-Caribbean groups that were being attacked in the same way, and worked to develop a response. Other efforts of hers from this time period, such as lobbying for vegetarian lunches, organizing the Hindu Pagua parade, and her more recent project of starting and running a Hindu senior center, are more directly the result of a self-awareness of her particular religious identity, its differentiation within a larger religious and civic ecology, the need for social recognition of this differentiation, and the ability to do so by navigating the public sphere through both religious and civic means.[17] In all cases, an awareness of religious plurality as part of the larger social and religious ecology is something Jamoona is aware of and responding to, and her doing so bolsters and builds on the claim made by Eiesland (2000) that an awareness of religious ecology benefits the ecological partners.

The examples of Jamoona's urgent actions on behalf of her community further demonstrate that civic structures and city social service agencies can appear neutral and accommodating within a religious ecology. However, when the religious ecology of the neighborhood is diversified, as this example of

Hinduism shows, we see that accommodations need to be made – and they were made, through the assertions of Hindu spokespeople like Jamoona. Jamoona is the provocateur who leads to a change in the civic accommodation to her faith tradition, but she does so through these very structures, which, because of citizens like her, have a built-in awareness that religious ecology is something changing and something that they must respond to.

Far from being critical of the civic structures, Jamoona used them or, we might say, was drawn into them, to navigate the problems she faced. Without these civic structures, Jamoona's programs could not have developed as they did, in terms of her ability to increase neighborhood safety, adjust laws, change school policy, and in turn educate her own community about the laws and social mores of the city. Civic life in Richmond Hill has for decades maintained vibrant community boards, as well as a connection to the Queens borough president's office. When Jamoona began her work, first with the Hindu Pagua parade, she took her case to community board meetings; she was also serving as the NYPD's Hindu liaison. Jamoona frequented many Hindu mandirs and met with the various children who were being bullied, and the families that were under attack during the basement crises were members of other temples and mosques. When she began organizing around these issues, it galvanized pre-existing religious voluntary organizations, such as these religious communities, to interact with long-established secular associations. The president of Community Board 9 was happy to meet Chan, because she had seen "people like her in our neighborhood, but I didn't know any of them." Likewise when Arty Storch at the 91st Precinct convinced Chan to be his Hindu liaison, he was able to break up the small-time but dangerous gang violence harassing her community.

These are important examples of the way a religious ecology and the larger civic ecology interact and further stretch the definitions of religious ecology beyond the "congregation" model, to include lay leadership and religious-based groups, such as senior centers, concerned parents, and home owners.[18] In fact, as Madhulika Khandelwal (2002) has observed, the Indian and Hindu populations in New York have a higher rate of organization creation than other immigrant groups, starting small groups that respond to the social and cultural needs of their communities in ways that of course parallel the Tocquevillian theory of association creation. Many of these associations are religious based, or have a religious orientation such as Jamoona's, and it will be the future work of congregational studies to incorporate this reality into new research.

A second and related way to understand Jamoona's entrepreneurship is through the lens of civic participation and social capital, which emphasizes the outcome of the interaction among these various groups within the social ecology. When I asked Jamoona how she came to do this work and what her motivation was, her first answer was, "I've always been civically minded." What exactly she means by this is bound to be different in the new Queens context that she finds herself in than it was back home in Trinidad, but Jamoona is clear about her own sense of citizenship and its value to her own identity and the larger community. Putnam (1993) has argued that the social networks and associations of trust that develop through civic groups build social capital, which resides in the relationships themselves. He is following the Tocquevillian idea that social groups that form in response to social issues and problems are by nature civically minded, build civic skills, and therefore help citizens develop habits of democracy, and thus help democracy at large. Indeed, we can see that Jamoona's civic participation develops her own citizen skills, helps her community adapt to its new setting, and helps the range of diverse voices in the public be heard, thus fostering civil society. Putnam (1993), again following Tocqueville, argues that the formation of such groups leads citizens to reach out across differences. While there are many important critiques of Putnam and others who use Tocqueville's ideas in this way, in the case of Jamoona, we can see how groups are formed in response to local problems, how the groups create networks that are then in place to respond to new problems as they arise, how these groups can be a conglomeration of different religious and ethnic groups themselves, and how their work empowers local citizens to shape local governmental structures.

Furthermore, while it is rarely addressed by proponents of social capital theory, we can see the role that social capital plays in a religious leader's ability to act as a social entrepreneur, both in terms of the way thick social interaction with one's community (called bonding social capital) would lead one to better know what kinds of programs and responses to develop, and in terms of the pragmatics of social action itself. Chan's detection of serious problems that her community faces, as well as her ability to organize overlapping citizen groups, demonstrates a long-term daily social commitment to these very communities, and argues for the value of indigenous leadership. It also explains part of the framework in which improvisation is successfully triggered and steered. Religious improvisation on a local level requires social capital both of the bonding (internal to one's community) and bridging (external to one's community) types, and the interrelation between the two. Jamoona demon-

strates her immersion in both forms of social capital with her ability to gal-
vanize a response to social problems with her community members (through
bonding) and to leverage this form of social capital in working with religiously
diverse leaders as well as civic and government leaders (through bridging). The
important point to emphasize for this chapter is the way in which citizenship
as a moral role, civic participation as a moral social activity, and social capital
as a moral social field act as pragmatic overlapping subfactors in a religious
leader's ability to develop new and creative programs.[19]

A third factor in Jamoona's work is her personal and community identity as a Hindu. Her own understanding of the role that Hinduism plays in
her work varies depending on the questions she is asked and the situation
she finds herself in. As mentioned above, at times, Jamoona denies the importance for her work of her being Hindu. Indeed many leaders, including
a Presbyterian minister and a program officer at the Queens borough president's office, see her as a civic leader, not a religious leader. They point to her
not being clergy or a temple president as evidence. These examples stand next
to others in which Jamoona asserts that her religious identity is important.
For example, the NYPD specifically hired her as its Hindu liaison. Likewise,
she can also talk about her work as Karma yoga, the Hindu spiritual path
of social service performed to reach higher states of being. Perhaps most
importantly, when I ask Chan how she had the idea to create a senior center,
she explains that the idea came through prayer.[20] Chan is a devout Hindu,
prays every morning, and asks particular deities for help when she is having
trouble. When she finds solutions, she understands them to be the manifestation of her prayers.

Are Jamoona's projects Hindu per se, or manifestations of Hinduism?
Chan's opinion aside, this may depend on the project, her audience, and
on our definition of religion. Clearly her negotiations on behalf of a Hindu
parade were for a Hindu activity. Lobbying for vegetarian lunches sought religious accommodation on behalf of a particular faith. An interfaith coalition
to respond to bullying cannot be stamped as Hindu per se, yet for Jamoona,
all three activities are the same basic response to situations on behalf of her
community. Is her Hindu cultural center a Hindu place? She often argues
that it is not. She developed the project with Muslim and Christian Caribbean leaders. She called it Hindu, because "Hinduism is universal. Everyone
can eat vegetarian food." While the center is for everyone and a few Muslims
do come, by and large it is a center that caters to and primarily serves Hindus,
with Hindu songs, prayers, and yoga as the organizing activities. In any case,

we can see the role of Hinduism as both motivating and explaining Jamoona's work as she understands it, though Hinduism's role does seem to change.

Jamoona's emerging position as a Hindu leader, and the way in which she shapes her senior center to be a Hindu space, is an example of what Orsi (1999) calls religious improvisation. Orsi has argued that when religious communities come to new urban settings, they are often faced with new social and physical structures that challenge the ways that they would ordinarily go about their religious practice. In response, they must improvise to continue their practice. For Jamoona this has meant creating a Hindu senior center. While she originally developed the center with Muslim and Christian religious leaders, she finally decided that the identity of Hinduism, with a focus on vegetarianism, was critical, though she knew it would upset some of her interfaith partners. At the same time, she also discusses her Hindu-based work (be it the senior center or the parade) as secular and civic in nature. Orsi tends to talk about religious improvisers who alter particular practices, but Jamoona's case serves as an example in which the very identity of her faith is both brought forward and emphasized, as in the case of the senior center, and at times discussed in entirely secular terms. Both are examples of religious improvisation within a changing urban cityscape that lead her to be understood as a community leader – in a religious or civic sense.

The fourth factor is the role that Jamoona's identity as a mother, daughter, and home owner plays in her work. In fact, the central programs she has organized developed directly out of these particular social locations: as a mother, she defended her children by organizing against bullying; as a home owner, she organized other home owners in the community across religious lines to work with the borough president's office; and as a daughter, she founded a senior center to take care of the aging Hindu population that did not have facilities that fit their needs. Her day job and parallel vocation as a nurse also continue to help her with this work, in terms of working with the elderly.[21]

The literature on civic participation and social capital does help explain how Jamoona organized her work, but it says nothing about the social location that one comes from or about the role that this too can play; in all three cases, Jamoona's social capital was the direct result of the particular role of being a mother, daughter, and home owner. Yet it is clear from following Jamoona's story that these roles, two of which are gender-related, are critical to understanding both how she detected the problems in her community and what resources she mobilized. Likewise, while the notion of religious improvisation as developed by Orsi (1999) helps explain the way Hinduism has developed in Queens, it does not detect the very different way Hinduism has developed in these cases because of Chan's familial context. Indeed, an example such as Chan's bolsters the claim of feminist philosophers who argue that situating the self in her or his personal narrative is critical for better tracing their rational response to moral problems.

CONCLUSION

The purpose of this chapter is to provide a single case study of how Hinduism operates in the religiously plural ecology of Queens, and to argue that the complex and particular context of individual religious actors matters when making sense of how leaders develop and improvise to engage and lead their communities. The factors I have highlighted – religious and social ecology, civic participation and social capital, one's religious identity, and one's situated self – provide a basic, though certainly incomplete framework for making sense of how this kind of religious improvisation takes place. Highlighting these factors does not preclude the importance of others. Rather, I seek to open a conversation to attend to the multiple social factors that help make sense of religious social entrepreneurship in a changing urban setting.

NOTES

The foregoing case study is derived from a much longer version in my dissertation, "Interfaith in the City: Religious Pluralism and Civil Society in New York," 2009.

1. My larger interest is in public religion and the role that civil society plays in creating it. The study of civic participation and democracy in America cannot be separated from the historical role that religion has played in its development.

2. While Bourdieu (1985) observed the "benefits accruing to individuals by virtue of participation in groups and of the deliberate construction of sociability for the purpose of creating this resource" (248), it is Coleman who explicitly articulates a form of capital that "inheres in the structure of relations between and among actors" (Coleman 1988, S98). Also see Portes 1998, 4. The choice of the term "capital" to explain this complex theory, while accepted among scholars, is perhaps unfortunate: too easy, ultimately clumsy, and somewhat misleading, because it risks reducing the subtle normative value of groups and relationships to quantitative results. Yet if it is recalled that social capital is a creative and unpredictable social phenomenon, most often the *unintended* result of relationships, and that the value received is always greater for the community at large than for the individuals who "give in" to the reciprocal process through their participation, then the dangers of simplifying the theory are reduced.

3. To position his theory, Coleman critiques the traditional sociological and economic understanding of agency: the former emphasizing socialization over

agency, the latter emphasizing agency's independence over social factors.

4. Nancy Ammerman (1997, 365) draws on Putnam's use of social capital to explain how social capital is built within communities.

5. Besides this twofold typology, Coleman also identifies how social capital, within a network or organization, can be applied to a new situation if the network is recontextualized through a changed situation. He calls this an "appropriable social organization" (1988, 108) and explains that the recontextualized activity of the network creates an awareness of itself as a resource. While I do not explicitly analyze Chan's case for this aspect of Coleman's theory, it is definitely applicable.

6. Drawing on Tocqueville's thesis that American democracy is built on volunteerism and civic participation, and on Verba, Schlozman, and Brady's definition (1995) of "civicness" as measurable forms of behavior such as trust, volunteerism, and communication skills, Putnam argues specifically that social capital emerges from the civic behavior of associational involvement, which fosters democracy.

7. The most notable critics of his assessments are Skocpol (1999); Foley and Edwards (1998), and Edwards and Foley (1998b). Others who build on Putnam and focus on areas more directly related to this project are Wood (2002) and Lichterman (2005).

8. Even critics such as Foley and Edwards (1998) who find Putnam's national scope to be problematic because of its inherent lack of attention to detailed particular situations are not specifically critical of what I am calling the social capital civil society dynamic, though they suggest a return to Coleman's framework. In this way Putnam's critics tend to focus on methodological issues and overarching claims, rather than on his analytical shift, which understands social capital as "in

relation to" civil society and democracy. The debate over his methods and thesis does not challenge the dimension he adds, except in the grandness or simplicity of its effect.

9. I understand agency along the lines described by Sewell (1992) in two important respects: first, that agency can be defined as the capacity to understand, extend, and transpose rules to new contexts; and, second, that agency is in a reciprocal and cocreating relationship with structure.

10. In both my ethnographic case study and the analysis that follows, I am influenced by the methods and theory of what is being called lived religion. For a definition of lived religion, see Hall (1997, introduction). Also see Robert Orsi's chapter "Everyday Miracles: The Study of Lived Religion" in the same volume. Leonard Primiyano's definition (1995) of "vernacular religion," though emerging from folk religion, seems remarkably close to lived religion. Courtney Bender's *Heaven's Kitchen* (2003) is an important sociological study of lived religion. The orientation of lived religion has greatly advanced how scholars understand religious practice, but it tends overwhelmingly to focus on heterodox and nontraditional religious actors and practices. Rarely does it attend to those who understand their practice as traditional or orthodox. More rarely yet does it address the lived religious lives of religious leaders. My case study of Chan Jamoona is a small attempt to do both.

11. Since the late 1970s Queens has been the epicenter of migration for South Asian communities in general and Hindus in particular. In fact, Queens may very well have the most diverse Hindu population on the planet, as there are sizable Hindu populations from all across India, Nepal, Afghanistan, Pakistan, Bangladesh, Sri Lanka, Trinidad, Guyana, and Jamaica. Richmond Hill and

Ozone Park have become the central location for Indo-Caribbean Hindus, who
are primarily from Guyana and Trinidad,
but also from Surinam, Jamaica, and
the Virgin Islands. For the best account
of the Hindu diaspora to Queens, see
Khandelwal (2002).

12. During another conversation, Chan
talked about the need to do community
work by first being part of the community
and having a long-term commitment.
She referred to the need not only for
long-term commitment but also for time
investment that was based on relationship building. She cited as an example
the problem with so-called community
organizers who would come in, try to "do
something," and then run for office "on
what they had done." Once in office, or
once they lost, they often dropped the
relationships or the particular cause and
"caused more trouble than anything else."

13. Chan was part of a community outreach project that included buying bicy-
cles for police officers, so that they would
be more accessible to the community.

14. For example, Chan was recently
part of a group of senior centers resisting
a new rule that would limit where seniors
who wanted to attend particular centers
could come from. Chan is very much in
favor of seniors being able to come from
anywhere in the city, because her particular *target* population (the Hindu community and the Caribbean community) are
spread throughout the city.

15. Here Chan is referring to the
Hindu belief that every person and crea-
ture has an atman, which is related to the
ultimate godhead, Brahman.

16. Chan is referring here to a passage
from the *Bhagavad-Gita*, in which Krishna, a manifestation of the God Vishnu, is
explaining to Arjuna, a warrior, why he
must go to battle, even against his rela-
tives. Krishna explains this in terms of
dharma, the Hindu concept of duty.

17. Civil society can be defined as the
overlapping associations that interact
in the public sphere, the zone between
private space and the government. Civil
society is understood to be separate from
but influencing the government. It can
be further defined as the social realm
that creates recognition between groups
and citizens, through their difference.
Jamoona's work is a good example of a
citizen, with her organic civic associations, participating in and cocreating
civil society. According to civil society
theorists such as Tocqueville, Michael
Waltzer, and Charles Taylor, when we
think of civil society's effect on government, it is important to attend to its local
nature: in this case the micro example of
a neighborhood in Queens with diverse
religious communities that interact and,
in doing so, shape the understanding and
responses of the police department, the
Department of the Aging, and the borough president's office.

18. An aspect of the relationship between religious ecology and the agency of
particular groups that is not covered by
religious ecology theory, and that can only
be pointed to here, is the impact of the
previously existing ecologies on particular
religious communities now present in
Queens. For example, the Indo-Caribbean Hindu community existed in a very
different religious ecology, one where it
was a minority, compared to Indian Hindus, who were new to being a minority
community here. In this way, experience
in the previous religious ecology informs
how leaders like Jamoona may navigate
their new religious setting. I wish to thank
Madhulika Khandelwal (2002) for this
important insight, one that I think de-
serves greater attention from anyone mapping how different communities respond
to their particular religious ecologies.

19. While the literature on social capital has grown exponentially in the past

decade, too little research has been done on the role of social capital in religious communities, and even less on the role of leadership in understanding the dynamic of social capital. This paper is a small effort to demonstrate the importance of social capital in the work of grassroots religious leadership, in which leaders have little economic leverage. One way to think about leadership in these communities, especially when leaders emerge from the community as a result of a social problem and their interaction within the community, is that such leadership is one of the dividends of the social capital the community develops. This insight is a result of a conversation I had with Lowell W. Livezey.

20. Bakhtin's notion of double-voiceness, and of the way in which each context calls for its own unique response, is useful here.

21. I am thinking here of Seyla Benhabib's idea (2002) of the situated self. Benhabib is concerned with demonstrating that the public sphere as described by Jurgen Habermas and others is not a purely neutral place in which citizens share a common space, location, and symmetrical and level rational playing field; instead, individuals are situated through their personal narratives and social situation, and rational discourse is necessarily and rationally colored, or situated, by these factors. Here I am arguing that Jamoona's situated self should be attended to, as we look at how she is embedded in, creating, and applying social capital. I am further suggesting that when tracing the religious innovation of individuals, we should likewise attend not only to the structure that agents finds themselves in but also to their situated selves, in terms of gender, identity, and personal narrative.

REFERENCES

Ammerman, Nancy Tatom. 1997. *Congregation and Community.* New Brunswick, NJ: Rutgers University Press.

Benhabib, Seyla. 1992. *Situating the Self: Gender, Community, and Postmodernism in Contemporary Ethics.* New York: Routledge.

Bender, Courtney. 2003. *Heaven's Kitchen: Living Religion at God's Love We Deliver.* Chicago: University of Chicago Press.

Bourdieu, Bourdieu P. 1985. "The Forms of Capital." In *Handbook of Theory and Research for the Sociology of Education,* ed. J. G. Richardson. New York: Greenwood.

Coleman, James. 1987. "Norms as Social Capital." In *Economic Imperialism,* ed. Gerard Radnitzky and Peter Bernholz. New York: Paragon House.

———. 1988. "Social Capital in the Creation of Human Capital." *American Journal of Sociology* 94: 95–120.

———. 1996. "Social Theory, Social Research, and a Theory of Action." *American Journal of Sociology* 91: 1309–35.

Edwards, Bob, and Michael Foley. 1998. "Social Capital and Civil Society beyond Putnam" (editor's conclusion). *American Behavioral Scientist* 42, no. 1: 124–39.

Eiesland, Nancy. 2000. *A Particular Place: Urban Restructuring and Religious Ecology in a Southern Exurb.* New Brunswick, NJ: Rutgers University Press.

Foley, Michael, and Bob Edwards. 1998. "Beyond Tocqueville: Civil Society and Social Capital in Comparative Perspective." *American Behavioral Scientist* 42, no. 1: 5–20.

Granovetter, Mark. 1973. "The Strength of Weak Ties." *American Journal of Sociology* 78, no. 6: 1360–80.

Hall, David D. 1997. *Lived Religion in America: Toward a History of Practice.* Princeton: Princeton University Press.

Khandelwal, Madhulika S. 2002. *Becoming American, Being Indian.* Ithaca, NY: Cornell University Press.

Lichterman, Paul. 2005. *Elusive Togetherness: Church Groups Trying to Bridge America's Divisions.* Princeton: Princeton University Press.

Livezey, Lowell W. 2000. *Public Religion and Urban Transformation: Faith in the City.* New York: New York University Press.

McRoberts, Omar. 2003. *Streets of Glory: Church and Community in a Black Urban Neighborhood.* Chicago: University of Chicago Press.

Orsi, Robert, ed. 1999. *Gods of the City: Religion and the American Urban Landscape.* Bloomington: Indiana University Press.

Portes, Alejandro. 1998. "Social Capital: Its Origins and Applications in Modern Sociology." *Annual Review of Sociology* 24: 1–24.

Primiyano, Leonard. 1995. "Vernacular Religion and the Search for Method in Religious Folklife." *Western Folklore* 54: 37–56.

Putnam, Robert D. 1993. *Making Democracy Work.* Princeton: Princeton University Press.

———. 2000. *Bowling Alone: The Collapse and Revival of American Community.* New York: Simon & Schuster.

Sewell, William H., Jr. 1992. "A Theory of Structure: Duality, Agency, and Transformation." *American Journal of Sociology* 98: 1–29.

Skocpol, Theda. 1999. *Civic Engagement in American Democracy.* Washington, DC: Brookings Institution Press.

Tocqueville, Alexis de. 2000. *Democracy in America.* Trans. and ed., Harvey C. Mansfield and Delba Winthrop. Chicago: University of Chicago Press.

Verba, Sidney, Kay Lehman Schlozman, and Henry E. Brady. 1995. *Voice and Equality: Civic Voluntarism in American Politics.* Cambridge, MA: Harvard University Press.

Warner, Stephen R. 1993. "Work in Progress toward a New Paradigm for the Sociological Study of Religion in the United States." *American Journal of Sociology* 98, no. 5: 1044–93.

Wood, Richard L. 2002. *Faith in Action: Religion, Race, and Democratic Organizing in America.* Chicago: University of Chicago Press.

Contributors

MOSES BINEY is Assistant Professor of Religion and Society and Research Director for the Center for the Study and Practice of Urban Religion (CSPUR) at New York Theological Seminary. He is the author of *From Africa to America: Religion and Adaptation among Ghanaian Immigrants in New York.*

RICHARD CIMINO received his doctorate in sociology in 2008 from the New School for Social Research. Since then he has been a research fellow at the Ecologies of Learning and Changing SEA projects. He is the co-author of *Shopping for Faith,* author of *Trusting the Spirit,* and editor of *Lutherans Today.* He is Adjunct Professor of Sociology at Hofstra University and also editor of *Religion Watch,* a bimonthly publication reporting on trends and research in contemporary religion, which is published by Religioscope Institute in Switzerland.

WEISHAN HUANG received her doctorate in sociology from the New School for Social Research and is currently a research fellow at the Max Planck Institute for the Study of Religious and Ethnic Diversity in Göttingen, Germany. Her work focuses mainly on immigrant communities, gentrification, religious movements, and transnational networks. Among the articles she has published, her "Immigration and Gentrification: A Case Study of Cultural Restructuring in Flushing, Queens" appeared in the journal *Diversities.* Her current research focuses on immigration and religious movements in urban Shanghai.

SHEILA P. JOHNSON, MPS, is a licensed minister and a Psychoanalyst Candidate at the Harlem Family Institute in New York City. Reverend Johnson is a graduate of New York Theological Seminary and of a four-year training program in child and adolescent psychoanalysis at Harlem Family Institute. Her chapter was conceived as a way to honor the senior pastors of

The Father's Heart Ministries, Charles and Carol Vedral, and to bring attention to their brainchild, Alphabet Scoop. By dynamically presenting Christ in culture, whether through an ice cream business or psychoanalysis, she believes that the faith community can bring a godly influence to bear upon every discipline and sphere of human experience. A talented pastry chef, she lives in College Point, New York, with her husband, Guy Johnson, and Roc, a rescue dog.

NADIA A. MIAN received her Ph.D. from The New School for Public Engagement. She is an adjunct professor at Polytechnic Institute of New York University and sits on the Planning Board for the city of Hoboken, New Jersey. Her research interests include faith-based development, urban redevelopment, and historic preservation.

KEUN-JOO CHRISTINE PAE is Assistant Professor of Religion at Denison University in Ohio. She received her Ph.D. in Christian ethics at Union Theological Seminary after earning an M.DIV. degree from Yale Divinity School. Her research interests include the dynamic lives and social characteristics of Koreans and their churches in Metropolitan New York.

DONIZETE RODRIGUES received his doctorate in social anthropology from Coimbra University in Portugal and is Associate Professor (with Aggregation in Sociology) at the University of the Beira Interior and Centre for Research in Anthropology in Lisbon. He was a Visiting Fellow in the Department of Religion at Columbia University, New York (2009–2010), and Visiting Fellow (2000–2001) and Erasmus Fellow (2002–2005) in the Department of Sociology at Bristol University, England. He has taught master's and Ph.D. seminars in sociology and anthropology in Spain, Sweden, France, England, Romania, Italy, India, Brazil, the United States, and Canada. Among his books are *The Religious Phenomenon: An Inter-disciplinary Approach* and *The God of the New Millennium: An Introduction to the Sociology of Religion.* He is completing a book manuscript titled "Jesus in Sacred Gotham: Brazilian Immigrants and Pentecostalism in New York City."

HANS E. TOKKE, MPS, is Program Director and Professor of Non-profit Management in the Campolo School of Graduate and Professional Studies at Eastern University in Pennsylvania. He has more than twenty-five years' experience in teaching and practice in the nonprofit sector, having served in Vancouver, British Columbia, as a director of urban ministries and programs with Campus Crusade for Christ, Here's Life Inner City, and the Alder Foundation, focusing on inner-city youth and children at risk. In New York City he served with Here's Life Inner City in various capacities, reaching people in the largest metropolitan area in the United States. He has taught at the State University of New York, the City University of New York, Thomas Edison State College, and Alliance Theological Seminary. He is a Ph.D. candidate in urban sociology and culture at The New School for Social Research and holds an M.A. in sociology and M.DIV. and M.P.S. in urban community development from Alliance Theological Seminary.

MATTHEW WEINER is Associate Dean of Religious Life at Princeton University. He holds a Ph.D. from Union Theological Seminary and an M.T.S. from Harvard Divinity School. He writes about public religion, interfaith and civil society, and engaged Buddhism.

Index

7/2013